God and Gadgets

God and Gadgets

Following Jesus in a Technological World

BRAD J. KALLENBERG

With a Foreword by Nancey C. Murphy

CASCADE *Books* · Eugene, Oregon

GOD AND GADGETS
Following Jesus in a Technological World

Cascade Books
An Imprint of Wipf and Stock Publishers
199 W. 8th Ave., Suite 3
Eugene, OR 97401

www. wipfandstock.com

ISBN 13: 978-1-60899-399-4

Cataloging-in-Publication data:

Kallenberg, Brad J.

God and gadgets : following Jesus in a technological world / Brad J. Kallenberg ;
foreword by Nancey C. Murphy.

xvi + 172 p. ; cm. 23 — Includes bibliographical references and index.

ISBN 13: 978-1-60899-399-4

1. Technology — Religious aspects — Christianity. 2. Communications — Religious
aspects — Christianity. 3. Computers — Religious aspects — Christianity. 4. Internet —
Religious aspects — Christianity. I. Murphy, Nancey C. II. Title.

BR115 .P74 K36 2011

Manufactured in the U.S.A.

To Elena, Lizzie, Isak, and Hannah whose upcoming world will be far more technological than mine: may you wear the garments of technology loosely and follow Jesus with undivided hearts.

Contents

Foreword

Theology as grammar.

—Ludwig Wittgenstein, *Investigations*, remark #373.

I T IS WIDELY AGREED that Wittgenstein had little to say about theological language. Yet this parenthetical remark within a remark—the full text reads: "Grammar tells what kind of object anything is. (Theology as grammar.)"—has inspired what some would say is one of the most important recent developments in philosophical theology. George Lindbeck's cultural-linguistic account of doctrine in *The Nature of Doctrine* (1984) is probably the best known and also the most controversial contribution. Less well known are earlier applications of Wittgenstein's work to theology such as those by Dallas M. High, in *Language, Persons, and Belief* (1967), and Paul Holmer in *The Grammar of Faith* (1978). More recently there is Fergus Kerr's critique, in *Theology after Wittgenstein* (1986), of significant twentieth-century theologians for their Cartesian starting points, long after these had been so effectively criticized by Wittgenstein. Wittgenstein's work has had an impact in philosophy of religion as well.

Why rehearse this history in the Foreword to Brad Kallenberg's book? Wittgenstein did not set out to *write* philosophy in the usual sense; he saw his job as that of "curing" his students of ways of thinking and speaking that gave rise (and continue to give rise) to philosophical perplexities. So teaching philosophy is a practice. Wittgenstein's goal for his followers was not that they be able to repeat what he'd said, but "to go on"; that is, to learn the practice from him, but then to extend and improve it by means of their own participation.

Kallenberg made his academic debut in *Ethics as Grammar: Changing the Postmodern Subject* (2001). Here he presented Stanley Hauerwas as the theological ethicist who has best fulfilled Wittgenstein's hopes that others could go on—best so far, at least. Kallenberg himself now rivals Hauerwas in this regard.

In *God and Gadgets: Following Jesus in a Technological World*, Kallenberg explains Wittgenstein's understanding of the nature of language, especially his recognition that the meaning of language can only be grasped by participation in the social practices of which it is a part. Kallenberg's examples are not only convincing, but so clever that you'll not want to skip over any even if you've already gotten the point.

Another of Kallenberg's major achievements was his *Live to Tell: Evangelism for a Postmodern Age* (2002), in which he applied his work on language and communal practices in order to develop an account of Christian evangelism that is at once practical and exciting. I believe Kallenberg's account of evangelism in *God and Gadgets*—now called the practice of "Gospelizing"—represents a further step in his ability to "go on" in re-thinking the practice.

The novelty of *God and Gadgets,* of course, is its concern with technology. Kallenberg incorporates an enlightening account of the ways in which technology, often without our consciousness, has reshaped human life. The very fact that I found the term "enlightening" to be appropriate here harkens back to the invention of artificial lighting. Kallenberg provides a brilliant account (metaphor intended) of the difference it made to the whole structure of human life when we became able to break from the natural rhythms of night and day—and in the process to have forgotten why ancient prayers included thanksgiving to God for preserving us from the terrors of the night.

Kallenberg's central concern is to evaluate the role of technology in the church. What we might expect for the structure of such a book would be a set of conclusions on the *content* of Christian ethics, followed by a list classifying various technologies as good, bad, or indifferent, according to their effectiveness in pursuing the aforesaid Christian goals. The book is, however, much more complicated. First, rather than a "propositional" account of Christian oughts and ought-nots, we have Kallenberg's analysis, mentioned above, of the communal practice of Gospelizing, with its Wittgensteinian claim that no church can speak the words of the Gospel meaningfully unless they are already living (at least to a noticeable extent) the Good News. So Christian "ethicizing" (if I may coin another verb form) is both illustrated and focused here.

So which technologies *work* to assist the church in its central call to Gospelize? Wrong question! To put matters in this way is to have bought into the *instrumental* worldview, which subtly standardizes, measures, and evaluates everything on the basis of its effects. The irony is that it was the development of technology itself that created this worldview—one so pervasive that it has become nearly invisible to us, including us in the church. Kallenberg contrasts an instrumental society with a (now rare) gift society, in which the technology (say, the ability to create beautiful necklaces from shells) is primarily for the purpose of creating gifts, which in turn are for the purpose of creating and sustaining bonds among disparate peoples. Christianity is meant to be a gift economy, so we need to learn how to evaluate technology on the basis of its contribution to a gift society. How do we do this? It is a learned ability; it requires communal discernment. But how does the process of communal discernment work? Most churches have long forgotten.

Now the book comes full circle. Kallenberg, who teaches engineering ethics in a Catholic university, uses the process of teaching engineering itself to illustrate the process of Christian ethical discernment. It involves apprentices and masters. It is embodied; engineers become masters by participating bodily in the tasks of designing and building things. Kallenberg emphasizes that the critical difference between a beginner and a master is the *tacit* knowledge that the master has acquired. This knowledge may sometimes, in well-practiced areas, be condensed into textbooks. But textbook directions will be taken by apprentices to be exceptionless *rules,* whereas in practice they are meant to be used as *heuristics*—general guidelines that tacit knowledge will finesse in practice.

Thus, Kallenberg argues, all Christian practices, including ethical discernment and Gospelizing, will appear to beginners to have cut and dried instructions printed on the pages of Scripture. But our task between now and the Eschaton is to acquire the tacit knowledge that allows us to perceive the "rules" as heuristics that will open our eyes to more and more imaginative ways to approximate the Kingdom of God.

A final note: Kallenberg's caution with respect to technology echoes that of Wittgenstein. Wittgenstein's speculation:

> It isn't absurd, e.g., to believe that the age of science and technology is the beginning of the end for humanity; that the idea of great progress is a delusion . . . ; [or] that there is nothing good or desirable about scientific knowledge and that mankind, in seeking it, is falling into a trap.[1]

1. *Culture and Value,* 56e.

Thanks to Kallenberg's careful work, we can still retain caution, but can look for signs of God's grace within the development of technology as well.

Nancey C. Murphy

Preface

I REMEMBER MY CHRISTMAS wishes as a fourteen-year-old Minnesota boy. For me, getting a copy of the newly published "New American Standard Bible" oddly ranked higher than getting new ice hockey equipment. My fervor seems to have been part of a broader cultural turn. America was in the throes of an amazing "revival" (in the religious sense of this term) among its youth: a widespread conversion to Christianity within the hippie subculture. These "Jesus People" not only read their Bibles with zeal, they created an entirely new genre of religious music. Although I was too young to have been a hippie prior to this revival, I bought into Jesus People music lock, stock, and barrel. It seemed only natural that I read the Bible daily while playing vinyl albums of *Love Song* or *Second Chapter of Acts* or *Maranatha! Music* in the background. As music became more portable, my peers and I brought JP music on the go in the form of homemade cassettes. On a long bus ride to a religious convention in another state, my batteries died. Oddly enough, as the music faded, the experience of reading my Bible seemed to lose its sheen. This marks the first time I recall feeling that the quality of my faith could be threatened by a hiccup in technology. How silly of me! I later went through a romantic phase where I insisted on absolute silence and solitude when reading the Bible. When others were seeking a patch of sunshine and the chirping of birds in order to get close to God, I set up a small table, chair, and light in my clothes closet in imitation of Matthew 6:6. The pains I took to purge my "Quiet Time" of technological noise had the by-product of making me blind to the encroachment of technology on the rest of my day, and thus on the rest of my Christian practice. How equally silly of me!

To give a sense of the state of technology in my youth, I should mention that one of my high school friends was the first in our large suburban school to purchase one of Texas Instruments' first hand-held scientific calculators. What now sells for $20 then cost my friend $279

... or the equivalent of $1,300 in today's dollars! Most of us thought he was crazy to spend that much. Who needs a hand-held calculator when the real heavy lifting is done by actual *computers*. When I enrolled at the Institute of Technology at the University of Minnesota, I remember a computer programming class for which punch cards was the preferred way to backup one's program. I was awed by the graduate students who needed whole boxes of cards to carry their scholarship! By humiliating comparison, my homework only required a rubber band. (The "happening" computer language of 1976 was Pascal. But the semi-colon used to mark the end of a line of code was not even on the keyboard of the card punch; it had to be generated by a tedious combination of keys, "+789" while holding down the multipunch key!)

Despite being technologically primitive by today's standards, these were probably the best years of my life. I married my high school sweetheart and joined the fulltime staff of a nondenominational parachurch ministry that focused on university students as its "mission" field. Working with college students kept my fingers on the technological pulse of each new generation. In 1983, the year my first child was born, I purchased my first personal computer: an Apple 2e. My "printer" was a converted electric typewriter with a nifty changeable typing ball for varying fonts! By the time my second child was born, varying fonts was a matter that the best computers handled internally; laser printing was becoming available to the public in special shops (for the equivalent of about $16 per page in today's dollars). Five years later I was purchasing kid's software for a Macintosh and had convinced myself that I needed a laptop to make it through grad school. That was 1992.

During the thirty-five-year period from 1972 to 2007, I was still reading my Bible the old-fashioned way: by turning pages. Yet all around me the practice of Christianity seemed to be changing. Some of my friends need to boot up their computer first thing in the morning in order to read the Bible. More than one person in a recent adult Sunday School class stopped carrying Bibles altogether because they had multiple and *searchable* translations on their PalmPilots. (I owned a Personal Desk Accessory briefly ... until I clumsily dropped it in a toilet!) Fellow seminary students even boasted of having the entire Greek New Testament on a PDA. Music went digital, and buds went into everyone's ears. Then came the information super highway. When the world went online, it became increasingly commonplace for believers to download a worship podcast or join a live stream of evening prayer on sites like modernpsal-ter.com, genevanpsalter.com, psalmistry.com, pray-as-you-go.org, and so on endlessly.

Today things are changing ever more rapidly as computer chip speed is said to double every eighteen months. Churches find them-selves competing with entertainment culture to win fans. Across the country pastors wrestle with tough questions: "Why would anyone take the trouble of *driving* to our church building, when he or she can travel by avatar into a more entertaining venue, such as the virtual 'worship' services in the virtual world of SecondLife.com?" And this question, "How do we help believers understand that the best way to handle James' injunction to 'confess your sins to one another' (Jas 5:16) is *not* to do so anonymously at absolution-online.com or via any number of online confession sites?"[2]

The contrast between what I understood as "personal devotions" in 1974 and the form that it sometimes takes today is but one reason for wondering what sort of impact the technological revolution has had and will have on the practice of Christianity in the affluent West. I don't simply mean that technology has created innovative ways to sin like "sexting" (the sending of explicit sexual pictures of oneself to one's peers via cell phone[3]) or like "AdultWork" (a sort of eBay for people wanting to start part-time careers in prostitution[4]). Technological innovation has *always* brought with it new ways to sin. But I mean that something more nefarious may be afoot in the present age, nefarious because it is invisible.

This book is an attempt to help us see what is invisible. It has grown out of several decades of ministry among, and education of, college students first as a campus minister and more recently as a professor of theological ethics. Early versions of chapters 1 and 2 were given as the Staley Lectures in February of 2005 at Cedarville University. Chapter 1 tells the story of the bewitching nature of technology, particularly the cultural enticements of *standardization* and *instrumentalism*. Chapter 2 considers the effect the technological explosion has had on the Christian practice of witness.

2. Banerjee, "Intimate Confessions Pour out on Church's Web Site."

3. Almost one in seven teens practice sexting. See St. George, "Sexting Hasn't Reached Most Young Teens."

4. Walsh, "England's Ebay for Sex."

Chapter 3 tackles the question of the role technology might play in the fulfilling of Jesus' Great Commission (Matt 28:18–20) by looking carefully at biblical texts concerning evangelism, evangelization, and witness. This chapter is a revision of a presentation I made at the Evangelism Roundtable, *Issues of Truth and Power: The Gospel in a Post-Christian Culture*, convened by the Billy Graham Center in 2004 at Wheaton College.

Chapter 4 began as an address given to the Region-at-Large division of the National Association of Baptist Professors of Religion in June of 2009 (Chicago). It argues that the practice of Christianity and Christian theology follows "the logic of gift" rather than the logic of tools.

A portion of chapter 5 originated as "Weight-bearing Crosses and Trusses: Christian Ethics and Engineering," my portion of the presentation series, *Contested Allegiances: Christianity in an Era of Permanent War*, at DePaul University (Chicago) in 2003. The chapter undertakes a decidedly positive turn with respect to technology by thinking about whether and to what extent technology might participate in redemption.

Chapter 6 was also part of the Staley Lectures given in 2005. In it I consider what positive lessons sincere Christians might gain from understanding the nature of the practices on which technology depends, particularly the practice of engineering.

I am very grateful to Cedarville University, the Billy Graham Center, Mike Budde of DePaul University, and the Region-at-Large of the NABPR for providing the concrete occasions (not to mention deadlines) for thinking through this material. But my deepest thanks are reserved for the many colleagues and friends without whose conversations my thinking would be much less clear: Andy Black, Michael Cox, Curtis Freeman, Tim Furry, David Gushee, Derek Hatch, Aaron James, Kelly Johnson, Rod Kennedy, M. Therese Lysaught, Damon Martin, Tim Meador, Jeff Morrow, Bill Portier, Ethan Smith, Terry Tilley, Sue and Bill Trollinger, Nikki Tousley, Ed Wingham, and Telford Work.

Above all, I am grateful to my wife, Jeanne, without whose holy encouragement and patient understanding—especially during those meals when my mind was miles away!—these chapters would have never been completed!

1

Bewitched by Technopoly

CONSIDER THE PRAYER FOR morning from the 1790 version of the Book of Common Prayer. The words are very good. But there is a surprise, so watch for it.

> Almighty and everlasting God, in whom we live and move and have our being; we, Thy needy creatures, render Thee our humble praises, for Thy preservation of us from the beginning of our lives to this day, and especially for having delivered us from the dangers of the past night. For these Thy mercies we bless and magnify Thy glorious Name, humbly beseeching Thee to accept this our morning sacrifice of praise and thanksgiving, for His sake who lay down in the grave and rose again for us, Thy Son our Savior, Jesus Christ. Amen. (577)

I happen to own a copy of this prayer book. It looks as old as it is. The spine is broken and the cover would fall off, were it not for the miracle of duct tape! I bought it in a used bookstore for a dime! The elderly woman who ran the shop raised her eyebrows when she saw the price, because she knew the book's real worth.

The Book of Common Prayer is not a collection of lofty niceties. The Book of Common Prayer is a resource for people who take seriously the Psalmist's cry "*seven* times a day I praise Thee" (Ps 119:164). The prayer I just cited is a family prayer—one intended to be used by parents each morning in the crucial task of training children to pray and to speak well the language we call "Christian." Moses spoke of this, did he not; instructing Hebrew parents to teach their children the Word while out for a walk, when they are sitting around, as they fall asleep and—as in our case—when they rise up in the morning (Deut 6:4–9).

But the prayer sounds odd, doesn't it? Its not just the "Thees" and "thous" that betray the eighteenth-century English. It is rather the surprising gratitude in their voices: ". . . especially for having delivered us from the dangers of the past night." Most of us hit the sheets wearily, tuckered out from the day's activities. But, how many of us climb into bed *warily*, with a sense of dread, because of the dangers that lurk in the darkness? How many of us climb out of bed the next morning with a sigh of relief: "Whew! *That* was close! I could have died during the night."

Look again: ". . . especially for having delivered us from the dangers of the past night." This phrase sounds childish even, as if the pray-er is still afraid of the dark. What's going on here? Was the Christianity of our great-grandparents so different from ours? They prayed to the same Lord of the Universe as we. So, what gives?

I have a hunch—but you're probably not going to like it. The single most important difference between their lives and ours, between their prayers and ours, between their Christianity and ours, lies in the fact that we have electric lights. The Book of Common Prayer eventually dropped the line about the dangers of nighttime.

Think about it. By the time this eighteenth-century prayer was penned, clocks had achieved an astonishing accuracy of 1/5 second per day.[1] But there were only so many hours in a day, and that number was fixed around twelve, give or take, according to season and latitude. Once the sun set and darkness descended, human activities shifted. Fine detail work was curtailed by the dimness of firelight or the glow of a kerosene lantern. By our modern standards of productivity, the hours of evening and nighttime were virtually a total loss.[2]

However, God created us to live by *reciprocal* rhythms. In the words of Genesis 8: "As long as the earth endures, seed time and harvest, cold and heat, summer and winter, day and night shall not cease" (Gen 8:22). The hours between dusk and daybreak were crucial to human flourishing. All creation takes a breath and lets out a collective sigh. Only when the detail work is set aside, is there time for conversation, for storytelling, for contemplation, for prayer, for tenderness and lovemaking, for sleep; even for dreams. "It is in vain," writes the Psalmist, "to rise up early,

1. Staudenmaier, "Denying the Holy Dark," 185. My account, maybe even my style of writing, is indebted to John Staudenmaier, whose friendship is very important to me.

2. Even mechanized labor was shut down as light fails, for machines became doubly dangerous to human operators when dark descended.

to retire late, to eat the bread of painful labors; for the LORD gives to his beloved—sleep!" (Ps 127:2 NASB).

Not only was nighttime built into the created order, darkness has forever been a metaphor for limits of human understanding. Thus the mind of God is "dark" to us because it is mystery. Moreover, "dark" also may indicate those forces that provide the resistance necessary for building spiritual muscles. Only the soul that has faithfully endured its "dark night" firmly trusting the Savior makes real progress toward deeper communion with God.[3] For this reason we ought not lump all "darknesses" together and vilify each as evil. For if each "dark" is unequivocally bad, then we may be tempted to brand any means by which dark can be vanquished as unequivocally on the side of good.

Are electric lights unequivocally good? What if the "dark" they chase away is broader than the dark of night? In 1910 Fillipo Tommaso Marinetti proclaimed to the very religious town of Venice: "It is time for electric lamps with a thousand points of light to brutally cut and tear your mysterious, enchanting and seductive shadows."[4] Evidently Marinetti expected technological change to drive away the "holy dark" as well as the darkness that our body needs for quality sleep.

Twelve hours of daylight? Not any more! Since Edison's first successful test in 1879 and the first standardized electrical system in 1882, *twenty-four* hours of daylight has become normative. High quality, artificial light means that every form of detail work imaginable—measuring, reading, planning, traveling, manufacturing, road repair—all proceed in unending fashion. As the Starbucks billboard along the interstate proclaims, "Open 24 hours—Plan accordingly!"

My grandfather was born into the earlier, simpler age. His son, my own father, now 87, belonged to the last generation who not only understood how every technology they encountered actually worked, they also knew how to repair virtually everything they owned. Such knowledge gave my father's generation a measure of power over their surroundings. However, things have changed for the ordinary citizen. Today's world has been dubbed "technopoly."[5] Technopoly is like a monopoly, except

3. The term "dark night of the soul" is widely misunderstood. Curious readers are urged to study the sixteenth-century original in order to mine the gems there. Saint John of the Cross, *Ascent of Mount Carmel*.

4. Cited in Staudenmaier, "Denying the Holy Dark," 175.

5. See Postman, *Technopoly*.

instead of a single individual exercising complete control over an industry, commodity or infrastructure, technology itself exercises the control. And just as ordinary folk like L'il Orphan Annie of the 1930s were once at the mercy of rich power-mongers like Daddy Warbucks, in our own age, ordinary folk knuckle under to an entire technological system.

So, the greatest difference between our Christianity and that of our great-grandparents may be a *technological* one. Am I saying that all technology is bad? Of course not. But I am saying that technology is as ubiquitous as it is incomprehensible—it is everywhere and we understand less and less of it! And for that reason it is invisible. And here's my point today: technology is shaping our discipleship in ways we do not easily recognize. We are under its spell, and we barely notice our bewitchment. To help us better see that which is invisible, let me describe some historical context for understanding a revolution in technology called "standardization."

THE STORY OF STANDARDIZATION

There are a number of ways scholars of culture explain how we got to where we are today. Sometimes a string of events—wars fought or avoided, economic boon or collapse, elections won or lost—are depicted as links in a chain that produce today. Other times credit is given to important books or movements that generate revolutionary ideas. The office cubicle, for instance, is generally conceded to be the result of Frederick Winslow Taylor's book, *The Principles of Scientific Management,* published in 1911. But what is sometimes overlooked is the role that change in the technology sector plays in altering society. Even a common cultural descriptor like the word "tolerance" has technological undertones. In fields of engineering, "tolerance" indicates the range within a measured part that is acceptable ("Three plus or minus 0.001 inches"). Outside these specifications or "specs" the part is entirely rejected. (Ones that are 2.998 inches are thrown out; ones that might be 3.002 are re-machined and measured again.) Surely this is how tolerance functions in society too. Not every person or every idea is really acceptable. We are a people who are tolerant within limits, although no one wants to specify precisely what the specs are.

It is difficult to pinpoint when the winds of change first began to blow.[6] But for our purposes, the real action began long before Taylor's book, ninety-six years earlier, around 1815. Historians tell us that the battles and skirmishes on either side of 1812 (from about 1806 to 1815) were but a continuation of the Revolutionary War. The real action happened not on the battlefield but at the treaty table, at which the British finally relinquished the military outposts they held on American soil. These concessions were the byproduct of a shift in British foreign policy; they more or less decided to move on and turn their attention elsewhere. That is to say, despite Jackson's impressive victory at the Battle of New Orleans, the American colonies "lucked out," especially considering the relative disarray of the U.S. military at the time.[7]

Pointing to insufficient supplies, tactical errors, and faulty arms, leading voices in the U.S. military expressed loud concerns over the sloppy state of U.S. forces.[8] In order to address these problems, in 1815 Congress passed an Act that empowered the chief of the U.S. Army Department of Ordnance "to draw up a system of regulations for the *uniformity* of manufactures of all arms ordnance, ordnance stores, implements, and apparatus...."[9] Thus "a system of uniformity and regularity" became the oft-repeated catch phrase of industrial revolution in the military sector.

The uniformity principle demanded sweeping changes not only in the military, but also for those engineering and manufacturing firms whose services were contracted by the military. For example, prior to 1815, weapons—such as the percussion musket—were assembled by skilled craftsmen who filed, shaped, and fine-tuned each part to mesh with a given set of parts to form a complex working whole—the rifle. These parts were never interchangeable between muskets. Each broken

6. The shift may have its origin in the invention of the clock. In its original form, clocks were simple tools, adopted by clergy for more easily dividing the day into divine hours. School children still sing of poor Freré Jacques who is in danger of sleeping past the moment he is expected to ring the bells announcing the predawn prayer service. The early clocks that would have kept Freré Jacques on track were crude devices that displayed only the hourly hand, because they were not very accurate. Staudenmaier, "Denying the Holy Dark," 185. In 1370 King Charles V mandated that all Parisians "regulate their private, commercial and industrial life by the bells of the Royal Palace clock." Postman, *Technology*, 27.

7. I am grateful to my friend, historian Bill Trollinger, for keeping me straight on the history of this period.

8. Smith, "Army Ordnance and the 'American System,'" 43.

9. Ibid., 44; emphasis mine.

musket was unique and could only be repaired by a skilled craftsman. The only way to certify the reliability of the repaired musket was an actual "proof-firing." In other words, it would be the gunsmith, rather than the soldier, that got blown up by a faulty weapon. Dangerous business indeed!

The fifteen years it took to complete standardization of weapon production required an enormous expenditure of coercive force to achieve the necessary degree of cooperation and communication. And in the end, the transformation of the practice was striking. Originally, a skilled craftsman had an entire tool shop at his disposal (and surely before 1815, it was always a "his") for handcrafting each musket as a unique, complex system. But after the changes of 1815, craftsmen were replaced by unskilled assemblers requiring at most six hand tools. The thing that made the craftsmen obsolete was the invention of hardened steel gauges, sixty-three in all, that were applied *not* to the device as a whole but used to create each individual part to spec *in isolation* from the gun as a whole.[10]

It took another dozen years (1841) before the private sector serving the military completed standardization and produced the nation's first fully-interchangeable firearms. But this success came at a price: the private sector had to reproduce the militaristic manner that typified production at the governmental armories, namely, *regulation*, *inspection*, and *compulsion*. Workers who might have labored for sheer love of the craft chafed against the demands for uniformity. Objectors were first chastised, then fired and blacklisted. But in the end, uniformity was achieved. Merritt Roe Smith reports,

> The accuracy of these methods received an unexpected test in 1852 when, as a result of a flood at Harper's Ferry [manufacturing firm], 9000 percussion muskets with unmarked parts were stripped, cleaned, and randomly reassembled "with every limb filling its appropriate place with perfect exactness."[11]

And we all mutter, "Of course! That's how it *should* be." But whence the "should"?

The trained eye can see that more was being engineered than musket parts. Managers coerced workers away from former customs and habits

10. Ibid., 60–62.
11. Ibid., 64.

(ironically on the grounds that such managerial force was required *by Christian love!*[12]). In this respect, the uniformity principle, which first described the new way workers viewed the *material* stuff of engineering, began also to infect the way *human workers* themselves were viewed. To say the same thing differently, managers and inspectors became to their employees what gauges were to mechanical parts.

There were two consequences stemming from the application of standardization to workers themselves. In the first place, just as gauges related to parts but never to wholes, neither managers nor workers retained the former skill set of relating to the artifact in its entirety. Workers comprehended one or more parts, but never the device as a whole. And the managers measured each worker for their conformity to regulations while giving scant attention to the working environment, much less to the device itself.[13] In short, the know-how that once permeated the small gunsmith's shop was removed at least one step farther away from the manufacturing process. Second, these living "gauges"— the managers—related to the workforce as if to machines. Managers and inspectors measured workers for regularity while forgetting the humanity of workers whose lives consisted not in production but in living well. One historical snippet from the era suffices to drive this point home.

The oft-spoken praise of industrialism holds some truth: precision machinery enabled workers to produce more widgets in less time. Yet here is the surprise. With the aid of labor-saving devices, most workers "chose to limit their output to customary levels and carry home approximately the same monthly wages."[14] Why would they do such a thing? The managers complained that the workers took unjust advantage of labor-saving machinery to work fewer hours while turning out the same number of widgets. In the eyes of the managers, such behavior showed a "lack of internal discipline" and posed a serious "labor problem."[15] They

12. Ibid., 79.

13. Today, engineers rarely rise beyond middle management; the real power is reserved for managers with business rather than engineering background.

14. Smith, "Army Ordnance and the 'American System'," 82.

15. One manager penned the following letter: "The men have been paid high prices & were in the habit of working 4 to 6 hours per day—& being absent whole days or a week. At the end of a month their pay was generally the same in amounts as if no absence had occurred. They are now required to work full time and during fixed hours . . . and the master of the Shop keeps a time account showing the time *actually spent in labor*. Here is the *great oppression* [workers] complained of. At the end of a month

reasoned that any hours that could be spent in production *ought* to be spent in production. In this manner, the workers were accused of defrauding the firm. The managers responded by clamping down, requiring fixed work hours, and compelling compliance by paying less and less for each widget produced. In the end, precision machinery greatly increased productivity but *did not save labor for anyone*. Ironically, the secret "fraudulent" practices at which workers supposedly frittered away their free time were often focal practices that made life worth living, such as farming, fishing, and raising children.[16]

It took thirteen years of heavy-handed, authoritarian control to inculcate a quite different form of life. In Smith's words, at the coercive insistence of their military supervisors, "workers gradually abandoned the task-oriented world of the craft ethos and reluctantly entered the time-oriented world of industrial capitalism."[17] Smith goes on to conclude:

> That the large scale manufacture of interchangeable firearms paralleled this change [in the workers] was no mere coincidence. Early on, ordnance officers had recognized the importance of work rules, clocked days, and regularized procedures in stabilizing the complex physical variables present in the workplace. *Experience had taught them that there was no other alternative—a factory discipline characterized by rigid bureaucratic constraints had to be inculcated and absorbed by all employees.*[18]

Not all manufacturing firms adopted the austere stance that came to characterize the much later theory of "scientific management" or the Ford assembly line. Nevertheless, standardization became a movement that, once inaugurated in national armories, went on to infect the whole of American engineering. Beginning with the U.S. Army Department of Ordnance Act of 1815, the practice of the armory at Springfield, MA,

---

the *quantity of labor performed* . . . and the *time* during which it is effected, are seen by a simple inspection of the Shop books. The degree of diligence used by each man is also known and hence results a knowledge of what is the *fair price* to be paid for piece work!!! The Armorers may attempt to disguise or hide the truth under a thousand clamors . . . but this is the *real cause* of their objection to a Military Superintendent. He enforces the Regulations which lay bare their secret practices (frauds—for I can use no better term)." Cited in ibid., 84–85; emphasis in original.

16. On the categorical difference between "focal" practices like playing the violin versus playing the stereo, see Borgmann, *Power Failure*.

17. Smith, "Army Ordnance and the 'American System,'" 83.

18. Ibid., 83–84; emphasis added.

and the private armament firms in New England "spread to technically related fields and by the late 1850s could be found in fields such as factories that made sewing machines, pocket watches, railroad equipment, wagons, and hand tools."[19] Even the nuts and bolts of engineering— I mean actual nuts and bolts—succumbed to standardization in 1864.[20]

To summarize the story, a thirst for efficiency in warcraft spawned a vision of control-by-uniformity fueled by fear. Manufacturing firms were thereafter governed with military rigor, because manufacturing became part of the war effort in times of peace as well as war. Workers themselves were treated as interchangeable units that must conform to a preset standard or face permanent rejection from the industry. For their part, the workers grumbled loudly, with good reason, about compulsory hours, relentless productivity pressures, blind enforcement of stringent regulations, and the installation of time clocks. And they complained bitterly about the injustice of *lowering* piece rates—that is, managers lowered the amount they paid per widget in order to force laborers to increase the number of hours worked simply to earn the same wages. Last, the dwindling number of "older artisans bemoaned the disappearance of traditional skills."[21]

NAMING THE EFFECTS OF THE TECHNOLOGICAL MONOPOLY

The lessons of these two stories—the takeover of darkness by electric lights resulting in a "modernized" prayer for morning in the Book of Common Prayer and the standardization of percussion muskets—can be illustrated in many other ways. If we were to make a detailed study

19. Ibid., 78.

20. On the standardization of threads, see Sinclair, "At the Turn of the Screw."

21. Smith, "Army Ordnance and the 'American System,'" 84. Eventually some manufacturers experimented with quantifying and recording the tacit skills of the expert craftsman. Most famously, General Electric developed a "record-playback" system aimed at capturing human skill in order to reproduce it tirelessly by machines. Kurt Vonnegut Jr., who worked as a publicist for G.E. at this time, immortalized the record-playback experiments in his novel, *Player Piano*. But the record-playback system was a bust and was rapidly replaced by numerical control technology. Not only could human skill not be captured in fine enough detail to drive machines, since the intended output was the manufacture of standardized parts, what was deemed more useful than a "skilled" machine that could only do one skill perfectly, was a versatile machine that by simply altering the numerical stipulations do anything (within set tolerances). Thus is born the field called "numerical control." Noble, "Social Choice in Machine Design."

of the history of technology, we might be able to better understand the
ways that technology has a monopoly on the way Christians see the
world. For the sake of time, let me briefly name three inter-related effects
of technopoly, explain how these run against the grain of God's reign,
and then issue a challenge. These three consequences might be thought
to constitute the "World View" of technology, except they are less visible
than World Views are sometimes construed.[22]

Reductionism

The first effect of technopoly is reductionism. I think I can explain reductionism with a simple illustration. Many college students, working
on a PowerPoint presentation for a class, have snagged the perfect digital
image off the internet only to find out that when the picture is enlarged,
it's too jagged? What's the problem? Not enough pixels in the original
image, right? So how many pixels is enough?

Technological modeling and computer simulations are like digital
photos. They "[break] reality into chunks, as many as possible but always too few."[23] The more pixels, or chunks, the larger the file and the
slower the computer processes. In the end, we compromise: we opt for
the largest file our laptop can handle without slowing down too much.
This lesson can be generalized: *every* computer model has already made
decisions about (1) the number and size of chunks reality is to be broken into and (2) what relations between the chunks are most worth
troubling about (and which relations are to be ignored). (3) The only
kind of relationships a computer can model are numerical ones. And the
only numerical relationship that can be observed by external modelers
is that of cause and effect. What results is always (4) an *approximation*
of mechanical causes between *approximate representations* of objects,
whether these objects be cars about to crash or people about to fall in

---

22. Teachers often teach by means of ideal types in order to get points across
to students. In this light, Christian philosophers who want to educate us about
Weltanschauungen, or wordviews, often teach them by listing a cluster of propositions
(or tenets) said to summarize the logic of said worldviews. This becomes a little mis-
leading when one realizes that the most nefarious aspects of worldviews is what cannot
be put into a brief list of summary sentences. Such is technology.

23. James Gleick cited by Ferguson, "How Engineers Lose Touch," 18.

love. Yet the model is presented to the rest of the population as factual, even infallible.[24]

Can God's world be "pixelized"? We used to think so. But since the advent of quantum mechanics, physicists now say the world is seamless.[25] What appear to be lumps of discreet stuff called atoms are really more like probability distributions knit through time and space. Do all interactions within this world reduce to mechanical cause and effect? No again. Not only is it seamless, God's world is unpredictable, non-linear, chaotic, complex.[26] As such it will take practical wisdom (what the ancients called *phronēsis*) rather than computer simulations to live well.

If God's world cannot be "pixelized" without loss of important detail, how much more does the spiritual world we inhabit resist "pixelization"? Yet we are tempted to oversimplify the spiritual landscape because technology has revolutionized the way we navigate physical space; because it revolutionized the way the surface of the earth is modeled.

Today the word "map" denotes a bird's-eye representation of a plot of land. We are convinced that maps are simplified pictures because we know how to shuttle back and forth between a Google map and the corresponding Google satellite photo. And of course, cartography has undergone its own standardization so that whether one uses a paper map from AAA or a "zoom-in-able" Google map or a Tomtom GPS navigator mounted on the dashboard, the driver is supremely confident of not getting lost.

Now recount all the times you have heard the Bible referred to as a "roadmap" for living. Is this a safe metaphor? No! The technological revolution has tricked us into forgetting all sorts of other kinds of maps.[27] As a first-order approximation to a spiritual map, consider the sport of

24. In the summer of 2007, a large bridge over the Mississippi river fell down during rush hour traffic in Minneapolis, Minnesota. Some thirty people were killed. When the bridge was constructed in 1967, civil engineers simply did not think fatigue cracking was possible in steel bridges. As a result, they built single-fail bridges: if one part goes, the whole thing falls down. Retrospectively, their smug optimism appears foolish.

25. At least, it is seamless down to the level of observability. Eventually Heisenberg tells us that observation ceases.

26. For an account of the reduction of all forms of causation to mere mechanical linkage see Juarerro, *Dynamics in Action*.

27. There are topographical maps, symbolic representations of subway lines (for a bird's-eye view, were it possible, does *not* mirror the subway guide!), even a map that represents the stress level of pedestrians (see http://www.biomapping.net)! All such maps require *skill* more than a printed legend in order to use them successfully.

orienteering. In this sport, competitors race to navigate a wilderness region armed only with a compass, a topographical map of the terrain, and instructions to the first of several landmarks. Each of the landmarks needs to be found in order to complete the course. This is a very demanding activity, requiring both stamina and skill—both of which can be improved by practice.

The important feature of orienteering is that one's knowledge is progressive. What counts for a "map" (the set of instructions between successive landmarks) must be followed in a particular order. Only if one finds the first landmark will directions to the second make any sense at all. There is simply no possible way to jump ahead and anticipate the final destination. One only learns of the destination and the means to arrive safely by journeying through all the landmarks.

In an earlier era, long before satellite imaging, human life in general and Christian life in particular was understood as a journey guided not by a roadmap but by orienteering an itinerary. Life was a quest for which safe arrival required both finding each landmark along the way and acquiring of skills by completing each character-building task along the way. Since the directions from the penultimate landmark only made sense to the one who had completed every leg up to that marker, each traveler or pilgrim humbly accepted as a God-given task the responsibility simply to move from the present marker to the next one on the itinerary.

The "itinerary" approach to spiritual growth will get more attention in chapter six. Bit for now it should be abundantly clear that so-called technological "advances" in cartography have actually introduced reductionism into the contemporary Christian outlook. If this reductive set of expectations has leaked into our practice of Christianity, we have thereby been impoverished by technological progress.

Standardization

The second effect of technopoly is that the standardization revolution in engineering has infected the whole of culture. Our culture has almost religious-like reverence for technology. The myth that the West has committed to memory combines (1) technical prowess for controlling nature, together with (2) the expectation of inevitable progress before which

(3) human beings are taught passively to conform.[28] Typically, this conformity takes the form of cultural standardization. Of course, standardization is ubiquitous. Cell phone clocks nationwide are in sync. Forty hours per week is the standard measure of labor. The quality of air, water, and food are measured against pre-set standards by the EPA and FDA. Daily temperature is reported as higher or lower than average. Children are measured for height and weight and IQ against standardized averages. Every slice of bread in a loaf is of identical thickness. Printer paper in the U.S. comes in reams of 500 sheets, no more, no fewer, and always 8.5 by 11 inches. SAT, ACT, GRE, MCAT, LSAT, and other tests constitute entrance standards to colleges and graduate schools. English is our standard language and the dollar our standard currency. Gas stations deliver gallons of gas, not liters. Credit ratings of individuals are accessible to everyone from the mortgage lender to the car dealer. Chemical solutions are measured against the universal concentration called "1 Normal." Water pressure is measure everywhere as P.S.I. (pounds per square inch). Cream is always sold by the pint. And if I am fifteen pounds overweight in Dayton, moving to Boston won't help matters; a pound is a pound is a pound. And for all these reasons and more, we get along quite efficiently.

However, the cultural embrace of standardization cost us something. It is self-evident today that church growth gurus are tempted to speak of growth in quantifiable terms. Mathematics is the ultimate form of standardization. But the cost to Christians may be even deeper. Again I draw on the work of historian John Staudenmaier to help us see what may have been lost in the standardization of society since 1815. A clear example of the start of this cultural shift can be found in the contrast that existed around the turn of the twentieth century between pre-standardized grain-shipping facilities of St. Louis and the standardized processes of Chicago.

For grain shipped from St. Louis, hand-bagged sacks of grain were loaded onto train cars. At the outer edge of the city, where the train tracks ended, the sacks of grain had to be loaded by laborers onto horse-drawn carts. Teamsters then drove these carts through the city to the river's edge where the sacks of grain were loaded, again by human laborers, onto riverboats for shipment.

28. Staudenmaier, "Perils of Progress Talk," 271.

In Chicago the system was quite different because the company that
owned tracks outside of town also owned track that ran through the city
all the way to the docks. Bulk-loaded grain cars could then be off-loaded
directly onto grain boats. In other words, the Chicago system rendered
human interaction and negotiation obsolete. Old-school St. Louis took
human interaction as a given and relied on face-to-face negotiation to
get work accomplished all along the route. "If the Chicago system was
a model of integration, speed, and efficiency, . . . the St. Louis market
preserved the integrity of each man's transaction and employed a host of
small entrepreneurs at every turn. . . ."[29] Staudenmaier raises the interesting question of whether the influence of standardization has resulted in
a culture-wide *atrophy* of human skills for navigating the social terrain.
His question is a good one. Once we are out of practice, who is to say we
do not lose altogether our former skills for negotiation?

This cultural shift is today being reproduced within the walls of
our churches. At stake are two different modes of living within Christian
community. One makes the assumption that, with a little tweaking, the
church is a well oiled machine, one that can run with little maintenance.
The other assumes that in order to get along, we'll have actually and
constantly to talk to each other, face-to-face, not about the weather, but
about things that matter most deeply to us and over which things we will
inevitably disagree. Because agreement on matters like politics, religion,
ethics, and the like is not guaranteed, our ability to "stay at table," to listen
charitably, to persuade with grace, and to compromise without full surrender, is a reflection of our maturity. To the extent we succeed, we are
living well. To the extent we can keep the conversation flourishing, we
are achieving what Paul describes to the church in Philippi: the mind
(*phronēsis*) of Christ. The corporate mind of Christ is possible because
we are, as the Body of Christ, an integrated whole. I may be a nose, and
you an arm, and your neighbor a big toe (!), but *together* we comprise
the single temple that God's Spirit inhabits. Paul writes, "for we [plural]
are the temple [singular] of the living God. . . ." (2 Cor 6:16). Conversely,
to the extent we live isolated from the living temple, we hamstring the
entire body.[30]

29. J. L. Larson cited in Staudenmaier, "Denying the Holy Dark," 192; emphasis in
original.

30. 1 Cor 12:26 employs indicative verbs: if one member suffers, all in fact do suffer
on account of the suffering of the one. See Kallenberg, "All Suffer the Affliction of the
One."

In contrast, a *standardized* mode of living within Christian community has about as much soul as a bag of marbles. Each marble is identical to all the others. Marbles roll with gravity and careen off their neighbors and other obstacles in their way. But on this view it simply makes no sense to speak of marbles "negotiating" their world. Rather, the standardized view presumes that the path followed by any marble is simply a function of cleverly arranged environment. And if all marbles are interchangeable, then the arrangement of the environment can be done from the outside via "scientific" principles that supposedly apply whether we are talking about running a business or growing a church.

Instrumentalism

The third effect of technopoly is instrumentalism. The technological world proceeds on the assumption that every technological artifact is just a tool. A hammer is a technological artifact. Someone had to design it. When it is used to build a house, it is good. When it is used to bash in someone's skull, it is bad. By itself—or so this first view goes—a hammer is morally neutral.

Of course the greatest champions of instrumentalism are the technologists themselves—the scientists, the engineers, and the manufacturers. If each artifact is neutral, then technologists need not have many moral scruples about what they make. Sadly, Christians have increasingly signed on to an instrumental view of the high-tech world. A particularly disturbing example was reported in 2007 by *The New York Times*. The story involves the use of a popular video game as the instrument for luring young men back to church. The game is "Halo 3," a war simulation game given a "M" (mature) rating by the entertainment industry for its graphic violence. Explains one twelve-year-old who comes to play: "It's just fun blowing people up."[31] Admittedly the end, namely church attendance, is good. But is the means (a violent video game) a morally neutral instrument, or one that is out of sync with the Sermon on the Mount? Or is it more acceptable or less to produce an explicitly "Christian" version of a violent video game? The *Left Behind* video game series was reviewed by *Newsweek Magazine* as characterized by top-shelf design but "a level of violence reminiscent of Grand Theft Auto."[32] For those unfamiliar

31. Richtel, "Thou Shalt Not Kill, except in a Game at Church."
32. Ness, "Culture: Gamers' Good News."

with the comparison, one version, *Grand Theft Auto: San Andreas*, was banned in Australia for its violence.

And, obviously, some technological artifacts *can* be used for good or evil ends. However, we get a skewed view if we insist that the moral quality is entirely and always the use to which a given technology is put. If it is the case that each technology is morally neutral by nature, then when we study culture and study the moral character of a culture, we could ignore the technological particulars. Technology would be nothing more than an add-on.

The opposite of instrumentalism is the view that technology *has* moral and political properties.[33] There are at least three reasons to not treat technology as morally neutral. First, there are some *inherently* political technologies that by the very nature of their political character raise moral questions about right and wrong exercise of power.[34] The clearest examples are nuclear technologies. Obviously a country in possession of a nuclear weapon necessarily has to have a matching hierarchical, authoritarian form of government capable of overseeing such dangers. The same is true of countries that do not have nuclear weapons but are powered by nuclear reactors. In real life, you'll never find Homer Simpson working in a nuclear power plant! No, nuclear plants employ only those who are capable of following strict protocol, protocol that has been designed and enforced by the brightest nuclear engineers and backed by a powerful government, which for its part has designed armed responses for possible terrorist scenarios. But the question of freedom restriction may be moot for countries relying on renewable energy such as wind or solar power. Rulers of countries driven by renewable energy probably do not lay awake at night worrying, "What if a wind turbine fell into the wrong hands?!"

A second reason we ought not consider technology neutral is that in solving practical problems in a particular time and place, certain local artifacts display community-shaping properties. Sometimes the effects can be very positive and widespread. For example, during the 1970s the nation undertook enormous transformation to become handicap accessible. Wider sidewalks, specialized bathroom stalls, ramps, and elevators are now standard in all public buildings. From sidewalk ramps to

33. There is a difference between assigning blame and locating evil. Even when blame cannot be assigned, we are still able to tell that something is deeply wrong.

34. The following argument is from Winner, "Do Artifacts Have Politics?"

extra-wide café tables at Starbucks, each handicap-accessible innovation resonates with Jesus' admonition to care for the marginal members of society. Even if these artifacts are designed, built, installed, and maintained by non-Christians, followers of Jesus say these artifacts are morally good precisely because the artifacts themselves embody Jesus' own care for the "least of these" (Matthew 25).

Conversely, particular technological artifacts can foster local evil as well as good. In 1936, Robert Moses (1888–1981) was awarded the Cornelius Amory Pugsley Gold Medal Award "for his services in extending and developing the parks and parkways in Greater New York."[35] Moses held as many as twelve different New York City and State jobs simultaneously and earned a reputation for being "the man who gets things done." During his reign, he more than tripled the number of playgrounds in NYC—a good thing. But by all accounts he was a power-hungry, egocentric, violent, and racist man capable of great harm. Under Moses' watch, clumsy intersections were replaced by scenic overpasses and elegant throughways that allowed traffic to flow smoothly. Two hundred of these overpasses were constructed over the beautiful parkways that led to the parks and beaches. Now the nefarious part: these two hundred overpasses were built with a maximum clearance of only nine feet. Because city busses were twelve feet tall, low bridges effectively *excluded* those who rode busses, namely poor people, especially blacks and Latinos, from having access to the posh parks and beaches. This outcome was not an oversight. Moses *intended* these overpasses for evil, and as such, the use to which they were put *was* evil. Moses is long dead, but the overpasses remain standing, perpetuating moral evil without any human agent willing it so. It is almost as if these overpasses were living minions carrying forward the evil designs of their maker.[36]

A third reason that technology is not morally neutral is that technologies are "addictive." Not all successful technologies are addictive. Staudenmaier compares dental floss to asphalt roads. Consider dental floss.[37] As a plaque-removal device, floss is highly successful. In recent

35. Online: http://rptsweb.tamu.edu/Pugsley/Moses.htm.

36. The suggestion I just made, that technology can take on a life of its own, was very much at home in the New Testament. I will take up this discussion in more detail in chapter 5.

37. I am indebted to my friend, John Staudenmaier, for the contrast between floss and asphalt in displaying two different notions of "successful" with respect to technology.

years, floss evolved from string to waxed tape. And the dispenser itself has improved in a number of ways. But let's be honest: if all the floss in the world were to disappear overnight, no one would notice! So, floss may be as successful as a technology can be. But few if any are "addicted" to floss.

But now consider asphalt roadways. Growing up in Minnesota, we had two seasons: winter and road repair. As a technological artifact, asphalt roads are barely adequate. They buckle in the summer sun while shrinking, cracking, and crumbling during the frigid winters and relentless pounding of large trucks. So, road crews repair asphalt roads endlessly.

But could we do without them? Before 1900, yes. But not since then. Of course, our dependence on asphalt has grown hand in hand with the role the automobile has come to play in our lives. But let's just think about asphalt for now. Consumer spending makes up 70 percent of America's Gross Domestic Product.[38] Nearly everything we purchase and consume comes from somewhere farther away than can be reached by walking. The vast bulk of it is delivered by trucks that depend on asphalt highways and service roads to get their goods to shopping areas. Then when a consumer wants to make a purchase, how do we reach the shopping areas? I recall as a child in the 1960s watching a little old lady—Grandma Anderson—*walk* the two blocks to the Red Owl grocery store and back again carrying a sack of groceries. She did this every day as long as I can remember. But anymore big chain grocery stores model themselves after the indoor malls. And which of the malls are accessible by foot? I mean, not only are they located far away from population centers, most malls are inaccessible to pedestrians. High speed multi-lane traffic whizzes around the shopping property. Traffic lights control the cars, but many intersections lack pedestrian crossings! The mall itself is surrounded by a sea of asphalt. While cars are zigzagging across the lot, pedestrians, stranded without sidewalks, are left to their own wits to get inside safely. You might think I exaggerate, but try walking safely from one end to the other of a mall parking lot with a stroller and a couple of five-year olds in tow! Ironically, the mall parking lot that is so vast only makes full use of its capacity on two days a year: Black Friday and December 26.

Whether for good or ill, American Christianity has accommodated itself to the automotive culture. A century ago, churches were built in

38. Siegel and Langfitt, "Wholesale Price Jump Dampens Good Retail News."

urban areas, because that's where the people lived.[39] The front doors of these churches not only faced the city welcoming all passers-by, the front doors were just steps from the sidewalk. But since the "mallification" of America, churches are now *designed* with their backs to the city. And the front doors of the church open up onto what?—a parking lot large enough to accommodate the two big "shopping" days of the year: Christmas and Easter. Of course, a healthy megachurch fills the lot many times a year; some do it more than once a week. But because of the immensity of the asphalt lot, megachurches cannot be built downtown.[40] They are built far from the heart of the city and thus far from those who are too poor to own cars. Megachurches are no longer suburban phenomena, but "exburban" ones, breaking ground for the next donut of development outside the suburbs.

You'll notice that I've yet to issue an explicit criticism. I've only attempted to describe what is so often invisible, because it seems there's no other way it can be: if you want to attend a *growing* church, you've got to get there by car. But now consider this: I once was a member of a growing church. This church had recently abandoned their suburban location for one further out, a newly-constructed "campus" in the exburbs. I already lived in the suburbs, and for me it was only a seventeen-minute drive farther away from the city. The church quickly grew. So I proposed an outreach aimed to help the poor who lived across the river in the poorest, most segregated sections of the city. In effect, I was advised to drop my idea, not because it was a bad idea, but because church leaders fully expected no one to volunteer for a ministry *so far away from the church building*.[41] It was asphalt that made it possible to hold so many commuters in the lot. But it was also the great quantity of asphalt involved

39. For one fascinating moral account of change in church architecture, see Bess, "Building the Church."

40. The church I attended had approximately 2,000 attenders on a Sunday—1,000 for each of two services. The parking lot had approximately 850 spaces.

41. In Luke 14, Jesus tells a parable in which the master urges his servants to comb not only the highways, but also the roads less traveled. They were to work their way along the hedges, where the homeless, and the poor, blind and lame, and all the people who in today's world cannot drive cars, "and compel them to come in, that my house may be filled." (Luke 14:23). I've since transferred my membership to a downtown church. Everyday we give out sack lunches to homeless folk who walk up to our doors in hope of food. (Last month we gave out nearly 800 lunches.) Some of these walk back to the church on Sunday and sit through the service. At least two of these have joined the church.

that required them to locate the church so far away that the distance prevented ministry to the very population that was too poor to own cars needed for attendance.

THEOLOGICAL REFLECTION

The Gospel is a powerful and adaptable virus, capable of inhabiting and transforming any host culture! So my dark reflections are not intended to scare us but to alert us to a "worldview beneath the worldview." When I presented some of these thoughts to a conference of Christian colleagues, one of them (a historian at Duke) blurted out: "So, what are we supposed to *do*?!" I think the question is best answered this way: we respond to technopoly by being the church.

Three passages of Scripture issue calls to "come out." First, in John's *Revelation*, Christians are warned of the world order called "Babylon" and are called out: "Come out of her my people, that you may not participate in her sins and that you may not receive her plagues" (Rev 18:4).[42]

In Genesis 19, the penny drops for Abraham's nephew, Lot. He sees clearly the imminent doom of Sodom and pleads with his sons-in-law to "come out!" "Get up and out of this place, for the Lord will destroy the city." And then the ominous words: "But he appeared to his sons-in-law to be jesting" (Gen 19:14).

To his sons-in-law, Lot's warning was mistaken for a joke. Why? Could it be that they were already enslaved by the habits of Sodom, Babylon, Technopolis? For them it was too late: they saw the situation with cosmopolitan eyes.

Between these two biblical eras, between *Genesis*, the Beginning, and *Revelation*, the Ending, Paul wrote to the church at Corinth: "we together are the [one] temple of the living God; just as God said, 'I will dwell with them and walk among them, and I will be their God, and they shall be my people. . . .' Therefore," Paul continues, "come out from their midst and be separate" (2 Cor 6:16–17; internal citation is Isa 52:11).

The crucial term in Paul's plea is the tiny word "midst." We are called out of the midst of Technopolis into a different "midst"—the "midst" of

---

42. Are we complicit in Babylonian sin simply by driving through a Robert Moses underpass? YES! Distantly so, but the answer must still be "Yes" for any who ever drives a car. For it is the entire automotive industry that gave rise to the need for roads that became the occasion for Robert Moses's sins and the ongoing evil of his racist bridges. Who then shall escape being tainted? Thus the call goes forth: "Come out of Babylon."

Christian community. This midst is where God's Spirit dwells; this midst is where the mind of Christ is imitated; this midst is where God walks. God dwells in the realm of the in-between.

But in the in-between is also the place where we walk and work and worship and pray and love. The tiny word "midst" connotes how we structure our lives together. When Paul in another epistle writes "conduct your interactions among yourselves in a manner worthy of the Gospel,"[43] he uses the verb *politeuomai*. Those of you who remember your Greek will recognize the similarity of this verb to the word for city, *polis*. Our corporate conduct, our whole pattern of interactions with each other and as a group toward the outside world (and not merely our individual behavior), is what makes us into the *polis* or community of God.

So the way we "come out of their midst" is not by physically leaving Western culture. Rather, it is by restructuring our lives together in ways that show that we "keep in step with the Spirit" (Gal 5:24) of the Gospel rather than with the spirit of technological determinism.

---

43. Phil 1:27: *Monon axiōs tou euangeliou tou Christou politeuesthe.*

2

Is Technology Good News?

I T IS MY HABIT to pray a Psalm every morning. At the time I was preparing this chapter, I was praying Psalm 92. The Psalm opens with a declaration that of all the goods we might pursue, one of the goods worth living for is the giving of witness. "It is good to give thanks to the Lord," writes the Psalmist. It is good "to sing praise to thy name," it is good to declare "thy lovingkindness in the morning," and it is good to declare "thy faithfulness by night" (Ps 92:1–2). If you've ever wondered what human life is *for*, the Psalm answers in no uncertain terms: the just man, the righteous woman will flourish—here it comes—"in order to declare that the Lord is upright; declare he is [our] rock, and declare there is no injustice in Him" (Ps 92:15).

I begin with the presupposition that the purpose of human life is, at least in part, giving witness to the character of God. In this chapter we will consider the effect of technology on evangelism by looking at the nature of human communication. In the next chapter we will consider the effect of technology on evangelism by looking very closely at the biblical texts concerning evangelism.

THE BROKENNESS OF HUMAN LANGUAGE

Evangelism is a challenging task. It is hard to imagine anything more daunting than trying to express the Infinite One in paltry human words. To make matters doubly problematic for us as *human* witnesses, the prophets tell us that we, both speakers and listeners, are shrouded by darkness. Isaiah wrote,

> Therefore, justice is far from us, and righteousness does not overtake us; we hope for light, but behold, darkness; for brightness, but we walk in gloom. We grope along the wall like blind men, we

grope like those who have no eyes. We stumble at midday as in the twilight, among those who are vigorous we are like dead men. (Isa 59:9–10 NASB)

Under these two conditions, clumsy language and darkened souls, the prophets declare that the glory of the Lord would one day shine: "For behold, darkness will cover the earth, and deep darkness the peoples; but the Lord will rise upon you and his glory will appear upon you" (Isa 60:2). These are the Scriptures of Christmas. And John's Gospel reports that the light shone spectacularly. Still, there is that lingering problem on the receiving end. "The light shines in the darkness, but the darkness did not comprehend it" (John 1:5).[1]

How is this possible? How did the light shine and the darkness successfully repel it? Part of the reason may be that the Gospel comes in the form of good news. And it belongs to the inherent nature of the news, even good news, to be rejectable if it is to remain *news* rather than, say, propaganda.[2] The Lord Jesus himself did not coerce others to understand. He was met by blank stares time and time again when he told his disciples plainly that he was to suffer and die and rise again (Luke 18:34 *et passim*). Think of what this means for ordinary human witnesses like you and me: ordinary human witnesses have no guaranteed method for compelling comprehension from those whom we evangelize.

Now, let's be honest. We all *hanker* after a means to coerce others to believe our witness. But not only are such means unavailable to us so long as it is news that we are sharing, God also entrusted the ministry of reconciliation to us as humans, who have no better tools with which to work than frail *human language*. Come to think of it, human speaking virtually never *compels* assent from a listener.

Maybe this weakness is simply the product of our fallen state. Sin has tainted every dimension of human existence. We neither reason clearly nor speak clearly. A great theologian of the last century wrote of our fallen state:

> . . . [I]t saddens us that we are so cut off from each other, that there are always such different worlds—you in your house and me in mine. This is simply not the way life is meant to be, this separate life we all lead. But with one single change we could have

---

1. I take the *kai* as contrastive.
2. See Yoder, "On Not Being Ashamed of the Gospel."

infinitely more joy and good fortune and righteousness among us, if we could open our hearts and *talk* with each other.

And then we experience the fact that we are mute. Yes, we certainly talk with each other, we find words all right, but never the right words; never the words that would really do justice to what actually moves us, what actually lives in us; never words that would really lead us out of our loneliness into community. Our talk is always such an imperfect, wooden, dead talk. Fire will not break out in it, but can only smolder in our words.[3]

I've been studying philosophy of language for many years. One thing I've learned is that when thinking about human language, we must remember Pentecost. It is easy to forget Pentecost. Perhaps we forget in part because we have grown uncomfortable with the exuberance of some believers in the Lord Jesus. And perhaps it has become easy to overlook the Day of Pentecost in the church calendar, because Mother's Day often falls on the same day. But we *must* remember, because Pentecost is God's ongoing response to the inescapable contingencies of human language.

The brokenness of human language is emblematized by the story of Babel in Genesis 11. There we read that God saved people from their idolatrous designs by confusing their language. In our fallen state, human beings are worse off in a pack than they are in isolation.[4] So, as an act of grace, God weakened and confused human language until the day when their corporate sinfulness can be healed.

When would such corporate healing take place? Here's the good news: it has already begun! Luke the Evangelist makes sure we don't miss the fact that the curse of Babel begins to be reversed at Pentecost. At Babel, people from the same place began speaking in different languages. But in Jerusalem, fifty days after Jesus had risen, people from every sort of foreign country—Parthian and Medes and Elamites and you name it—all heard the praise of God in their native tongue.

The event called Pentecost is a single coin with two sides. On the one side is the amazing fact that God's Spirit came in a brand new manner, and came to stay. Good thing, too. For,

3. From Karl Barth, "Lukas 1:5–23," from *Predigten* 1917, 423–31 of the original German version. Cited in *Watch for the Light*, December 13; emphasis added.

4. This was an oft-repeated theme in Reinhold Niebuhr's theology. See, for example, Niebuhr, *Moral Man and Immoral Society*.

Without the Holy Spirit, God remains distant, Christ remains in the past, the Gospel remains a dead letter. Without the Spirit, the Church is merely another organization, authority becomes tyranny, mission is only propaganda, the liturgy is a simple remembrance, and Christian life takes on the atmosphere of slavery. But in the Spirit, in an indissoluble synergism, the cosmos is freed and becomes a foreshadowing of the Reign of God, humans struggle against the flesh, and the Risen Christ is already present. The Gospel becomes a vivifying force; the Church echoes the Trinitarian communion; authority is Pentecostal; the liturgy is a memorial and an anticipation; and human activity is divinized.[5]

On the other side of the coin, Pentecost is the perpetual reminder that the Holy Spirit so animated a motley group of ordinary human beings that the Incarnation was *extended* because of them. Wow! Make no mistake, Christ is the Head. But because of Pentecost, we have become Christ's body. Paul's words are unmistakable: "you all [together] are the body of Christ and individually each of you are members of it."[6]

Does this mean that human language has been completely repaired? Alas! No. We eagerly anticipate a day when every knee shall bow and every tongue confess that Jesus Christ is Lord (Phil 2:10–11). But it is not this day. We live in the church era, between Pentecost and the Eschaton. And in this present age, even with the enduring presence and repeated fillings of the Holy Spirit, we cannot escape difficulty and contingency in our living and speaking.[7] That is why New Testament writers call our sojourn a struggle, even a war.

What then is the advantage after Pentecost? Great in every respect! Speaking narrowly about language, language has *begun* to be repaired. It is just that we are still in process. What does this mean for that very particular act of communication called evangelism? Here's a road map for the rest of this chapter. I'll begin by describing a problem that technology poses for evangelism and one church's attempt to deal with this problem. Second, I'll discuss three weaknesses of human communica-

5. The words are those of Ignatius IV (Hazim) of the Eastern Orthodox Church. He is currently the Patriarch of Antioch and All the East. Cited in Aguilera and Arnaiz, *Enfleshing the Word*, 221.

6. 1 Cor 12:27: *humeis de este sōma Christou kai melē ek merous.*

7. John Bowlin argues persuasively that contingency and difficulty are good things in the hands of the Spirit through whom a virtuous character can be formed precisely because life is difficult. See Bowlin, *Contingency and Fortune in Aquinas's Ethics.*

tion that God was pleased *not* to remove at Pentecost. And finally, I'll draw some practical conclusions about our relationship to technology with respect to evangelism and discipleship.

The Non-Place called "Second Life"

I've recently read a series of disturbing news reports involving a site in cyberspace called "Second Life." Its not really a Web site (at least not in the Web 1.0 sense of the term), but more of a "3-D virtual world built and owned by its residents."[8] Everything is a cartoon, but because it is repeatedly remade and re-remade by visitors it spookily has come to mirror the real world to the smallest detail. Inhabitants get jobs, earn and spend money (called "lindens"), buy property, and so on. So realistic is this virtual world that psychologists tell us that relationships between online characters (called "avatars") are mimicked even down to the smallest unconscious norms we follow in real-life, such as not crowding another's "personal space." Not surprisingly, real-world persons often form deep attachments and find their own emotional dispositions being shaped in response to avatars they meet and situations in which they find themselves in Second Life.[9]

The headlines of one article asked "Is this Man Cheating on His Wife?"[10] The story details the daily life of a real-world man named Ric.

> While his wife Sue watches television in the living room, [Ric] chats online with what appears on the screen to be a tall, slim redhead.
>
> He's never met the woman outside of the computer world of Second Life, a well-chronicled digital fantasyland with more than eight million registered "residents" who get jobs, attend concerts and date other users. He's never so much as spoken to her on the telephone. But their relationship has taken on curiously real dimensions. They own two dogs, pay a mortgage together and spend hours shopping at the mall and taking long motorcycle rides. This May, when [Ric], 53, needed real-life surgery, the redhead cheered him up with a private island that cost her $120,000 in the virtual world's currency, or about $480 in real-world dollars. Their bond is so strong that three months ago, [Ric] asked

8. Teague, "Give Me That Online Religion."

9. On the ability of human beings to form *bodily* dispositions in response to non-bodily realities such as ideas or virtual worlds, see Harak, *Virtuous Passions*.

10. Alter, "Is This Man Cheating on His Wife?"

[Janet], the 38-year-old Canadian woman who controls the red-head, to become his virtual wife. The woman he's legally wed to is not amused.[11]

Like other active Second Life users, Ric typically spends between twenty and forty hours online each week. Ric's avatar owns a mall, a private beach club, a dance club, and a strip club. He oversees twenty-five "employees," each employee avatar being controlled by a single real-life gamer somewhere else on the planet.

The draw of Second Life seems to be the way it enables players to improve their alter egos without any of the fuss that real-world living involves. Avatars need not be caught by the surprise of traffic delays. They can simply teleport between locations. And while money can be made or lost, physical characteristics don't require self-control, exercise, and perseverance. One can simply *purchase* ripped abdominal muscles or big biceps without any of the daily grind of working out. Male-pattern baldness can likewise be solved by simply purchasing special long wavy hair that sways when you walk. Chest hair is also for sale. In other words, everything that goes into character development in real life—difficulties, genetics, contingency, a time-tested way of wisdom—are all rendered obsolete in Second Life.

The question I want to consider is whether the prerequisites for successful human communication fatally hinders virtual evangelism. Of course, some churches are trying to give witness within Second Life. One church in Oklahoma City has reportedly sunk *thousands* of real-world dollars into establishing a virtual church in Second Life, one whose services are simulcasts of the real-world services. In other words, users teleport their avatars to the front door of the church and search around until they find the auditorium. While the avatars sit in theater seating, the real-world user can consume the digital video streamed live from the real-world church service in Oklahoma City.

The Second Life version of church is a "come-as-you-are" affair. One of the avatars attends this virtual church in the form of a six-foot cheetah dressed in Hawaiian shorts and a T-shirt. The corresponding real-world operator said that he liked a church in which he could really "be himself."

11. Ibid.

So here is the question: Can the Gospel be communicated in Second Life? If the same message is preached live in Oklahoma City and digitally streamed in Second Life, isn't the message the same?

Prerequisites for Human Communication

My thesis is that the Holy Spirit didn't finish repairing human language at Pentecost because certain conditions for human speaking must still be met in order for us to communicate with nonbelievers so desperately in need of Good News. There are three conditions for successful communication.

HUMAN COMMUNICATION TAKES TIME

First, human communication is timeful, it requires time. There is a beginning, a middle, and an end to every sentence. There is a beginning, a middle, and an end to every paragraph. To move from the beginning to the end takes time. This is not a deficiency of language; this is the crux, the very thing that makes it work. For in the time it takes to move from the beginning to the ending, crucial relationships are built up between the words of a sentence, and between sentences of a paragraph, and between paragraphs of a chapter, and so on. If we managed to purge speaking of its timefulness, we wouldn't have to read textbooks anymore! We could just read a dictionary. Boring, to be sure. But hey, all the words every author uses are in the dictionary. So if the order of the words—the part that requires time—doesn't matter, the dictionary becomes the ultimate shortcut to knowing everything!

But human communication, whether written or spoken, *does* require time. How much time does it take? If it takes twenty hours to read a book, who wouldn't want to be able to read it in ten or even five hours? Isn't trimming waste and reading more efficiently part of "redeeming the time" (Eph 5:16)? Maybe. But is efficiency always our friend? My wife and I just invested in a nifty device: a microwave fireplace. That way, we can have a relaxing evening at home in just three minutes! You get the point.

How many here want to go on an "efficient" date? After all, you're busy. Why not cut out all the waste by eliminating all the pauses in your conversation. After that, we can work on speeding up delivery. I'm sure with practice you can compress and entire evening's worth of conversation into about fifteen minutes.

Of course, I'm being ridiculous. But isn't the pace of delivery crucial to communication? Listen to the words of Psalm 46: "*BestillandknowthatIamGod!*" . . . "Be-still-and-know-that-I-am-God" vs. "Be . . . still . . . and . . . know . . . that . . . I . . . am . . . God." It makes a difference, doesn't it? Do you remember what Treebeard said to Merry and Pippin in the movie version of Tolkien's *Lord of the Rings*? ". . . you must understand, young hobbit. It takes a long time to say anything in old Entish, and we never say anything unless it is worth taking a long time to say." What holds for Ents also holds for human beings. For each message we want to convey, there is a pace that is just right. Successful communication means finding that pace.

Technology threatens the timefulness of communicating. Think of how fast news traveled in our great-grandparents' day. The operative word is "travel." News was like people or cargo. It had to be *carried*.[12] For example, when did Californians find out what Lincoln said in his 1860 Inaugural Address? This story had to be carried by horseback. The Pony Express set the land-record for that particular 2,000-mile journey in seven days, seventeen hours at an average speed of almost eleven miles per hour—which, incidentally, was still faster than trains! It took just over a week. When did Europeans learn of Lincoln's address? Well, how fast can the Atlantic be sailed?

Less than a year later, the first transcontinental telegraph line was completed (1861), forever putting the Pony Express out of business. News was still carried to Europe by ship for another five years, until the transatlantic cable was completed (1866). Keep in mind that in those days, a single telegraph cable could carry a single message at a time. So, even though the two continents were linked by the speed of light, only the most important news was sent by telegraph to Europe: . . . one . . . letter . . . at . . . a . . . time.

How fast does news "travel" today? The metaphor doesn't even work any more. News doesn't travel; information distribution is instantaneous. Rather, we have to speak about news "spreading"—indicating that human beings themselves are the rate-determining step. *We* bog down

12. There were early systems of visual transmission that predated the pony express. They operated much like the Beacons of Minas Tirith in Tolkien's *Lord of the Rings*. For example, Claude Chappe invented a system of visual semaphores in the early 1790s. By it he was able to transmit a message ten miles. Since the experiment depended on two perfectly synchronized pendulum clocks, the transmission of data—letter by letter— was very cumbersome. See Holzmann and Pehrson, *Early History of Data Networks*.

the works because of lag time on our end—*we* log on to computers, *we* download emails, and it takes us a second or three to click "reply."

So how fast has information distribution become? In April of 2007, hackers sent a spoof email to Apple employees, disguised as an internal Apple news alert, claiming that the release of the iPhone would be delayed by four months. Within two hours, Apple corporate office calmly posted a rebuttal, exposing the fraud and assuring employees that all was well. But it was too late; the false rumor had been leaked and ended up as a post on a reputable techie blog site (called *Engadget)*. How long did it take before Wall Street felt the effect of this post?

Seven minutes. Within seven minutes, Apple stock lost $2.8 billion. In this case, the truth spread more slowly than the rumor.[13] When the market closed four hours later, Apple stock was still down by $512 million.[14]

Does technology help or hinder our evangelism? If technology is neutral, there is nothing to worry about. And in some instances, technology is clearly advancing evangelism. My college friend Ed has spent twenty plus years with Wycliffe Bible Translators, living in the foothills of the Himalayas creating a written language for the "T" people. Computers are invaluable to his work there. And because he uses computers, a translation of the Gospel of Mark (and others) is for the first time available to this preliterate people.

However, if each message that humans speak requires a pace that is just right, we should at least ask the question of whether the sheer speed of technology threatens to distort the Gospel message by delivering it at the wrong pace. Now, I'm not so dense as to overlook the fact that *people* usually supply the right pace as they *read* an online message. But the timefulness of communication is more than just pace. The just-right pace is the pace that allows a *reciprocal* flow, a give and take, of words. When communication is instantaneous, we think we have to put the whole thing, the entirety of the Gospel—pearls and all (Matt 7:6!)—out there in cyberspace for grazers to stumble across. We would not want them to miss anything. But in this dump-truck approach, what is lost is the give and take of evangelism.

13. For an interesting account of the enduring character of falsehood on the internet, see Nakashima, "Harsh Words Die Hard on the Web."

14. Diaz, "Little E-Mail Prank."

By "give and take," I mean that evangelism, like all human communication, is an ongoing process. Possibilities for misunderstanding are endless, especially when the topic may be entirely unfamiliar to the friend with whom we are trying to share the Gospel. The philosopher Ludwig Wittgenstein's illustration is apt for what can happen in evangelism: "In a conversation: One person throws a ball; the other does not know: whether he is supposed to throw it back, or throw it to a third person, or leave it on the ground, or pick it up and put it in his pocket, etc."[15] Successful communication is like teaching someone a more complicated game than catch. So, give and take, moves and mismoves, false starts and course corrections. Remember that when Paul preached in Athens, a significant number of his audience were still "in process" when he finished speaking. They could not digest any more if they'd wanted to. They told Paul quite honestly in Acts 17:32, "we will hear you again." They weren't being shifty or evasive. They simply needed time to process.

In addition to threatening the pace and flow of human communication, the drive for speedy delivery of information has pedagogically backfired. Instead of creating an Information Superhighway, human beings have been dazzled by the sheer volume and speed of information so that they have retreated into tiny information neighborhoods where they only talk to others like themselves and read from an abbreviated list of pre-selected news sources.[16]

Let me offer a story that seems more in keeping with Christian identity. The University of St. Thomas is producing a new "Illuminated Bible." Before there were printing presses, monasteries considered it their calling from God to make copies of Scriptures by hand. Great care went into the accuracy of transmission. And great care went into the artwork in the margins so that the pictures both expressed worship and resonated with the content of the written word.

One of my colleagues had a chance to view some of the pages. Obviously, the pages that she looked at were very beautiful. But it wasn't

---

15. Wittgenstein, *Culture and Value*, 74e.

16. Cass Sunstein observed that information is so ubiquitous and is delivered so blindingly fast that assessment of any given Web site's quality is de facto left to *consumers* who, looking for shortcuts, simply pre-select their favorite *sources* of information. Unfortunately, consumers unwittingly select sources that tend to conform to their already unschooled prejudices. If our goal is evangelizing the unchurched via information technology, why would this group ever migrate away from their prejudicial favorites to read our pages? See Sunstein, "Daily We."

the ornamentation that arrested her attention. She realized that she had never seen such a large block of biblical text painstakingly written out in longhand. She realized how precious a gift it would be to receive hand-written Scriptures from a parent or a friend or a spiritual mentor who'd have taken so much time and tedious energy to pen the words.

Of course, handwriting was how it always used to be done. When Paul tells Timothy to pass on the things he had received, Paul wasn't only being metaphorical (2 Tim 2:2). Included in the list of what Timothy had received were large portions of Scripture. And in passing these on to faithful others, Timothy would have to take a great deal of *time* to write out copies longhand.

Imagine staring at a manuscript that could trace its lineage through the handwriting of actual Christians all the way back to the original that Paul penned for Timothy. Nothing magical about this. The point is simply the organic connection that we have through generations of Christians stretching all the way back to the first century. So, my colleague told me that she was *mesmerized* by these hand-written pages. And, more importantly, she felt palpably in touch with the entire Christian tradition.[17]

Human Communication takes Location

Human communication takes time. Second, and closely tied to the time-fulness of witnessing, is the role of *location* in successful human communication. Without place, hearers cannot tell if a sentence is truth or fiction.

Is the following sentence true or false: "France is hexagonal." How do we decide? Don't we need to know *where* such a sentence was spoken? If it was overheard at a map-makers convention, it would be obviously false. In point of fact, it was spoken in a war room by a French General who advocated six lines of defense against Hitler's advancing army, because "France is hexagonal."

How about this sentence. True or false: "All men are evil beasts." Doesn't it matter whether it is overheard in a tea shop where a bevy of women are recounting times they'd been jilted by jerks? All *males* are evil beasts. Then again, maybe it was spoken at a Billy Graham crusade. Now it becomes a statement about human depravity, and a very true

---

17. Obviously, those who use a writing utensil on paper or vellum or parchment are still using technology! But there is a difference in degree when we employ technologies in collaboration with human labor and when we use it to displace human labor.

one at that. For we are each and all evil beasts in need of rescuing from ourselves.

One more. True or false: "In the absence of women, men will not burn." How can we know whether this is true or false? Was this sentence found in a sexual psychology text or perhaps in the rulebook for a monastery: "In the absence of women, men will not burn." The actual *place* of this sentence was a German concentration camp. Soldiers were having trouble cremating batches of emaciated male corpses, because of their low percentage of body fat. After all, no one wanted to deal with leftovers, partially cremated body parts. Their solution was to make sure that each batch of corpses had a sufficient number of females, because of their higher percentage of body fat, for "In the absence of women, men will not burn."[18]

My claim is that location, place, is crucial for human communication to succeed. Some may object that my examples are not only in poor taste, they are far-fetched. "These aren't ordinary sentences." One response I'm tempted to give is that to non-Christian ears, virtually every sentence we speak is out of the ordinary. Listen: "God was in Christ reconciling the world to himself." Is that an ordinary sentence, plainly understood by anyone?

But I have a purpose deeper than defending a particular batch of examples. My deeper purpose is to draw attention to the bewitching way that technology tricks us into confusing the universal offer of the one true Gospel with a uniform mode of delivery.

In chapter 1, I described a revolution in engineering that I called "standardization." What resulted was a sort of one-size-fits-all approach to innovation and manufacturing. In their masterful book, *Cradle to Cradle*, William McDonnough and Michael Braungart illustrate the problem this way.

> In product design, a classic example of the universal design solution is mass-produced detergent. Major soap manufacturers design one detergent for all parts of the United States or Europe, even though water qualities and community needs differ. For example, customers in places with soft water, like the Northwest, need only small amounts of detergent. Those where the water is hard, like the Southwest, need more. But detergents are designed

18. Katz translates the sentence this way, "Men won't burn without women." Katz, "Technology and Genocide," 213.

so they will lather up, remove dirt, and kill germs efficiently the same way anywhere in the world—hard, soft, urban, or spring water, in water that flows into fish-filled streams and water channeled to sewage treatment plants. Manufacturers just add more chemical force to wipe out the conditions of circumstance. Imagine the strength a detergent must have to strip day-old grease from a greasy pan. Now imagine what happens when that detergent comes into contact with the slippery skin of a fish or the waxy coating of a plant. Treated and untreated effluents as well as runoff are released into lakes, rivers and oceans.[19]

These authors conclude that "one-size-fits-all" is really "design for a worst-case scenario." In order to achieve a baseline efficiency, "they design a product for the worst possible circumstances" and use that single product on every occasion.

Once technology embraced standardization, the rest of culture followed suit. To add to the list from chapter 1: driver-side airbags are now "standard"; living room wall sockets always deliver one hundred and twenty volts and accept the standard electric cord plug; newspapers report temperature in degrees Fahrenheit; the same postage stamp will deliver a letter anywhere in the U.S.; manufactured goods must meet ISO specs; electrical devices must conform to UL standards; emotional conditions of patients are assessed by standard psychological tests such as the MMPI; and if I purchase a lamp in Seattle and light bulbs in Amarillo, I expect the thing to plug in and give light in Memphis.

Fortunately, not every human practice adopts a one-size-fits-all approach. For example, if you've got strep throat, the doctor doesn't put a cast on both your legs, take out your appendix and give you chemotherapy! The physician tailors treatment to the disease and to the person. But if one-size-fits-all doesn't work in medicine, why do we so unblinkingly lean toward a one-size-fits-all approach in so much of our living? There is even growing evidence of a disturbing trend toward one-size-fits-all Christian ministry.

I think you know what I mean. Technology sometimes tricks us into ignoring *place*. For example, we sometimes think that because we *can* pipe in a superior preacher from far away on a Sunday morning, we *ought* to do so. I realize I'm stepping on some toes, but hear me out. Let

19. McDonough and Braungart, *Cradle to Cradle*, 29–30.

me offer a couple of extreme examples. I'll leave it to you to discern the local applications.

First, I read an early draft of chapter 1 to a group of colleagues, all Baptist ethicists. In our discussion of my paper, a nationally known author told the group that he and his family recently visited the satellite campus of a megachurch in Atlanta. He was stunned when the sermon came in the form of a "hologram." At least that's what it looked like to my friend. The pastor was projected onto no visible screen and positioned so realistically on the stage that it looked like he was actually standing there. But he wasn't. (By the way, is this truth-telling or a form of deception?) My friend reports that he was able to detect that it was a projection only because he was seated at extreme stage left. But he heard from others that some visitors don't realize that the speaker isn't really there.[20]

If that weren't enough, he was even more dismayed by what happened outside the auditorium. He asked several volunteers, important folk who wore nametags and directed people places, "Who is the pastor here? I know that so-and-so does the preaching by video, but who is the pastor if you need something or someone?" You see the problem, right? The "preacher" shows up as a hologram for thirty minutes every Sunday morning. So, who fills the role of "pastor?" Their answer? *They did not know the answer.* Not one of those whom he asked could identify a living, present pastor. I wonder what St. Paul, the author of those great texts about the Body of Christ and the body-ness of Christianity (1 Corinthians 12 and Ephesians 4), would have to say. Incidentally, in 2005 churches in the U.S. spent $8.1 *billion* on projection equipment.[21]

Story number two. While in Minneapolis over Christmas break, I visited an evangelical church with whom I've stayed in touch for thirty years. The pastor, fairly recently called to this church, was very upbeat in his announcement of a conference that the church would host. Not a conference with live speakers, mind you. But rather, a DVD conference. In fact, the pastor endorsed the conference "by faith," since he had

20. As it turned out, it wasn't a genuine hologram. However, the technology is now available to use spinning mirror screens to generate 3D images at twenty frames per second. I fear that it is only a matter of time before a church pays out to have one of these.

21. Dickson and Rampell, "Worship Goes Big-Screen and Hi-Fi, with Direct-Deposit Tithing." For an important analysis of the role of technology in worship, see Schultze, *Habits of the High-Tech Heart* and *High-Tech Worship?*

not previewed the DVDs. Later, I glanced through the rest of the bul-
letin and noticed three upcoming adult Sunday School classes that were
scheduled to start after New Year's. Two of the three were also classes
via DVD. You probably know the type: talking head and short dramatic
clips followed by group discussion to be facilitated by a well-intentioned
volunteer who may or may not be able to answer a *real* question. And
therein lies the problem, for authentic and genuine questioning belongs
to the very sort of conversation necessary for growth but not covered in
the prepackaged one-size-fits-all training manual.

To their credit, in this particular evangelical church, there *was* one
class scheduled that was to be taught by a live teacher. In fact, it was also
the *only* scheduled class that investigated a book of Scripture as the topic
of study. And this class was taught by an eighty-two-year-old man who'd
been filling this important role for at least thirty-three years. Please do not
misunderstand. This eighty-two-year-old man is the *hero* of my story. I
know him personally. He has studied the Bible diligently in large groups,
in small groups, and personally for the thirty-three years I've known
him. But where are his compatriots? Where is the sixty-year-old Bible
teacher? Where is the fifty-year-old Bible teacher? The forty-year-old
Bible teacher? I pray that I am wrong. But my fear for this congregation
is that readily available, pre-packaged, one-size-fits-all DVD classes have
made this church neglect the urgent need to educate several generations
of Bible teachers (or at least to flush them out of the woodwork). If ever
the church of the Lord Jesus needed heroes like this eighty-two-year-old
man, who, knowing both the Scripture and the local lay of the land, is
able to apply the Bible to this time and place and people, it is now. This
man is neither hologram nor "campus director" but what Paul termed a
pastor-teacher (Eph 4:11).[22]

HUMAN COMMUNICATION TAKES BODIES

What does it take for human communication to succeed? It takes time.
It takes location. Third, it takes physicality. By the term "physicality" I
mean that human language—no matter how abstract or conceptual—at
its deepest level is connected to our bodies and to the way our bodies
bump into each other!

---

22. I take the *kai* as emphatic since the particle *de* does the work of the conjunction
"and." Thus the term ought to be read "pastors even teachers" or more naturally, "pastor-
teachers": *tous de prophētas, tous de euangelistas, tous de poimenas kai didaskalous.*

Bodies are very important to God. We'll see this again in the next chapter when we consider the biblical texts about the nature of our witness. The apex of the redemption story is not the casting off of our bodies, but the resurrection of them.[23] If we could get along fine without bodies, God wouldn't take the trouble to resurrect them. There must be something inherently human about our embodied state and that without them we'd be something inferior. Doubtless, resurrected bodies will be a drastic improvement over the death-infested version we are now. Our new bodies won't break down or wear out. That wonderful promise also means that we'll be stuck with them . . . for all eternity!

The fact that bodies are important to God means that when God sent word announcing our salvation, he didn't send a philosophical treatise, he sent a body: "And the Word became flesh and tabernacled among us." And by means of this body, John continues, the first disciples were able to behold "his glory, glory as of the only begotten of the Father, full of grace and truth" (John 1:14). The properties of grace and truth were not perceived *in spite* of Jesus' body, but *by means of his body*! In his first epistle, the same John insists that the content of his witness is precisely "what we have *heard*, what we have *seen with our eyes*, what we *beheld* and our *hands handled . . .*" (1 John 1:1).

There is something about bodies that is crucial to human communication. Consider this sentence: "Last night my wife nuked some leftovers." Can anyone today be in doubt as to the meaning of this sentence? Yet thirty years ago, the sentence wouldn't have made sense. But since the microwave went retail in the 1970s, it has become a standard feature in every kitchen. Around the device a whole new speech pattern evolved.

Imagine trying to explain "nuking leftovers" to your great-grandparent. Until they'd seen it done, they'd never comfortably or naturally be able to use the phrase "nuking leftovers." Now imagine trying to translate the idea of "nuking" to aboriginal peoples who do not have the requisite

---

23. Perhaps the most unfortunate mark of Neo-Platonism in Augustine's theology is his equating soul with person (cp. Augustine, "Greatness of the Soul," 30.59 with Ennead IV 7 8). Not only is free will located in the soul (36.80) but the soul uses the body like a tool. The soul uses the body, rules the body, and eagerly waits to cast off the body: *"And that the soul may not be impeded from giving full allegiance to the fullness of truth, death—meaning complete escape and acquittal from this body—which previously was feared, is now desired as the greatest boon"* (33.76, italics added). Although Augustine gives lip service to the resurrection (33.76), in this early Augustine writing, the human body is not integral to the self.

background concepts such as "electricity," "refrigeration," and "radiation" needed for comprehending the phrase "nuking leftovers." Or to say the same thing differently, our concept of "nuking" is bound up with our complicated form of life,[24] here, now—in these bodies in this time and in this place.

Given the importance of the Incarnation, whereby the Eternal Word took on human form, it shouldn't surprise us to learn that as creatures of God *all* of our linguistic concepts[25] are extensions of bodily experience.[26] Now, I'll grant that this isn't the way that we normally think about language. Ordinarily, we think that language is learned by *pointing* and *naming*.[27] "Bottle," "podium," "chair," and so on. It is not by accident that perhaps the greatest insights in philosophy of language came from a philosopher who, between jobs, served the poor by teaching elementary school children. His first insight was simple enough: long before children learn that there are "physical objects" that need "naming"—both abstract concepts—they get *physically* involved with the particular things around them. His second insight was far more profound: *this process never ends.* Adults, like children, extend their fluency in their primary language not by naming but by doing. Thus Ludwig Wittgenstein carefully remarked that "It is part of the grammar of the word 'chair' that *this* [sitting down] is what we call 'to sit on a chair.'"[28] His point? We only truly understand how to use the word "chair" in a sentence by virtue of our dealings with chairs. Chairs are things we sit in, fetch, count, reupholster, stand on, trip

24. The phrase "form of life" is Wittgenstein's, *Philosophical Investigations*, 174e.

25. When I speak about language, I'm not talking about natural languages such as French or Chinese. I'm talking about *conceptual* languages. People who speak the same natural language, such as English, may be worlds apart because their English words embody different concepts. And vice versa.

26. The following seven paragraphs have been adapted from Kallenberg, *Live to Tell*.

27. As Augustine famously wrote: "When they (my elders) name some object, and accordingly moved towards something, I saw this and I grasped that the thing was called by the sound they uttered when they meant to point it out. Their intention was shewn by their bodily movements, as it were the natural language of all peoples: the expression of the face, the play of the eyes, the movements of other parts of the body, and the tone of voice which expresses our state of mind in seeking, having, rejecting, or avoiding something. Thus, as I heard words repeatedly used in their proper places in various sentences, I gradually learnt to understand what objects they signified; and after I had trained my mouth to form these signs, I used them to express my own desires." *Confessions* I.8, cited in Wittgenstein, *Philosophical Investigations*, §1.

28. Wittgenstein, *Blue and Brown Books*, 24.

over, stub our toes on, etc. Without these activities, "chair" would be a vacuous concept.

I'll admit that this claim isn't obvious. That's because the mode of our own fluency is transparent to us. Much of what goes for "extending our fluency" often boils down to translating a so-called "new" concept into something we already know. For example, having never seen the word "obdurate" before, I don't go out and interact with obdurate persons in order to get a hands-on sense of the term! Rather, I look it up in a dictionary and learn to swap "obdurate" for its synonym, "stubborn."

However, this coping strategy fails when we encounter a brand new field. For example, one can never supply a synonym for the term "partial differential equation!" One can only learn what partial differential equations are by hours and hours of learning calculus under the tutelage of a mathematician. When adults are faced by entirely foreign concepts, whether these come from mathematics or Christian doctrine, there may be no synonyms. Sometimes the only way to learn new concepts is by participation.

Think of how a small child learns a word like "shoes." Children learn to speak about the same time they learn to walk. Of course, children prefer to tool around on bare tippy-toes, and the wrestling match that is mistaken for getting a young child dressed isn't over until shoes are found, matched, wedged on (don't forget to straighten the child's toes), laced, tied, and double-tied. All the while, the parent is talking "Now then, where are your sho . . . Ah! Here they are. Let's put on your . . . sit still, please!, while we finish putting on your *shoes.*" And still some children manage to kick off their shoes before they even get down the hallway! Moving at full speed through a room whose floor is scattered with Lego blocks, the barefoot child winces with surprise and screams out in pain. After rushing to the rescue, the parent soothes the child with a word spoken with great tenderness: "shoes." Slowly the child begins to associate the word "shoe" with a variety of activities. Shoes are for wearing, throwing, dropping, losing, kicking off, finding, lacing, unlacing, mismatching, knotting, double-tying, and so forth. Apart from these activities, the word "shoe" has no meaning.

In the hurly-burly of each day, the child begins to pair the word "shoe" with all the activities associated with shoes. Sentences that include the word "shoe" come to have a sense for the child *because of the activities.* Without such activities, the word "shoe" would remain as enigmatic

for the child as the word "enigmatic"! We might even say that such activities imprint the child with the sense of the word "shoe."

If words of simple objects such as shoes are learned by their proximity to certain activities, then the basis of a child's fluency in a language
is *participation* in these activities. While wearing shoes is a simple activity that makes sense for its own sake, some activities are more closely
tied with *complex* behaviors that only make sense in community.

So, imagine asking a young child, "Who is God?" What will the answer sound like? Will the child say "God" is "the ground of our Being,"
"the First Cause," or the "cosmic Omega Point?" No. A child learns who
God is by pairing the word with those activities in which the word "God"
is at home. In other words, the child is apt to say, "God is the one we pray
to." "God is the one we thank before we eat." "God is the one we sing
songs about . . . and tell our friends about . . . and confess our sins to."
Only by virtue of these activities does the word "God" mean anything at
all to this child.

But now think of the atheist. I'll grant that there are atheists who
are theists in denial. And some have "converted" to atheism after years in
the church. Communicating with these folks is fraught with special difficulties. But there are also genuine atheists who have had absolutely no
contact with Christian practice over the course of their entire lives. This
second kind of atheist *never* prays. They never give thanks to God. They
never sing praise to God. They certainly don't tell their friends about
God. And while they likely know the pangs of guilt, they never confess
their sins *to God*. For these persons, the word "God" may be in their
vocabulary, but as far as we are concerned, it is not who we're talking
about. Same word, different Person. For this type of atheist, and perhaps
for many unchurched, the word "God" is an empty concept. And given
their lack of involvement in those activities in which the word "God" is
properly at home—praying, singing, witnessing, confessing, thanking—
they actually may be speaking the truth when they deny God's existence!
Why? Because what the atheist means by the word "God" is NOT what we
mean. For the atheist, the word is already an *empty* concept! Therefore,
its denial ought not offend us.

My point in this section is simply this: human words only have
meaning for those who are engaged in "doings." And this is extremely
important for those of us who take the Great Commission seriously.
Not just the word "God," but virtually all of our theological vocabulary

is intelligible only through its connection to bodily activities. The more complex the term, the more complex the interplay of human bodies is needed to convey its sense. For this very reason, the earliest apologists repeatedly drew attention to the *manner* in which Christians lived with one another.

Perhaps a beer commercial can clarify things. Although I hesitated to bring this up, I'm betting you've seen it . . . more than once. The ad consists in a single sentence repeated a dozen times. In fact, the sentence that is repeated consists in a single word: "Dude!"[29]

When our hero is hungry and finds an unexpected jar of peanut butter in the last cupboard, his cry "Dude!" means something like, "Hooray! I have found us some food!" But when he walks into a public toilet, his exclamation "Dude!" means something like "I find this overflowing toilet physically repulsive!"

Imagine taking this sentence—pop!—out of its context, and printing copies and handing it out on street corners, or posting it prominently in cyberspace. "Dude!" It is in English. Can anyone understand it? (Do we?).

What fixes the meaning of this sentence, "Dude!" is the fact that it is spoken by a human body in the presence of other bodies, all of whom have direct sensory contact with each other and their surroundings (the peanut butter or the toilet) in a particular time and a particular place. These are the conditions for successful communication. And these features are precisely what are missing from technologically tainted attempts to preach the Gospel.[30]

Someone will surely complain that this is not a fair comparison. After all, we can and do translate "Dude!" into something less ambiguous such as "Overflowing public toilets are physically repulsive." And that is

---

29. These Bud Light commercials have been immortalized by YouTube: http://www.youtube.com/watch?v=6xBQHA7ZKU4.

30. Thus have some compared cyber-evangelism with second century Gnosticism: for both, the human body, if not downright evil, is entirely unnecessary. My friend and colleague Jana Bennett directed me to David Kelsey's words: "If coming to understand God involves deep changes in personal bodies, then teaching and learning that aims at deepening understanding of God inherently involves the organic personal bodies of both teachers and learners . . . Are virtual space and virtual presence adequate media for communication among personal organic bodies, or is 'virtual' just a euphemism for 'bodiless'?" Kelsey, "Spiritual Machines, Personal Bodies, and God," 9.

correct. But such a translation, only works because everybody has been grossed out by a public toilet. So, the translation is straightforward.

In contrast, when we speak the truth of the Gospel translation is not straightforward. The two worlds are so entirely different. The terms in which the Gospel is framed have no accurate synonyms in secular lingo. And the less contact the unchurched person has had with authentic Christianity, the less leeway we witnesses have for finding near-matches for synonyms. The fact of the matter is that "sin" is not the same thing as a "mistake." Nor is "forgiveness" the same as having those mistakes "overlooked." (Otherwise, God who is infinitely patient and longsuffering could simply overlook everyone's sins and there would really be no need for atonement.) In stark contrast, the Gospel is an entirely new conceptual language, a language that becomes more and more intelligible the closer one stands to the body of believers who speak that Gospel well because they live with each other in highly particular (which is to say, "holy") ways.

The Real Place Called Church

In contrast to the no-place called Second Life, my third point has to do with the real place called "church."

How does worshipping with a hologram help us together to be the kind of community capable of embodying real forgiveness among ourselves and display it to the world? How does viewing a digitally streamed church service into a cartoon auditorium (while adopting any out-of-body camera angle one chooses) help develop my own character or, alternatively, make me aware of my sinfulness? If I'm in the virtual world, I cannot smell the pungent body odor of the person directly on my left. Nor am I distracted by the person sniffling so loudly on my right. Nor do I have to worry about controlling my own body—I can eat Cheetos, take a bathroom break, do pushups and more if worship is merely virtual.

Nor can a Second Life church do what an Amish congregation did in October of 2006 after a gunman strode into their schoolhouse and executed five children before killing himself. As you'll remember, the Amish responded in ways that only living bodies could. First, some elders visited Marie Roberts, the wife of the murderer, to offer forgiveness. Second, the families of the slain girls invited the widow to their own children's funerals. Third, these same parents requested that all relief monies intended for Amish families be shared with Roberts and her children. Finally, to cap these astonishing acts of reconciliation, more than thirty members of the Amish community attended the funeral of the killer.[31]

Is it pure coincidence that such a story of genuine Christian forgiveness comes out of a community that strictly limits their interaction with technology? The Amish refuse to use lanterns lest they be tempted to work into the night, thus surrendering precious hours meant for family and for rest. The Amish intentionally distance themselves from telephones for fear that it would tempt them to conduct fewer conversations face to face. These positions strike us as extreme. But it is at least logically possible that the intentional decisions to leave off lanterns and phones *contribute* to their ability to imitate Jesus when the heat is on.

CONCLUSION

To conclude this chapter, I've argued that there are three conditions, conditions not removed by the coming of the Holy Spirit at Pentecost, that must be met for human communication to work. These are the very three conditions—time, place, and bodies—that technology bewitches us into thinking we can ignore. If we really want to reach the unchurched, we'll have to cooperate with the Holy Spirit who has not opted to by-pass the three conditions of communication. In sharpest contrast, the Spirit wants to teach us how to take these conditions with utmost seriousness so as to communicate the most clearly.

What will evangelism look like if we cooperate with the Holy Spirit and take seriously these conditions? For one thing, this kind of evangelism proves to be intimately connected with discipleship and Christian practices.

In the following chapter I will look at the nature of human communication, and thus how technology might affect it, by examining closely the biblical record. In the meantime, let me conjure a snapshot from an earlier age, an age like ours in which Christians were not in the majority. Historian John Howard Yoder estimates that prior to 315 CE, Christianity never commanded more than five percent of the population across the Roman Empire. As a severe minority, Christian witnesses could never rely on cultural similarities with pagan polytheism in order to "translate" the Gospel into words anyone could understand. But this

31. Patterson, "Simple Truth in Power of Forgiveness."

did not slow them down. Their strategy was to pair evangelism and discipleship. In other words, they made sure that their words were always spoken at a particular time and place and from within a particular community with real live people who lived with one another in the most striking manner.

Aristides was one early witness.[32] Aristides knew that he could not make himself plain to Caesar Hadrian by translating Christian vocabulary but *by drawing attention to the way Christians actually lived with each other.*

> But the Christians. . . . show kindness to those near them; and whenever they are judges, they judge uprightly. . . . they do good to their enemies. . . . if one or other of them have bondsmen and bondswomen or children, through love towards them they persuade them to become Christians, and when they have done so, they call them brethren without distinction. They do not worship strange gods, and they go their way in all modesty and cheerfulness. Falsehood is not found among them; and they love one another. . . . And he, who has, gives to him who has not, without boasting. And when they see a stranger, they take him in to their own homes and rejoice over him as a very brother. . . . And if they hear that one of their number is imprisoned or afflicted on account of the name of their Messiah, all of them anxiously minister to his necessity. . . . And if there is any among them that is poor and needy, and they have no spare food, they fast two or three days in order to supply to the needy their lack of food. . . .
>
> Such, O King . . . is their manner of life. . . . And verily, *this is a new people, and there is something divine in the midst of them.*[33]

You want to know what "forgiveness" means? Look at how Christians live. You what to know what "service" means? Look at them. You want to learn what Christians mean when they say, "God"? Watch how they conduct themselves in the nitty-gritty business of living with bodies.

I've argued that evangelism does not escape the bodily constraints that our Creator placed on all human communication. It takes time, it takes bodies, and it takes location. In a bewitching contrast, technology

32. Aristides wrote in an age of enormous confusion. Christians were being charged with atheism, incest, and cannibalism: atheism because Christians worshipped no visible idols; incest because one's spouse is also one's sibling in Christ; and cannibalism because of the Lord's Supper: "This is my body. . . ." Of course, these charges seem so easily refuted.

33. Aristides, "Apology of Aristides the Philosopher," 9:276–78; emphasis added.

seems to offer a shortcut. But we must discern the point at which technology distorts Christian practices lest we end up with merely a "virtual" Christianity.

3

The Technological Evangelist

I ONCE SAW A Steve Kelley cartoon that showed two teachers, monitoring a hallway bustling with schoolchildren, overhearing one little girl say to her friend "And he's like, 'No way!' And I'm all like 'Duh!'" To which one teacher remarks: "Perhaps we shouldn't make English the official language."

This story satirizes a deep cultural problem. One day my wife returned from youth group at the church—at the time she was working with ninth-grade girls—and told me that the oddest thing happened. She had divided the girls into groups of three to exchange prayer concerns and to pray for each other. At the end of the meeting she instructed everyone present to remember during the coming week to "pray for their threesome." The girls exploded into giggles but were too embarrassed to let my wife in on the joke: today, fifteen year-old girls most often hear the word "threesome" spoken in the context of two-on-one sexual encounters.

If the shifting of culture has wreaked havoc with ordinary words like "threesome," what do you suppose it has done with the vocabulary with which we attempt to frame the timelessly true Gospel? . . . the Gospel that we received? . . . the Gospel in which we stand? . . . the Gospel by which we are saved? Namely,

> that Christ died for our sins according to the Scriptures, and that he was buried, and that he was raised on the third day according to the Scriptures, and that he appeared to Cephas, then to the twelve. After that He appeared to more than five hundred brethren at one time. . . . (1 Cor 15:3–6)

Well, for one thing, we ought not be surprised that evangelists get some goofy questions: "My religion prof told us that *Chrestos* was a common name for slaves—is that how Jesus got his last name?" or "How do

46

you mean 'died for our sins'? Did the coroner really put down 'sin' as the cause of death?" or "You say 'According to Scriptures'? Which scriptures? the Koran and the Bhagavad-Gita too?" In this present chapter I will revisit the question raised in chapter 2: "What role can technology be expected to play in the Great Commission?" In chapter 2 I looked at the tension between the bodiless nature of technology and evangelism as an instance of body-bound communication. In the present chapter we will look more closely at biblical texts of evangelism.

Paul wrote in Galatians that Christ appeared "in the fullness of time" (Gal 4:4). Some biblical scholars reason that Paul is alluding to the many cultural advantages for spreading the Gospel that were available at the turn of the first millennia that had not been available before. Because of the Jewish *Diaspora*, the notion of monotheism had representation in many corners of an otherwise polytheistic culture. As the Romans conquered and expanded Alexander the Great's Grecian empire, they built roads throughout the Empire and made them safe for travel. The roads became the arteries along which the Gospel spread. Moreover, before the Caesars, Alexander the Great had given the Empire Greek as its common cultural language. Thus the New Testament was penned in Greek. And so on.

One wonders whether our age affords similar, unique opportunities for the rapid spread of the Gospel. Some claim that the explosion of communication technology (telephones, radio, television, cell phones, the internet, texting, twittering, etc.) gives a distinct edge to the missional church of the twenty-first century looking to spread the Good News. In this chapter, I will look closely at the biblical text, especially at the verb "evangelize" and the noun "Gospel" to better understand our job description. Only then can we see to what extent technology might be our ally in fulfilling the Great Commission (Matt 28:18–20).[1]

THE GOSPEL WE PROCLAIM

In this era of growing biblical illiteracy I want to turn this section heading into a thesis. I will argue that in the phrase "the Gospel we proclaim," the verb *proclaim* governs the noun *Gospel* as much as the noun governs

---

1. An earlier version of this paper was titled "The Gospel we Proclaim" and presented at the 2004 Evangelism Roundtable conference, "Issues of Truth and Power: The Gospel in a Post-Christian Culture," convened by The Billy Graham Center in Wheaton, IL, April 22–24, 2004.

the verb. Not only does the content of the Gospel message determine the manner in which it ought to be proclaimed, but the fact that the message is one that we "proclaim" (rather than *peddle* or *joke* or *market* or *rumor*, etc.) provides clues as to the nature of the message.

The first part is straightforward enough. We admit readily enough that the content of Christian belief governs the *manner* in which the Gospel ought to be proclaimed. The Crusader who cries "Christ is Lord!" while cleaving the skull of the Turk has got something terribly wrong. Skull-cleaving is out of sync with the identity of Christ as the Prince of Peace.[2] As Christ offered good news of the kingdom without coercion, so ought we. As John Howard Yoder points out, in order for the Good News to remain *news*, it must be offered in a way that can be rejected. Granted, we don't like this stipulation. Instead, we hanker after ways to make the Gospel irresistible. We want that they *must* believe us. But there it is. If we offer in violent or coercive or manipulative ways, it ceases to be good *news* and becomes instead propaganda (or worse). It is not a willingness to cleave the metaphorical skulls of our opponents, but rather our readiness to bear their hostility against us, that validates our message.[3] This may be why prior to the fourth century, Christians instinctively refused to take up arms even in self-defense.[4] In fact, Irenaeus, an early and prolific pastor, theologian, and apologist, pointed out that the Father and the Son were *not* opposites with respect to violence (as if Jesus was the meek one while God the Father was violently vengeful):

> And though the apostasy [i.e., the devil] had gained its dominion over us unjustly, and, when we belonged by nature to almighty God, had snatched us away contrary to nature and made us its own disciples, the Word of God, who is mighty in all things, and in nowise lacking in justice which is His, behaved with justice even towards the apostasy itself; and He redeemed that which was His own, *not by violence* (as the apostasy has by violence gained dominion over us at the first. . .), *but by persuasion*, as it

2. See Lindbeck, *Nature of Doctrine*, 64.

3. Yoder, "On Not Being Ashamed of the Gospel," 285–300.

4. In the early 300s, the Emperor Constantine reversed the empire-wide prohibition against Christianity making it legal to be a Christian (the so-called Edict of Milan). By 391 CE, then-Emperor Theodosius made Christianity the *mandatory* religion of the empire. From then on it became increasingly difficult to distinguish genuine Christians from pretenders.

was *fitting for God* to gain his purpose by persuasion and not by use of violence. . . .[5]

So the fit between the content of our message and the style of our presentation is an extremely important subject. What holds for Jesus holds for us: we must offer the Gospel persuasively but gently, because it is *news* we offer. Only if the offer is accepted freely does it count as an instance of evangelism. As crucial as this topic is, I want to focus this chapter on the other perhaps less obvious side of the coin. I want to examine the senses in which the verb "proclaim" illumines the meaning of the noun, "the Gospel." This exercise has a point: only if we understand what it means to *proclaim* (literally, to "*gospelize*") can we assess the extent to which technology might assist or hinder evangelism.

Look back at the heading, "The Gospel We Proclaim." In the New Testament, the phrase "to proclaim the Gospel" is actually a single word: *euangelizō*. Fifty-four times the word shows up as a verb: *to gospelize*. That's an odd word, "to gospelize." Yet I want to use it for the time being rather than the more common word "evangelize" in order to help us get past what we assume it means and come to hear it in a fresh way.

Although by the time of the New Testament, the word had been around for hundreds of years,[6] the word "gospelize" was not very common. One might have heard it used to describe the report of a messenger-slave that a battle had been won or that so-and-so were to be married.[7] Good news in both cases. During the first century CE, the word became increasingly co-opted by a group of religious extremists. Members of the Jewish sect, contemptuously called *Christianos* by their detractors,[8] began using the verb "gospelize" to describe one of their most distinctive practices.[9] As a result, the word became more and more colored by

5. Cited in Aulén, *Christus Victor*, 26-27; emphasis added. Like their eastern Greek-speaking counterparts, early Latin-speaking pastors also pointed to Acts 15:29 as requiring abstention from violence. Unfortunately this was based on a mistranslation; the Greek word prohibits blood sacrifice rather than bloodshed per se. Nevertheless, this early Christian misreading is strong evidence that nonviolence was widely taken to be *the* Christian position.

6. Apparently, the Greek philosopher Aristophanes was the first to use it in print. Friedrich, "Euaggelizomai," in *Theological Dictionary of the New Testament*, 3:710.

7. Moulton and Milligan, *Vocabulary of the Greek Testament*, 259.

8. Wilkins, "Christian," in *Anchor Bible Dictionary*, 1:925-26.

9. For an account of how traditions are constituted by their cooperative practices, see ch. 2 of Murphy, Kallenberg, and Nation, *Virtues and Practices in the Christian Tradition*.

its close ties to Christian behavior than by its previous popular uses. In other words, Christian behavior seems to have shifted the semantic range of the word on the street. Consequently, we must look closely at these activities in order to get a handle on what the word "gospelize" means.

On the one hand, to gospelize did *not* mean to propagandize or even to proselytize if by these terms we mean something coercive or manipulative. As mentioned above, the very rejectability of the news is part of what makes it *good* as well as *news*. News that one was not allowed to reject was not news but propaganda. And in point of fact, even if the preacher was an Apostle, gospelizing was *not* irresistible. The author of Hebrews tells us that some who were gospelized "failed to enter" into the Sabbath rest of God for reasons of their own disobedience and unfaith, rather than for some failure on the part of the gospelizer (Heb 4:1–6). And Luke reports that in Athens some of Paul's listeners sneered while others just scratched their heads (Acts 17:32).

But on the other hand, for New Testament Christians, the verb could never mean a simple mundane recitation of the facts. Quite the contrary, both the noun (*gospel*) and the verb (*gospelize*) show up in biblical passages accompanied by other active verbs and participles such as "healing" (Luke 9:6; Matt 4:23, 9:35), "teaching" (Acts 5:42; Matt 4:23, 9:35), "solemnly testifying" (Acts 20:24) "announcing" (1 Cor 9:14), "boldly speaking" (1 Thess 2:2), and "preaching" (Matt 4:23, 9:35, 24:14, 26:13; Mark 13:10, 14:9, 16:15; Gal 2:2). The close proximity of these verbs to "gospelize" paints a complex picture: perhaps gospelizing cannot really take place if these other activities are absent.

Take "preaching" as a first example. I suspect it doesn't surprise us to learn that the word "preaching" normally accompanies "gospelizing." But by "preaching" do we mean what the New Testament writers meant? By his own admission, Paul arrived in Corinth full of weakness and fear and much trembling. In *this* condition, his preaching was persuasive. But how? Because he has a big brain? No. Paul's preaching was not persuasive because of its tight logic and rhetorical coerciveness. His preaching was marked instead by a "*demonstration* of the Spirit and of power" (1 Cor 2:1–5). If gospelizing involves preaching and preaching involves "demonstration," what sort of demonstration is Paul talking about?

The demonstration Paul has in mind is *practical* rather than theoretical in nature.[10] In other words, what authenticated Paul's preaching as "spiritual," "persuasive," and "powerful" was not some logic-chopping *apologia* or finely tuned argument, but *skills of living*. How do we know this? Perhaps an illustration can help. The *Tebtunic Papyri* dating from the second century uses the same technical term for "demonstration" (*apodeixis*) that Paul employs. This Papyri explains that when an Egyptian priest got "carded" outside the Temple of Isis, he or she would be asked to demonstrate their qualifications for entry by translating some sample hieroglyphics.[11] Nobody but cultic priests could do that. His or her skill at reading hieroglyphics *demonstrated* that he or she was in fact, the Real McCoy.

In a similar way, Paul offered *practical* evidence that his preaching was authentic. The twist is that the evidence Paul offered was not simply the set of skills that he possessed, but skills that he passed on and that the *Corinthians* now embodied. To say the same thing differently, *the evidence that Paul's message was true was the changed lives of the Corinthian believers.*

> *You* [plural] are our letter, written in our hearts, known and read by all men; being manifested that *you* [plural] are a letter of Christ, cared for by us, written not with ink, but with the Spirit of the living God, not on tablets of stone, but on tablets of human hearts. (2 Cor 3:2–3; emphasis added.)

Through Paul's gospelizing the Spirit of God was actually crafting the Corinthian community in such a way that the *character* of Christ himself could be read off the shape of their life together as easily as one reads a letter (*epistolē Christou*; 2 Cor 3:2). Remember, Paul explained in his earlier letter that what he sought to "detect among them" (*eidenai en humin*; 1 Cor 2:1) was precisely what he "proclaimed" (*katalangelōn*; 1 Cor 2:2), namely "Jesus Christ and him crucified." He preaches Christ crucified and looks to see if those seeds take root among the Corinthians, for example, by changing how they treat each other. In other words, it is the new shape of the corporate life (from the midst of which the Gospel

---

10. On the difference between practical and theoretical reason, see Joseph Dunne, *Back to the Rough Ground: Practical Judgment and the Lure of Technique* (Notre Dame, IN: University of Notre Dame Press, 1993).

11. Moulton and Milligan, *Vocabulary of the Greek Testament*, 60–61.

would continue to sound forth[12]) that demonstrates the validity of the message. This same expectation lay behind Paul's confident admonition in his later correspondence that they themselves look and see whether Christ was recognizable in their corporate life—"among you all" (*en humin*)—because if not, they failed the test (2 Cor 13:5). So, Paul's gospelizing of the Corinthians entailed a certain sort of "preaching" (*kerussō*) that by its very nature intruded into everyday conduct. Thus Paul spends chapter after chapter giving hard-hitting practical instruction for dealing with interpersonal problems in this new "cruciform" way, to the end that the Corinthian disciples might *together* slowly look more and more like Jesus. If this was what Paul was up to, then the very act of preaching was a declarative intrusion into the way people actually conducted themselves. In Paul's mind, anything less intrusive would have failed to be an instance of "preaching." And if preaching was properly invasive, by extension, so must gospelizing be.

Similar conclusions can be drawn for gospelizing from its proximity to three other verbs that are found nearby in the text. The giving of solemn testimony (*diamarturomai*), ordinary conversation (*laleō*), and teaching (*didaskō*), like preaching and demonstrating, are all, in the main, *linguistic* practices. But they are distinct from each other—as different as telling a joke is from arguing a case in court. So we must not be fooled into thinking that gospelizing reduces to word games or tricky strings of one-liners. Anyone can speak a sentence, but the mastery of this cluster of linguistic practices is perhaps the most demanding task we will ever face. In what ways do all these linguistic practices enrich our understanding of "gospelizing?"

I spent perhaps the best decade of my life "gospelizing" with an evangelistic parachurch ministry on college campuses in the Midwest. One of the advantages of this was that I became very comfortable talking about Jesus with a wide variety of people in a broad range of circumstances. Unfortunately, as my comfort level grew, I began unwittingly to think of evangelism as a simple, self-contained, relatively brief, solitary task. I did evangelism like doing up the dishes. But this kind of thinking is wide of the mark. To see why, let me draw out some contrasts between the linguistic practices involved in authentic gospelizing and the simple task of doing the dishes.

---

12. On the "sounding forth" of the Gospel by means of exemplary living, see 1 Thess 1:6–10.

According to my kids, Mom was in charge of food preparation, making her, in their lingo, the "food-in-charger." For my part, I was the "dishes-in-charger." As my children grew older, I began to enlist their help. And even though they had to stand on a stool, it only took one session to make them relative experts. By comparison, how long does it take to master a language?! As native speakers, we simply are not aware of just how difficult this process is . . . until we try to learn another language!

One of the hoops that seminary demanded was that of translating into English texts written in Greek (not to mention the ones written in Latin . . . and Hebrew . . . and French . . . and German!). After my basic Greek courses were out of the way, I spent an intensive six months preparing for my translation exam. Every morning I'd read devotionally in my Greek New Testament. But the cornerstone of my strategy was to take a pack of flashcards onto deserted mountain trails for long runs of an hour, sometimes two. Finally, after six months I could plod and stumble my way pretty well through most biblical passages. But of course I wasn't fluent. I could barely, and only, read. I could neither speak nor write nor hear much less *think* in Greek. My "fluency," so called, rode piggyback on my knowledge of English. Truth be told, what I did was more like decoding than reading. I'd look at a text and make the English substitution phrase by phrase. But I still *thought* in English—a language I'd spent a lifetime speaking. If I were to become *fluent* in Greek, it would take much longer than six months.

Of course the disciples didn't share my disadvantage; they had already learned Aramaic on their mother's knee and picked up Greek in the marketplace. But the real gap was not between their Greek and my English. Both Greek and English are natural languages. And as time-consuming as learning a second *natural* language is, a much tougher task is learning a new *conceptual* language. In acquiring this skill the disciples didn't fare much better than we! That's because a conceptual language isn't just about talking or reading. It is about *seeing* in entirely new ways. ("A whole new world!" writes Paul.[13]) And to see, think, describe, and act differently requires life transformation, which is neither automatic, nor speedy. For example, Luke reports that when Jesus spoke about a crucified Messiah the disciples did not and seemingly could not

13. 1 Cor 5:17 does not say "new creature" but "new creation." A more literal translation of Paul's semi-poetic line would be, "If any person is in Christ, a whole new world!"

understand what he meant (Luke 9:45; also John 12:16)! They, as well as we, needed to *learn* the new language—for which "crucified Messiah" was not an oxymoron!—and that took time.[14] Even those who traveled with Jesus for three years were still trying to wrap their minds around the implications that the Gospel held for race relations (to name but one example). By Acts 15 they made a pretty good go at sorting out what the Spirit was up to. But even after the letter mentioned in Acts 15 had been penned and mailed, that Peter was snared by the old way of thinking (i.e., that Jews eat with Jews and Gentiles with Gentiles). Paul, in turn, publicly confronts Peter.[15] And fortunately, Peter appears to accept Paul's correction. (One can imagine Peter slapping his forehead with a humble "Doh!" It is so easy to slide back into the old ways!) In correcting Peter, Paul acted out a living revision of the Acts 15 policy. Apparently it was not sufficient to direct only the Gentiles to curtail certain behavior, because Jewish Christians needed directions too! Paul's revision shows us that whatever progress toward fluency the disciples had made by Acts 15, they still had further to go!

The time intensiveness of learning this new conceptual language called "Christian" is brought to the fore by the verb "teaching" (*didaskō*) that, as we saw above, is sometimes associated with "gospelize" in the biblical texts about evangelism. When Paul visits Corinth for the first time (Acts 18:1–11), we read that he borrowed the home of Titus Justus in order to set up a school right next to the synagogue. This precedent of giving instruction to those in the process of converting is imitated by the earliest pastors and is one of the reasons that pastors are simultaneously teachers as well as shepherds.[16] They conducted pre-conversion instruction in order to help potential converts understand that to which they were converting. This instruction became known as "catechesis" and amounted to a sort of boot camp for thinking, acting, and talking in the way Christ-followers think, act, and talk. This became standard practice. Four centuries after Paul, a leading pastor in North Africa named Augustine (d. 430) reports that his own pre-conversion catechesis lasted

14. Time and Pentecost. But even the Holy Spirit does not *override* the natural ways we have learned to see. In the process of following Christ, there is as much to unlearn as there is to learn. See Hauerwas, "Church as God's New Language."

15. See Galatians 2.

16. The Greek text links "pastor" and "teacher" in Eph 4:11. These early pastors are referred to as the Church Fathers, and their earliest book of discipleship is called the *Didache*.

something like nine months. Nine months may have been shorter than was typical. To be on the safe side, one pastor (Hippolytus, d. 236) recommended three full years of pre-conversion instruction![17] The length of time our forebears devoted to pre-conversion instruction ought to give us pause. If, as some claim, we live in a post-Christian age of neo-paganism, yet an age in which the process of becoming a U.S. citizen requires *eight years,* how much time do we think should be required for gospelizing? Ten minutes? Ten hours? Ten days? Ten weeks? Learning the conceptual language of the Gospel takes time.

Second, one can do up the dishes alone, but learning a language necessarily requires a team effort. My fluency requires participation by other speakers. That explains why the Hebrew language all but abandoned me as soon as my last seminary exam was over: no one ever spoke Hebrew with me. Even during my coursework, when people did talk *at* me in Hebrew, I had no emotional engagement in the exercises. I only did what was needed to pass the exam. In contrast, the level of participation needed to attain fluency must go beyond simply talking *at* one another. It must involve a complicated interplay of reactions enmeshed in the whole hurly-burly of living together.

As an example of this complex weave of reactions and responses, think of how we learn pain language.[18] Babies cry when doctors poke them with syringes. Crying is an instinctive, primitive reaction to their environment—like blinking in the wind or sneezing at pepper or puckering at lemons. Later in this baby's life, after skinning a knee on the driveway, they will fight back the tears all the way into the house. But as soon as the door bursts open and Mom is visible in the kitchen, the floodgates open. This sort of crying is different than what a baby does. It is a different sort of primitive reaction; it is a kind of communication. And through the crying, the child hears the mother coo, "There, there, I know it hurts." Slowly the child learns that words like "it hurts" can go proxy for crying. So as an adult, when you or I trip on the sidewalk, we grab our knee and say "Wow! That really *hurts!*"[19]

---

17. St. Hippolytus, *Apostolic Tradition,* 43, 87.

18. Fiser, "Privacy and Pain."

19. For a more careful explanation of the connection between behavior and the learning of language, see Kallenberg, *Ethics as Grammar,* 101–12, 203–15.

But the hurly-burly doesn't stop at these first-order primitive reactions.[20] It belongs to the mother's own God-given primitive reactions
to respond sympathetically to the injured child. In a sense, the *visceral*
responses of all mothers everywhere is also bound up in our shared language of pain. But it extends even further than moms; a third party has
a certain reaction to the scene of a mother giving comfort (or failing to
give comfort). These third-party reactions are *also* part of the grammar
of the word "hurt." And then there's the fourth party who reacts to the
perceived empathy (or indifference) of the third party witnessing the
scene of injury and comfort (or neglect). And so on. And so on. All these
networks of reactions are tangled up with speaking a language fluently.
My point? Only by immersion into this body-involving web of relationship can one master the conceptual language of the Gospel.

Third, one can do up the dishes with a pretty short list of rubbing
motions. But one cannot master a conceptual language without simultaneously mastering a *vast web* of behaviors that constitutes a form of
life. For example, think of how children learn to use the word "chair."
Although it may sound counterintuitive, in point of fact a child does *not*
learn what chairs are by watching adults point to chairs while intoning
"chair." Rather, a child picks up what to do with the word "chair" by overhearing the word spoken in a wide range of *physical activities involving
chairs*. We stack chairs, stub our toes on them, reupholster them, buy and
sell them, stand on them, tip them over, paint them, count them, fetch
them, race around them, knock them over, set them back upright, and
sit on them. As the child becomes increasingly familiar with these *activities*, the child learns to use the word "chair" properly. When the philosopher Ludwig Wittgenstein wrote that part of the grammar of the word
"chair" is our actually sitting in them,[21] he meant that our familiarity
with the whole range of activities involving chairs is sort of put on alert
the moment we hear the word "chair" spoken. Conversely, to the extent
that someone is unfamiliar with these activities, that person will have a
proportionately thin understanding of the word "chair."

Not surprisingly, our fluency in *theological* terms is likewise bound
up with our everyday activities. Recall the point I made in chapter 2: If
a young child is asked who God is, the response is likely to include "He's
the one we pray to before bed," "we're supposed to confess our sins to

---

20. For more on primitive reactions, see Hertzberg, "Primitive Reactions," 24–39.

21. Wittgenstein, *Blue and Brown Books*, 24.

God," "We sing songs to him and visit him on Sunday," "He's the one we thank before we can eat," and perhaps "He's the one we tell our friends about." The richer this child's engagement with each of these activities, the richer will be his or her understanding of God and of how to use the concept "God" fluently.[22] But catch the significance for evangelistic conversations: You or I may talk with someone who neither prays to God, confesses sin to God, thanks God, worships God, sings to God, nor testifies about God. How then can we possibly assume he or she has even the slightest inkling of Who we're talking about? For them the word "god" is very nearly a null set. This is why the best way for someone to understand what we mean by the word "God" is to *watch how we behave*:

> I should like to say that in this case . . . the *words* you utter or what you think as you utter them are not what matters, so much as the difference they make at various points in your life. How do I know that two people mean the same when each says he believes in God? . . . *Practice* gives the words their sense.[23]

Let me take a step back. In defending the claim that the actions implied by the verb "gospelize" manifests important aspects of the Gospel message, I've tried to make two points. First, in order for one to be a proper gospelizer, one must be in the process of mastering a whole range of community-constituting linguistic practices, because these practices are associated with the word "gospelizing" in the canons of Scripture. Second, one cannot achieve fluency in these linguistic practices without being immersed into the community of believers for whom this conceptual language is fluently spoken, because we each need familiarity with their activities in order to shape our own en route to becoming fluent in the conceptual language of the Gospel. But how difficult is this?

A word about kinds of languages. As referred to above, there are *natural* and *conceptual* languages. But there are also *first* and *second* languages. Every child is born into a host language. A language, such as English or French, is absorbed by the child as he or she grows up in proximity to sentences spoken from within a form of life. This practice-rooted language becomes his or her "first" language. When one goes

---

22. George Lindbeck writes, "In short, it is necessary to have the means for expressing an experience in order to have it, and the richer our expressive or linguistic system, the more subtle, varied, and differentiated can be our experience." Lindbeck, *Nature of Doctrine*, 37.

23. Wittgenstein, *Culture and Value*, 85e.

about learning a second language, it remains a *second* language until it takes over as the primary language in which one thinks. Before that can happen, a person will dream in that language, make a pun, argue under duress, and cry out in pain all in that new language. To the extent these reflexes occur, the second language is becoming a first language.

The difference between natural and conceptual languages is a bit trickier. Two distinct natural languages (such as French and English) can constitute the *same* conceptual language. If so, sentences are easily translated from the one to the other and back again without remainder or loss of meaning. For example, both French and English speakers reflexively think that the world divides neatly into events and objects. This is because Western civilizations share a *conceptual* language that employs two primary parts of speech: verbs, relating to events, and nouns, relating to objects. Obviously, there are variations on verbs and nouns (like participles and gerunds, etc.), but the point is the same. So long as the French and the English use verbs and nouns, they will classify their experiences into *objects* and *events*. There are alternative natural languages. For example, the Native American language of Hopi has only verbs, no nouns. As a result, they see the world exclusively in terms of events.[24] How this works is beyond the scope of discussion. More germane to our task is that in addition to natural languages, there are also alternative *conceptual* languages that vie for the place of "first" or "second" in terms of the priority of their grip on our way of seeing.

Imagine an artist and an engineer admiring a bridge. Even if both share English as their first language, differing conceptual languages are in play. The engineer sees the bridge first in terms of structure. The engineer's conceptual language is a combination of mathematics (e.g., differential equations), pictures (e.g., technical drawings), and English words with special meanings such as *truss, footing,* and *flange.* The artist's natural language may also be English. But the artist instinctively employs a different vocabulary such as *form, color, beauty.* Lest we underestimate the uniqueness of the artistic language, we do well to remember Goethe's line that his painter friend had thirty-one different shades of "black!"

In many ways, learning to be a faithful disciple of Jesus resembles the time and effort that goes into learning to speak "engineering" or "art." Consequently, it is fluency in the *conceptual* language of Christianity that becoming a Christian entails. While we may never completely succeed

24. Whorf, *Language, Thought, and Reality,* #3069.

in making the Gospel our first conceptual language this side of heaven, we all understand that we *ought* to strive for this and that we *ought also* to repent each time our speech is displaced by secular, which is to say *non-Christian*, conceptual language.[25]

If the comparison between following Jesus and learning a language holds, then evangelism involves two conditions. First, in order for someone to be gospelized, we must assist them in mastering the Christian conceptual language. Second, this assistance cannot be "off-shored." Only by immersion into an actual living, breathing community of Christians will do the trick. Let me explain these in order.

George Lindbeck was not the first to suggest that the very heart of becoming a Christ-follower is learning to speak, think, and act in another language. But he did say it well: "just as an individual becomes human through learning language, so he or she begins to become a new creature through hearing and interiorizing the language that speaks of Christ."[26] If Lindbeck is right about this, then many contemporary gospelizing strategies are bound to fail. Why? Because these strategies presume the Gospel must be *translated* into terms anyone can understand, as if everyone already shared a single conceptual language. Yet one cannot master Chinese by reading English translations of Confucius. Neither can the unchurched learn the language called "Christian" so long as the Gospel is expressed in terms that secular society already buys. And while communication technology does make translation very, very rapid, it does not help much if translation is itself a fatally flawed strategy. Let's see why translation is such a bad idea.

As I discussed in chapter 2, translation is a very poor strategy for disciple-making. A piano teacher will not get very far with the novice by saying that playing the piano is a lot like typing . . . only different. Granted, keyboards are involved in both cases. But typing does not take

25. Admittedly, there may be some overlap between all conceptual languages that stems from some basic shared form of life. For example, the sun warms all people, so there is likely a large semantic overlap between "sun" in English and "soleil" in French. However, many of these basic terms are uninteresting—that is, until they are employed by conceptual languages. Thus "The sun is shining" has a quite different nuance that "The Lord God is a sun and shield." We ought not assume that because my neighbor understands the word "sun" as a fiery ball in the sky that he or she is able to comprehend Ps 84:11. Since conceptual languages must *always* employ natural languages, there is always danger of misunderstanding. This is why apologetics is forever ad hoc. See Werpehowski, "Ad Hoc Apologetics."

26. Lindbeck, *Nature of Doctrine*, 62.

rhythm into account, nor intervals, nor key signatures. There is simply little point in trying to explain one in terms of the other. Translation simply will not do. One can only learn piano from scratch, by *training* rather than translation.

The inapplicability of translation is one of the enormous problems with reliance on communication technology to spread the Gospel. Malcolm Gladwell once quipped that technology cannot solve every problem: if the toilet is backed up, no tech support from a phone bank in India will do the trick. I need a person, here, now, with a plunger or wrench or whatever. So too for evangelism. Someone fluent in the language called Christian needs to be here, now, on location to help the would-be convert learn to speak fluently. And of course, that will take some time.

Using translation is not merely a tactical error because it is inefficient. It is sometimes downright distorting. Some terms and phrases *ought not* be translated because they *cannot* be translated. To translate anyway will breed the wrong idea. Consider some of the contrasts between pop theology and the language of the New Testament. The New Testament authors do not as often describe a *"personal* relationship with God"—that notion of person doesn't emerge until after the sixth century—as they do a matter of being baptized into the body of Christ (1 Cor 12:13). This is a complicated topic. The Gospel clearly involves knowing God (John 17:3) as well as being known by God (Gal 4:9). But there is widespread confusion swirling about the idea of a "personal relationship with God." We must be very careful not to foist twenty-first-century psychology onto first-century texts. Christianity isn't so much about "going to heaven when I die," as it is the hope of being resurrected into an eschatological kingdom. It might not even be at all about "Jesus in my heart," though it certainly *is* a matter of being a brick, side by side with other bricks, together constituting the living temple, the *whole* of which is indwelt by God's Spirit (Eph 2:21–22).[27] The Gospel gets murkier when the "abundant life" (John 10:10) is marketed as the prosperous life; or when reconciliation is diluted to mere conflict resolution; or when "peace" becomes a way to make career decisions but no longer has anything to do with foreign policy.

27. For a discussion of holism vs. individualism in the New Testament, see Kallenberg, "All Suffer the Affliction of the One."

Fortunately, there is an alternative strategy to that of "translation." This brings me to the second condition: In order for those being gospelized to master the Christian conceptual language, they must be immersed into a community of believers (and their practices) for whom this conceptual language is the first conceptual language. Members of this community become trainers rather than translators of the Gospel. In other words, instead of translating the Gospel into modernese, the gospelizing community seeks to raise the fluency of potential converts to such a level that they can hear the Gospel on its own terms. Thus the gospelizer is at heart a language coach.

Suppose you and I are at an impasse in a conversation. You have advanced degrees in mathematics and I do not. You are eager to explain linear algebra to me, and I am eager to hear it. If I, because I lack sufficient education, expect you to explain linear algebra to me in terms I already am familiar with, our conversation will get nowhere. Granted, you might be able to give some inkling of what linear algebra is *for* ("You can use it to figure out how much lift an airplane wing has at a given speed"). But unless you are able to introduce special vocabulary, such as "partial differential equations," I'll never understand linear algebra itself. Moreover, I'll need more than a glossary of terms. I'll need a set of *skills* to build on. Before I can get an inkling of how to solve partial differential equations, I'll need to know how to integrate normal differential equations by having first mastered calculus. My achievement of understanding requires of me the listener *training over time*. But if linear algebra is worth knowing—if, for example, it is a matter of my salvation—then the training is worth the time, effort, and tutelage. Of course, linear algebra is not a matter of salvation. In point of fact, only 4 percent of Americans even understand my last illustration—a fact which underscores my point that some things can only be understood by training! But the Gospel is a matter of salvation. Therefore, we owe it to God to give up translating and take up language coaching.

Where have we gotten to? There's no way to understand *what* we are talking about except by more talking. It follows that how *well* we talk—what I've called fluency—sets the limits of *what* we can say. Moreover, how well we talk is in an important sense dependent upon the vitality of language practices in the speaker's host community. In our case, this means that communication of the Gospel is a function of the sort of community out of which we speak. This link may seem counterintuitive, especially in light of evangelicalism's recent history of lone-ranger evangelism. But I can bolster the case I'm making by showing how this conclusion resonates with other Scripture. Let me give three examples of surprising scriptural passages that become clearer when we assume that there *is* a close connection between gospelizing and the shape (or character) of the Christian community from which the gospelizer speaks. You'll want to have a Bible handy while you read.

In this case, I'll be using the New American Standard Version. The first surprise is the wordplay of 1 Thess 1:5. There Paul writes, "our gospel did not come to you in word only, but also in power and in the Holy Spirit and with full conviction. . . ." Paul deliberately uses a very bland verb—the word "to come" (*ginomai*) or "to become" or "to happen"—in order to highlight by contrast the powerful and divine and persuasive manner the Gospel *was* actually delivered to them. In point of fact, the Gospel didn't just "happen." Mere words ("in word only"; *en logō monon*) didn't simply fall from the sky. After all, mere words would have fallen flat. Here is Paul's pun: mere words didn't come, *we* did: ". . . just as you know what kind of men we became [*ginomoai*] in your midst for your sake."[28] By using the same bland verb, "come, become," Paul draws attention to the fact that the power of the Holy Spirit could not be conveyed by the mere words strung together ("in word only"). Rather, these words were crucially bundled with *actual, living, breathing messengers*. What was crucial was not *who* the messengers were, but what *sort* (*oioi*) of people they were. We know what sort a person someone is by tracking closely their activities, their responses to setbacks, their mindfulness of others, their spoken encouragements, and their unspoken body language. As always, words are made intelligible against the context of action ("*practice* gives the words their sense"). These gospelizers initiated with the Thessalonians a conversation in an entirely alien language and then stuck around long enough for the Thessalonians to gain fluency by listening to Paul and his cohorts speak and watching them behave. They remained on (as Paul's team typically did[29]) as trainers, conversation partners, language coaches. That's where the transforming power resides.[30] In reflecting on this process, Paul could not separate (as we

28. Here the difference in spelling is simply the addition of the pronominal suffix "we."

29. Paul and Barnabas spent an entire year in Antioch (Acts 11:26).

30. While God's Spirit is capable of acting without mediation, for some reason God

are seemingly prone to do today) the Gospel words themselves (i.e., "in word only") from the *manner* in which the gospelizers spoke, acted, and lived with each other during their tenure with the Thessalonians. This is because the communication of the Gospel is (1) a function of the *sort* of community who speaks it and (2) the reproduction of that form of life among and in the presence of the hearers. In other words, the Gospel can only be said to have been communicated when it has scooped up the hearers and made them part of the ongoing conversation.

A second surprise passage that can be untangled by applying the social nature of language is heard in the odd locution of Rom 15:19. There Paul says he has "*fully* preached the Gospel." One well-intentioned Christian organization once tried to take this text seriously by quantifying "fully preached" with a "70 percent exposure" policy. We have already met quantification as a temptation in chapter 1. The urge to have a number (70 percent) that tells the missional group when to move on is but an offshoot of technologically driven standardization. They reasoned that because so much of the world has never heard, Christians are obligated to move on to new ground after a goodly chunk of the population (70 percent) has had a reasonable chance to be exposed. So, for example, if an evangelist such as Billy Graham or Luis Palau comes to a town of 10,000 and the stadium holds 7,000, then the Gospel has been "fully preached." In their minds this conclusion holds even if only thirteen people showed up: since the stadium holds 7,000, then 7,000 were given the *chance* to be exposed to the Gospel, even if, sadly, it was not an opportunity they afforded themselves.

The trouble with this policy is that it is out of sync with the text itself. Romans 15:19 actually asserts that Paul "*fulfilled* [*peplērōkenai*] the Gospel." We are all familiar with the "filling" of the Spirit (as the verb is used in Acts 13:52) and with the "fulfilling" of prophecy (as the verb is used in Acts 3:18), but what can it possibly mean to "fill" or "fulfill" *the Gospel*?

The context provides clues for a better reading strategy. Let's back up and consider verses 18–19:

> For I will not presume to speak of anything resulting in the obedience of the Gentiles, except what Christ has accomplished through me by word *and deed*, by the power of signs and won-

is pleased to speak through people—thus the Psalms, thus the incarnation, and thus Paul.

ders, by the power of the Spirit; so that from Jerusalem and round
about as far as Illyricum I have fulfilled the gospel of Christ.[31]

Again we see that the Gospel cannot be identified with mere words, but
with the couplet, "word and deed" (not to mention "attesting signs"[32]).
The term "deed" (*ergon*) typically conveys the human response to God's
Spirit. For example, Acts 26:20 describes the turn to God as displayed
in the performance of "deeds in keeping with repentance" (*axia tēs
metanoias erga*). Perhaps nowhere is the Spirit's activity more clearly at-
tested than in the erasure of social divisions that have violently haunted
us since Babel. But now in the body of Christ, "There is neither Jew nor
Greek, there is neither slave nor free man, there is neither male nor fe-
male; for you are all one in Christ Jesus" (Gal 3:28). Believers across the
empire took this erasure very seriously. The second-century pastor in
Rome, Clement, wrote that *freepersons* were actually selling themselves
into slavery, thus becoming slaves, in order to ransom believing slaves,
thus transforming former slaves into freepersons.[33] This is amazing stuff!
Free persons surrendering civilian rights and privileges to embrace servi-
tude in exchange for elevating a non-person (i.e., a slave) to the position
of freedom and rights. Their reasoning? Simply this: Christians ought to
live in imitation of Christ, who though he was rich, for our sakes became
poor that he might make us rich. Their *actions* tell in miniature the story
of redemption. My point is this: because the brave deeds of these early
believers *embodied* (i.e., incarnated in imitation of Christ) the story of
Christ, their very deeds supplied the crucial backdrop for making sense
out of the language of the Gospel. John's Gospel reads, "You shall know
the truth and the truth shall set you free" (John 8:32). But these Roman
believers show what "free" really means: free to serve, free to sacrifice,
free to surrender freedom! Thus the communication of the Gospel is a
function of the sort of community out of which we speak.

---

31. My translation with emphasis added. The Greek is repetitive. The same preposition, "in" or "by," is used three times in a row. So it makes sense to reflect Paul's emphasis
with an identical English preposition: *by* word and deed, *by* the power of signs and wonders, *by* the power of the Spirit. Together all three point to the *means by which* Christ
worked through Paul. An alternate reading is possible: *in* word and deed, *in* signs, *in*
power. But the spatial metaphor "in" doesn't seem to clarify Paul's meaning as does the
instrumental preposition "by."

32. The term "signs and wonders" was used almost exclusively to signify the miraculous. The authenticating role of miraculous signs is beyond the scope of this paper.

33. Clement, "First Epistle of Clement to the Corinthians," 55.2.

A third and most difficult puzzle. Paul once described the Gospel as literally "the word of truth" (Col 1:15). But Paul throws us a curve ball in 1 Timothy 3:15:

> in case I am delayed, I write so that you may know how one ought to conduct himself in the household of God, which is the church of the living God, the pillar (*stulos*) and foundation (*edraiōma*) of the truth.

In the first place, we are surprised to hear that the truth needs a pillar and foundation. Even more troubling is the identity of the foundation. Where we'd expect to see God named as the foundation, we discover that Paul means the *church*; the *church* is the foundation of the truth and not the other way around.

Admittedly this sticks in our craw. Our instinct is instead to say that the word of truth, the Gospel, is the foundation of the church. How then can Paul deliberately reverse the order? If we think for a minute, we see this actually makes sense. We saw above that the Gospel is not the Gospel unless it is a living language actually spoken and lived by a real community. Without this community the message is reduced to gibberish, or worse, it becomes a wax nose that can be twisted in any direction. Infamously, the Bible has been used to defend slavery in the Deep South as well as justify mid-century Nazism. But when it becomes a living language, when the Bible becomes Scripture,[34] the *community* of speakers itself becomes normative for the use of that language.[35] Once

34. I do not mean to imply that the Scriptures are nothing until believers embrace them. That would be philosophically wrongheaded and historically false. Each Scripture is a speech-act and therefore already presupposes a group of people involved in conversation. Scripture, community . . . chicken, egg. Neither preceded the other; God initiated both the community and Scripture with the same breath of the Spirit.

So, while no community gives life to the Scripture by believing them, there clearly are communities for whom our Scripture is simply good literature and nothing more. To them the Bible is dead, for they do not speak its language.

35. This claim is difficult to substantiate. It is more of a faith claim than an empirical one. As a colleague reminded me, "When it came to Biblical defenses of slavery, that defense came out of a community of churches, not only in the deep South, but in the upper South and even in parts of the North. It was a language lived by these churches, with Christians who really did believe that the Bible made clear that the best social order included slavery. I agree, this is a 'gibberish Gospel', but this gibberish Gospel came out of communities where people cared for each other, prayed together, worshiped together, and so on. What do we do with this?"

I'll admit I was nervous about including reference to the culture of slavery in the U.S. Yet there is good reason for doing so: A graduate thesis some years ago by Danielle

again, onlookers only discover what the Gospel means in tandem with watching the lives of those who speak it. We need not worry about the specter of relativism. This is not relativism, but a logical extension of the incarnation. The truth of the text is not at stake, although its clarity is. For if the community lives poorly, the timelessly true message will not get through, here and now, in this place, for these people. And that is a great loss.

The idea that the local believers anchor the clarity of the message is a conclusion that is corroborated by the other term used to describe the church: *pillar*. The pillar (*stulos*) was the ancient equivalent of a showcase.[36] It was a pedestal whose use was the holding up of something of value for all to see. This is the sense that Paul intends in his letter to Timothy. How the church behaves is crucial because it is the pedestal, the showcase, the plausibility structure, as it were, of the Gospel.

Together the dual roles of the church as foundation and as pillar evoke an image of *incarnational evangelism*: the Gospel is embodied in the life of the believing community. Please don't misunderstand me, however. By "incarnational evangelism" I don't mean (as some apparently do) that the Gospel can be spread without words. Just the opposite: we *must* speak the words. However, there are two stipulations. We must speak the words with each other as well as with outsiders. (The words we

---

Harley included an example about slave holders allowing slaves to attend church but not be baptized, since baptism might compel them to release their slaves. This shows discomfort among slave-holders who claim to be Bible-following Christians. Harley, "Bishop Daniel Payne," 13–14. See also Raboteau, *Canaan Land*, 16.

Perhaps the misuse of Scripture by Nazism is less problematic: The Hebrew word "Adam" is also the Hebrew word for "red"; in other words, Adam as the original human being could blush. Since only Aryans can blush, Aryans are descendants of God's original creation; non-blushing races are contaminated, mutated, inferior.

But isn't this example also problematic? Afterall, leaders of both Roman Catholic and Lutheran churches had "agreements" with Hitler. Surely these two churches represented the majority of Christians in Germany. And the breakoff "confessional churches" (lead by Niemoller, Bonhoeffer, and Barth's "Barmen Declaration") were really teeny by comparison. Does this imply that many German believers may have been sincere in their discipleship, but simply mistaken about the "Jewish question?" If so, doesn't that undermine my claim that when Scripture is lived, it is reliable? I do not know what to say. Nevertheless, something is terribly wrong with a form of Christianity that enabled a congregation to gather for "worship" within eyesight of the concentration camp fence.

So, there is more work to be done. For my part, I will choose to risk an error on the side of trusting too much in the power of the Scriptures and seek the fault in the exegesis and hermeneutics of those who consider hate crimes to be *biblically* justified.

36. Wilckens, "Stulos," in *Theological Dictionary of the New Testament*, 7:733.

must speak are many more than those that comprise a tidy summary of the plan of salvation.) And, the very words we use remain unintelligible to outsiders (and eventually fall into unintelligibility for us as well) unless spoken against the backdrop of a robust and distinctive form of life. In fact, it is this form of life—consisting in a complex web of deeds and words—that is itself an essential part of the Gospel message.[37]

In sum, getting to the truth of the Gospel requires a journey by the traveler into the very heart of the believing community. If one loses a coin in the basement, one does not search for it in the backyard simply because the light is better outside! Where one searches depends on what one is looking for. And the Gospel is found *inside* the believing community. Maybe this is what Augustine and Cyprian meant by the statement: "Outside the church there is no salvation." It is certainly why many early apologists, when they had their backs against the wall, instinctively pointed to the crazy cross-shaped way Christians lived with each other. Listen to their words:

> Most of our brethren, in their surpassing charity [in response to the plague] and brotherly love did not spare themselves and clinging to one another fearlessly visited the sick and ministered to them. Many, after having nursed and consoled the sick, contracted the illness and cheerfully departed this life. The best of our brethren died in this way, some priests and deacons, and some of the laity.[38] —Dionysius of Alexandria (d. 259 CE)

> We know many among ourselves who have given themselves up to bonds, in order that they might ransom others. Many too have surrendered themselves to slavery, that with the price which they received for themselves, they might provide food for others.[39] —Clement of Rome (d. approx. 101 CE)

> But among us you will find uneducated persons and artisans, and old women who, if they are unable in words to prove the benefit of our doctrine, yet by their deeds exhibit the benefit arising from

37. I do not deny that Gideon Bibles placed in hotel rooms and randomly read by non-church goers can and will sometimes result in salvation. That this happens is evidence of God's magnificent grace! But that grace also requires Christ-followers to use our heads to think clearly about the nature of evangelism rather than reduce it to one-size-fits-all technique. I thank God for groups like the Gideons, but surely—as they themselves agree—their strategy does not exhaust what Paul means by "gospelizing."

38 Eusebius Pamphilus of Caesarea, *Church History*, 7.22.9.

39. Clement, "First Epistle of Clement to the Corinthians," 55.2.

68 GOD AND GADGETS

their persuasion of its truth: they do not rehearse speeches, but
exhibit good works; when struck, they do not strike again; when
robbed, they do not go to law; they give of those who ask of them,
and love their neighbors as themselves.[40] —Athenagoras (d. late
second century CE)

This is the key to evangelism: speaking the right language from within a
communal life marked by grace and love.

WHAT ABOUT TECHNOLOGY?

When Christians dream about using technological tools to expedite the
Great Commission, we instinctively employ "efficiency" as the metric.
What makes the tool "good," supposedly, is calculated in terms of how
much information can be disbursed across a wide population in the
least amount of time and for the least amount of money. Granted, in the
West money is not always in this equation. We are so wealthy that we
seem happy to throw money at any hair-brained scheme that promises
to minimize human effort. (There is something demonic in the promise
of "efficiency" if we think it means getting something for nothing. We
would do well to consider the Psalmist's harsh condemnation of those
who have become wealthy without expending calories.) Thus a church
may happily spend hundreds of thousands of dollars to build and maintain a presence in "Second Life" (see ch. 2) as long as it doesn't take too
many man-hours.) In this chapter I've tried to show that efficiency is be-
side the point; those who couch evangelism in terms of efficiency grossly
misunderstand evangelism. Evangelism is decidedly not the simple dis-
bursement of information. Rather, when seen from the vantage of how
language works, evangelism is shown to be a performative act of communication that requires living bodies interacting over space and time
(ch. 2). In addition, seen from the vantage of biblical texts, evangelism
can be seen to be a complex, highly ramified linguistic act that requires of
the speakers a growing fluency that is itself a function of other complex
linguistic acts! Properly speaking, evangelism isn't so much "done" as it is
"lived." I don't mean to imply that St. Francis has the final word ("Preach
the Gospel; if necessary, use words"). Because my point is not that words
are unnecessary but that an evangelistic message is only fully intelligible
if heard against a backdrop of actions (mercy, generosity, self-sacrifice,

40. Cited in Bush, *Classical Readings in Christian Apologetics*, 44.

help, etc.) and yet *more* words ("teaching," "proclaiming," "praising," etc.). It is this web of background living—both doings and speakings—that makes the gospel click.

The New Testament uses the noun "gospel" and the verb "gospelize," or more commonly, "evangelize," one hundred and thirty times. I have touched on just a handful of these to make the case that both the evangelist and those being evangelized are engaged in learning a language and that the learning of this new Word requires a community of fluent speakers already to be in place in order to welcome a newcomer into the tribe. The central question that remains, therefore, is this: What sort of community must we be in order to properly execute the verb, *evangelize*? Three sub-questions come to mind. First, *Are we capable of sustaining the distinctive vocabulary of our new first language?* Or are we in danger of losing important concepts because we no longer use in everyday talk words like "holiness," or "propitiation," or "saint"? However far we are currently off course, the road back will require us to become intimately reacquainted with the text. Theologian George Lindbeck writes

> [I]t is questionable that the churches can seize the opportunities that this intellectual [milieu] provides.... Biblical literacy, though not sufficient, is indispensable. This literacy does not consist of historical, critical knowledge about the Bible. Nor does it consist of theological accounts, couched in nonbiblical language, of the Bible's teachings and meanings. Rather it is the patterns and details of its sagas and stories, its images and symbols, its syntax and grammar, which need to be internalized if one is to imagine and think scripturally.... What is to be promoted are those approaches which increase familiarity with the text.[41]

But he fears that the church in the West may not be up to the task: "Relearning the [conceptual] language of scripture is difficult, and at present there are no signs that the church can do it."[42]

Second, *Are we capable of sustaining the form of life necessary for making our language intelligible in a high-tech age?* It is of enormous importance that no apologist today writes in the manner of Aristides (and Clement and Mathetes and Athenagoras and Athanasius and . . .). Perhaps we lack an authentic church at which to point. I'm not suggesting that the early church was perfect—Good heavens, who'd want to worship

41. Lindbeck, "The Church's Mission to a Postmodern Culture," 51–52.
42. Ibid.

with the Corinthians! Nevertheless, even the Corinthians were marked by counter-cultural *deeds*; deeds that exemplified the message.[43]

Third, *Are we fit enough to tell ourselves the truth about the present unhealth of our churches?* One skill in particular seems to be lacking. It is called truth-bearing. Let me illustrate what I mean. In one church in my past, I served as part of the teaching leadership for an adult Sunday School class. (Of course, it had a fancier name than that!) It was my aim, so far as it lay in my power, to move this group of two dozen or so folk toward genuine biblical *koinonia* (fellowship) by cooperating with the Spirit when the Spirit's movement was obvious. Having learned that John and Melinda (not their real names) were going through a particularly bad financial patch, I took my cues from Acts 4 and spread the word among ourselves and raised a unspecified chunk of money—unspecified because we all blindly threw into an envelope whatever cash we were moved to give without knowing what anyone else gave. I can say this much, it was a thick envelope. We presented this gift to John and Melinda in class one Sunday morning and then thanked them for giving us the chance to practice imitating the church in Acts. They, of course, were deeply moved. And the rest of us were moved too—and also moved ever so slightly closer to corporately resembling Jesus. But there's a sting. . . .

For this act, or for fear of others like it, I was "corrected" by a member of the pastoral staff. I was told in no uncertain terms that "Under no circumstances may money be collected or distributed in class." Paul's example lept to mind, how he not only collected money from churches (such as Corinth), but that he was so resolute to deliver this gift to the needy saints in Jerusalem that when Agabus the prophet warned him that imprisonment awaited him, he went anyway (Acts 21:7–14). Evidently Paul thought that supplying financial care for poverty-stricken brothers and sisters was itself part and parcel of spreading the Gospel. As though he thought his preaching would be illegitimate unless he also was doing things like caring for the poor. But when I raised this counter-example with the pastor, I was snubbed. "Under no circumstances may money be

43. I fear that in contrast, the mega-church, currently so much in vogue for American evangelicals, has simply broadened the narrow way by reproducing within its walls a microcosm of *civil* society rather than a microcosm of God's peculiar people. I'm at odds with myself on this issue. I have been a member of a mega-church. But I find myself agreeing with Robert Jenson's conclusion that, if God be merciful our churches will of necessity get much *smaller* than they are. Jenson, "What Is a Post-Christian?," 29.

collected or distributed in class." The reason given? Collection of money might be off-putting to newcomers who might then stop attending.

I was aghast. I was angry. But I was also puzzled. What is wrong with this picture? It wasn't simply that the pastor and I didn't see eye to eye. The level of misunderstanding was deeper than that. It was as if we were speaking entirely different languages. Come to think of it, what *was* the conceptual language being spoken by this pastor in this congregation?

This returns us to the central issue of this chapter. Discrepancies between the conceptual language of the first-century church and that of this contemporary congregation must be under repair before there can be any hope of progress in faithful witness. That is why in a chapter on technology and evangelism I haven't written much about technology itself! When it comes to evangelism, what matters is not our tools but our form of life. And sometimes the tools that promise to spread the gospel most efficiently end up hindering our witness in ways that go unnoticed because the tools subtly shape the form of our lives together.

Consider something as benign as church architecture. As might be expected, the above pastor served a congregation that was "Gee Whiz!" about all things technological. And their building reflected their love of gadgets. The semi-circular room had a carpeted floor that sloped gently down toward the elevated center stage. The ceiling was high enough to make room for enormous projection screens visible above the heads of those on stage.[44] A single bank of windows to the west was kept covered by electronically controlled room-darkening shades. Thus the space was kept pitch dark, even at mid-day. House lights could be dimmed, but were often completely off whenever there was action on the stage. The stage, of course, was brightly lit by spotlights. Theater chairs substituted for pews, and pew racks were unnecessary since Bibles were absent. Paraphrases of relevant Bible verses were projected onto the screens for all to follow along as they are read orally by the speaker. Sermon notes are teleprompted to the speaker who comes across as folksy, spontaneous, and unstudied. I suppose that many pastors would cheerfully admit to being proud of the distance they have put between their communication style and that of the Reformers (who purposely wore academic

---

44. One church I have visited has seven such screens, sometimes with different images simultaneously. The church in the present illustration utilized only two—but they were gargantuan in size.

robes in the pulpit to remind parishioners to love God with all their minds as well as their hearts).

This scene is typical and replicated many times over across the country on any given weekend. The buildings owned by fast-growing congregations are invariably new. Some congregations began as storefront churches. Others were lucky enough to sell their inner-city buildings and build mega-churches to spec out in the suburbs or exburbs. Those who occupy one of these newer buildings are likewise proud of the fact that their buildings are "better" than the Baroque worship spaces that Luther and Calvin oversaw. But "better" in what respect? The criterion ought to be "better for forming Christlike community." Only if Christlike community is being nurtured at the level of the entire believing community can the conceptual language of the Gospel be fluently spoken. So the question of technology and evangelism is intimately connect to this question: Does our worship technology help or hinder community development? Specifically, does mega-church architecture help or hinder growth toward corporate Christlikeness? Since singing is listed as evidence of the Spirit's presence (Eph 5:18–19), we can focus the question even more sharply: does mega-church architecture help or hinder our singing? Despite the popular belief that mega-churches churches are marked by robust congregational singing, mega-church architecture may accidentally train us *not* to sing.[45]

During a worship service of the church described above, the sound system temporarily failed while the audience of 1,200 was singing. In the split second before everyone fell into stupefied silence, I was struck by the lack of volume coming from the chairs. The moment the stage volume vanished, why was the crowd unable to fill the silence? Perhaps they fell silent waiting for directions. Perhaps they didn't know the music. Perhaps they weren't singing to begin with. Whatever the reason, it became clear in a flash that the architecture was making things worse.

This church's architecture accidentally undermines Christian worship. The acoustics of many mega-church buildings are intentionally designed to maximize the clarity and volume of the PA system. One architectural assumption seems to be that the on-stage performers are of central importance. The performers must be clear enough and loud

---

45. I have, with Aaron James, previously recounted the following example in a previously published essay. See James and Kallenberg, "What Mega-Churches Can Learn from Catholics," 19–20.

enough to override the inevitable errant notes and hesitancy of people who are struggling to learn a new tune by ear. A second architectural assumption seems to be that, acoustically, the building structure must *swallow* all the ambient noise that a crowd of 1,000 (or 2,000 or 4,000) generates, so that everyone (including the television re-broadcast audience) can listen to the musicians and the speaker without distraction.

The impact of this architecture on corporate worship is in some cases crippling: the interior architecture ends up forming attendees to be little more than polite spectators. When the sound went out in our mega-church that Sunday morning, the silence emanating from the stage was taken as just one more cue to which spectators in the padded seats must politely respond in kind. Not that the acoustic vacuum could have been overcome had the crowd wanted to. But the real point is this: *it didn't dawn on us to try*, because the architecture had been forming us, over many Sundays, toward the assumption that we the audience are auxiliary to the real action taking place on stage.

IN TWITTER WE TRUST?

"Gospelizing" is one of the central practices of Christianity. And when the question of technology is raised in the context of this practice, it is very tempting to slide into list mode, approving those artifacts that help the evangelist (from microphones to blogging) and disapproving of those that hinder the task. But list-making defeats the purpose of this chapter.

My purpose has been to use a close reading of biblical texts in order to show how involved, how physically demanding, gospelizing is. In particular, the practice makes enormous demands on the *manner* of our life together. To the extent we live with one another in a way becoming the Good News about Jesus, our evangelistic words to outsiders gain traction. To the extent we fail to live the Gospel, or do so "in secret" (Matt 5:14–16), the evangelistic message becomes diaphanous, a wisp of smoke, and slips by unnoticed. Jesus tells us to pray in secret, but not to live in secret!

The church's record at "incarnating" the Gospel has been spotty at best. Heroes and villains abound. When medieval Italian Camillus of Lellis converted to Christianity after a long illness, he undertook to care for other sick in an age when the really sick were treated as aliens and forced to seek shelter in caves and catacombs rather than suffer mistreat-

ment at the hands of indifferent, sometimes sadistic, "hospital" staff re-
cruited from the criminal class.[46] Meanwhile, different religious (whom
Holbein lampooned as "warrior monks" in a woodcut) took up cudgels
with which to dash out the brains of the alien and foreigners.[47] Pretty
hard to share Jesus with someone whose brains have been dashed.

But today we face a different set of problems in addition to violently
conflicting examples of being "Christian."[48] Today's technology tempts
us to think that a Gospel shorn of human activity is still a message.

In 1960 Joseph Bayly published an insightful parable about well-
intentioned Christians who hired a "Gospel Blimp" to drop evangelistic
leaflets on the neighborhood rather than simply talk to their neighbors
in person. As a marketing ploy the idea was destined to fail; most of
the leaflets would be ignored and thrown into the landfill or blown into
the river. As an act of evangelism, the Gospel Blimp would be wrongheaded for a second reason: sentences need to be in close connection
with human bodies to be fully meaningful. Without bodies conversing,
sentences reduce to bumper sticker mottoes or ad slogans, which may
raise curiosity, but communicate little novel substance—the operative
word being "novel."

Just how radical is the Gospel? If we say, "not much," then the Gospel—like a billboard—might be paraphrased into terms anyone can understand. Optimism in this regard has been made all the more trenchant
by information technology. Inventors promise that very soon (although
not yet!) machines will flawlessly translate idiomatic sentences from one
language to another. An IBM version of one such project ingeniously uses

46. Ellsberg, *All Saints*, 300–302.

47. Historian Roland Bainton reports the words of one of the foreigners surprised
to be attacked by priests! "A certain Latin priest stood on the stern and discharged ar-
rows. Though streaming with blood, he was quite fearless, for the rules as to priests are
different among the Latins. . . . We are taught by the canonical laws and the gospel that
the priest is holy. . . but the Latin barbarian will handle divine things and simultaneously
wear the shield on his left arm and hold a spear in his right. At the one and the same
time he communicates the body and blood of God and becomes a man of blood, for
this barbarian is no less devoted to sacred things than to war. This priest, or rather man
of violence, wore his vestments while he handled an oar and was so bellicose as to keep
on fighting after the truce." Bainton, *Christian Attitudes toward War and Peace*, 114. For
Holbein's woodcut, see 134.

48. I used "violently" advisedly. At the time of writing, some pastors are calling for
overtly violent responses to the conviction of Scott Roeder of murder in the shooting
death of abortion doctor, George Tiller.

"crowd sourcing" (contributions of idiomatic translations volunteered from among 400,000 participants) to compile a huge database of *phrases* rather than words. Thus metaphorical expressions such as "he kicked the bucket" are not translated word by word, which would be a disaster, but by an equivalent colloquialism.[49] Computers make this search-and-swap very fast, although the delay time is still thirty minutes.

But the real problem is not to get idiomatic expressions correct—as important as this is—but to help others navigate the semantic range of the unfamiliar terms. Translators can substitute the French "Dieu" for the English "God" without pausing to wonder whether the god in question is Kali, Vishnu, Allah, Asherah, Jehovah, or a hundred other candidates. Who is meant can only be ferreted out by a series of questions and qualifications. But at some point, it is faster simply to become bilingual.[50] Thus we are back to the issue of evangelist as language coach. The real question, therefore, is can technology help us become better language coaches?

This question is best considered in two parts. On the one hand, there exist communications technologies (cell phone, texting, Internet, and so on) for which words are of central importance. On the other hand, is everything else (hammers, power grids, skyscrapers, and so on) that seem to have little or nothing to do with words. A clever reader may realize that since non-communicatory technologies affect bodily life, and the manner in which we use words is closely bound up with bodily life, non-communicatory technologies do have a role to play in getting the message out. We will consider how this works in chapter 5. The rest of this present chapter will consider the role of communication technologies, particularly the Internet, for evangelism. Our jumping off point will be a recent exhortation made by a high profile Christian, perhaps the highest profile Christian alive today, about the Christian duty to utilize the Web for gospelizing.

On January 24, 2010, Pope Benedict XVI made public his "Message for World Communications Day." He writes that "the explosive growth and greater social impact" of new media means that a fruitful response by Christians "necessarily involves using new communications technolo-

49. Cohen, "A Translator Tool with a Human Touch."

50. Rorty, "Inquiry as Recontextualization," 104. MacIntyre explains the categorical difference between translating and going bilingual. See MacIntyre, *Three Rival Versions of Moral Enquiry*.

gies." Priests and ministers in particular are "thus challenged to proclaim the Gospel by employing the latest generation of audiovisual resources (images, videos, animated features, blogs, websites) which, alongside traditional means, can open up new vistas for dialogue, evangelization and catechesis." In proportion to the closeness of these Christians to Christ, each minister will be able to "give a 'soul' to the fabric of communications that make up the 'Web.'"[51] The eighty-two-year-old Pontiff has increasingly said that a wise reading of the signs of the times constitutes "a challenge for the Church, called to proclaim the Gospel to [people] of the third millennium, keeping the content unaltered, but making it comprehensible thanks also to the instruments and means harmonious with the mentality and cultures of today."[52]

Techno-savvy evangelism, according to the Pope, means (1) proclaiming the Gospel, keeping the content unaltered (2) by means of the latest generation of resources. Is this possible?

Expert bloggers were quick to respond to news of the Papal message by offering advice to the Pontiff regarding protocol and etiquette of the current Websphere. There are "rules of reciprocation" which apply to those who do not want to be dismissed as rude: "if I link to you, you must link back to me." You must post every day (if only to set up a link to a favorite YouTube clip). Sentences ought to be short, and hot links must be substituted for academic footnotes. Finally, the Pope is urged to aim high: "He should try to get linked by the bigger blogs. He should try to be linked by, for example, Instapundit and the Huffington Post because if he gets the exposure there, then he can up his blog and ad rates."[53]

The expert bloggers are worried that the Pope doesn't know what he is getting into. Some of the problems that face the Pope's call to Web-based evangelism are a function of a shift in the way people use the Web. The contrast in styles has been dubbed as a shift from Web 1.0 to Web 2.0.[54]

51. Pope Benedict, XVI, "Papal Message for World Communications Day."

52. "Pope: Spread the Word Using New Media."

53. Madeleine Brand, "Blog Tips for the Pope: Give Us This Day Thy Daily Post."

54. I am very grateful to my friend and colleague, Jana Marguerite Bennett for her excellent paper on this subject. Bennett, "Thomistic Internet?"

Web 1.0

The way people initially conceived of the Web was simply an extension of the print- and imaged-based world we so long had inhabited. The Web afforded wider and cheaper accessibility, but the "content" still originated from a single computer operated by the author who owned the intellectual property of the posted material. Access could be restricted so that only those who successfully logged on could view the site. Material that was made public could be viewed by anyone who navigated to the site, whether intentionally or accidentally. The page(s) could be viewed but never altered by these visitors.[55]

Web 2.0

Web 2.0 represents a paradigm shift in using the Internet.[56] Tim O'Reilly has summarized the crucial differences by the following table that contrasts early read-only, full-control technology with its "open source" replacement:[57]

Web 1.0	Web 2.0
DoubleClick	Google AdSense
Ofoto	Flickr
Akamai	BitTorrent
mp3.com	Napster
Britannica Online	Wikipedia
personal websites	blogging
evite	upcoming.org and EVDB
domain name speculation	search engine optimization
page views	cost per click
screen scraping	web services
publishing	participation

55. It is a bit ironic to imagine the Pope blessing read-only use (Web 1.0) since an earlier message given to the University of Regensburg, Germany (September 12, 2006), by the theologian formerly known as Joseph Cardinal Ratzinger, contained one sentence in particular that was extracted from context, circulated around the Internet, and created quite a stir in the Muslim world!

56. For helpful introductions to this shift, see "Web 2.0," in Wikipedia, the free encyclopedia. Online: http://en.wikipedia.org/wiki/Web_2.0.

57. O'Reilly, "What Is Web 2.0."

content management system	wikis
directories (taxonomy)	tagging ("folksonomy")
stickiness	syndication

Of all the contrasts, Wikipedia is probably the easiest for novices like me to understand. In fact, the primary source for the explanation that follows was itself a Wikipedia entry! Wikipedia is a tool that epitomizes Web 2.0 because the articles are not only freely viewable by the public, *they are also editable by any viewer*. So, if a reader spots an error in an article, he or she can make the correction. The resulting post is immediately updated—without an editorial review process to bar malicious gossip or screen out any rhetoric intentionally slanted toward corporate profits.[58] While many express suspicion over what surely must be the low quality of the entries, at least one study has shown Wikipedia articles are of equal quality to those of the prestigious Encyclopedia Britannica.[59]

Imagine being a contestant on "Who Wants to be a Millionaire?" When stumped by a question about the year George Washington crossed the Delaware, you are permitted to employ a "lifeline." You might call a close friend. Then again, the chances of your friend knowing the answer are no better than your own chances. You'd be safer to query the audience. It turns out that most often the audience answers will cluster around the correct answer. Now imagine appealing to an audience of a couple hundred thousand people. The odds improve. The odds of getting a right answer are even better when only those who think they know bother to respond. This phenomenon is called "crowd sourcing" (or peer production or collective intelligence) and works quite well for general matters of fact.

The problem with the advice given by Benedict XVI is not that the Gospel will be tainted by the evils swirling around the Internet. Heavens knows there are plenty of those! But the "space" created by the Internet is every bit as sick as the real one we live in. The yuckiness of the dark corners of cyberspace is not what ought to give us pause when considering cyber-evangelism. What believers must come to terms with is that when we employ the latest generation of Web tools, we lose some control over the message. As one blogger puts it to the Pope: "Putting a message out

58. Hafner, "Seeing Corporate Fingerprints in Wikipedia Edits."
59. Terdiman, "Study: Wikipedia as Accurate as Britannica."

over the Internet is exactly the same thing as losing total control of your message. People take it up, they republish it, they make fun of it, they [re-] contextualize it. The simple message becomes incredibly complex."[60]

CONCLUSION

The Internet belongs to the class of communications technology. It enables fast, rich, image-based messaging in a variety of culturally enticing ways. We all know this. While a Gospel Blimp is laughable, and it seems patently ludicrous to imagine *tweeting* the Gospel (Twitter currently restricts each tweet to a mere hundred and forty characters), the latest generation of Web technologies seems to be a promising candidate for proclaiming the Gospel. But we have seen two difficulties that must be dealt with. First, Internet communications is *bodiless* (what former theologians would have called "Gnostic"). As we have seen in the biblical witness, genuine communication requires *bodies*. Thus Paul's exhortation is seen in a new light: "How can they understand without a preacher"— which is to say, without a living, breathing, eating, sleeping, sweating, sneezing, talking, walking preacher.

Second, early uses of the Web (Web 1.0) allowed evangelists to retain authorship and control over the message. This "read-only" approach faces the problem of traffic. How does a Web site generate sufficient hits by nonbelievers? If the site is packaged as entertainment, traffic to the site may increase. But the genre of entertainment undermines the seriousness of the Gospel as news. On the other hand, if the seriousness of the Good News is upheld, the traffic is likely to be only the closed loop of sympathetic believers who have bookmarked the page. Nonbelievers will not mistakenly stumble into a church Web site any more often than they mistakenly stumble into the church building. (Of course, they may visit both as a result of a friend's invitation. Once again, real people make all the difference.) Moreover, as a form of "read-only" communication, Web 1.0 reproduces the plight of the Ethiopian court official to Candace, Queen of Ethiopia, who puzzled over Isaiah. When Philip jogged up to the caravan, the court official complained, "How can I understand what I am reading, since I have nobody to converse with?"

Web 2.0 brings an entirely different set of problems for evangelism. Napster caught on because it was free. (Its freeness evidently was too

60. Brand, "Blog Tips for the Pope."

countercultural for it to survive legally.) Wikipedia works because when it is info that is needed, the opinions of a concerned crowd converges on the facts.[61] Google works because it provides (for free) a valuable set of services.[62] But will Web 2.0 work for evangelism if our message becomes disconnected from us and floats around in cyberspace to fend for itself? And what then of the 27 percent of U.S. adults do not use the Internet or the 30 percent who, perhaps due to poverty, do not have access at home?[63]

Second, the Internet in particular, and all communication technologies in general, only work insofar as they can be parasitic on communication that is connected to real bodies. Much of the time we get along well enough all by our lonesome. But should confusion arise, we need bodies—eye contact, body language, give and take dialogue, physical imitation, and so on—to supply context.

In some areas of Southern California, the eight lane interstate rushes past people's back yards. One enterprising soul had painted a very crude sign on a panel of wood and affixed it to a pole. The sign was brief enough to be read by speeding drivers: "Jesus saves." But what does this mean? Given the high percentage of Hispanics in the area, Jesus might be the name of a neighbor, a gardener, or a relief pitcher for the Dodgers. And "saves?" The neighbor saves at PNC Bank; the gardener saves a rose bush from disease; the relief pitcher saves a victory. Like those who zip along the Information Super Highway, my fellow commuters on I-10 were unable to ask "How do you mean?" Even worse, the commuters may not even have realized that the sign might not have meant what they think it meant. How could they, without a preacher?

In this chapter I have tried to highlight what needs to be our focus if we hope that our forays into evangelism will be fruitful: we must attend to how we live with each other in our church communities. So, how *are* we doing at this business of living well? This question almost entirely

61. Note that "information" does not exhaust all the categories of learning. Some truths can only be mastered by those who, being inside a practice, are shaped to see the world in a particular way.

62. Googledocs is one of the most recent. For an introduction to the newest trends, Web 3.0, see the various presentations posted online: http://www.labnol.org/internet/web-3-concepts-explained/8908.

63. These statistics are the result of a study funded by Pew Internet and American Life Project: "The Digital Divide." See also Gowen, "Lack of Computer Access Hampers Some Students."

eclipses the question of "Which technologies ought we use when spreading the Gospel?" Almost, but not entirely. At some point we need to ask about the proper role technology ought to play in fulfilling Christ's Great Commission (Matt 28:18–20). It will be the burden of the next chapter to consider this latter question on three levels: (1) What technological tools aid or hinder evangelism? (2) What technological "doings" occlude or manifest the Message? and (3) In what ways does technology as a "principality and power" impede the Gospel?

Many Christians do not pause very long over the first question. It's a matter of "full speed ahead!" Build that "virtual church" in cyberspace! Get busy blogging the Gospel! But I hope that my description of the biblical characteristics of "gospelizing" sensitizes us to the built-in limits to indiscriminate use of technology. There simply are no technological surrogates for actual human beings living with each other in a cruciform manner transparent enough for the neighbors to see.

As to the third question, throughout this chapter I've hinted at something troubling inherent in the technological world view of the West. If these inherent troubles can be blocked and countered, it will happen by Christians acting in concert. Such intentional action falls under the second question. To these three questions we turn next.

4

What Good Is Religion? Or, If I Had a Hammer . . .

S EVERAL YEARS AGO I attended a conference in Berkeley for first-time teachers of courses in theology and science. One of our conference events was a field trip to the animal cloning labs up the road at UC Davis. At one point, the tour halted in front of TV monitors that displayed a real-time image of the technician's view through her microscope. Astounded and amazed we watched her denucleate a mouse ovum and prepare to inject. . . . The atmosphere was electric, on the verge of applause. The tour ended in a self-congratulatory mood, as though being witnesses made us contributors to some sort of victory. To a person, we each walked away saying to ourselves, "Shazaam! *That* was really something!"

Technology has a wonderment about it that charms us, despite some very dark applications. But technology has a more insidious way of bewitching us than by simply being marvelous. It controls the way we think. It has become the single lens through which we struggle to bring the world into focus. For example, imagine an old-fashioned wind-up alarm clock. If asked to describe it more completely, you might identify its make and model. If pressed for a general definition, you would likely resort to explaining a clock in terms of its innards: cogs, gears, flywheels, springs. The real action, in fact what we take to be the *essence* of the clock, is here, in the mechanical interplay of these parts.

Since Isaac Newton, the clock has provided a fruitful metaphor for conceiving the entire cosmos. The universe is like a clock, mathematical in its regularity and mechanical in its interconnections. But we have come to mistake the metaphor for the thing itself. No longer do we think that the universe is *like* a mechanism, the universe *is* a mechanism, and the only explanations of its workings is that of mechanical linkage. So powerful is this technological metaphor that it can be applied to virtually everything, from enzymes to the economy, from psychology to cabinet making. Thus the machine metaphor tempts us to always and only look for explanations in this form: external causes and their correlative mechanical effects.

However, technology did not come to exercise control over human thinking by virtue of the fact that we put innumerable technological gadgets to good use. Rather, technology has locked its grip on us because it is more than a collection of useful tools. Of course, technological artifacts are instruments for doing work. And in this instrumental vein, technology begs for commentary from theologians. But technology is also more than instrumental. In chapter 5, I will argue that technology is additionally a "human doing" and (mysteriously) a "revealing." But first things first.

#1. TECHNOLOGY AS TOOL

Unsurprisingly, when we raise the question, "What is technology?" in order to understand ways in which Christians ought to relate to technology, we instinctively apply the tool metaphor and thus conceive technology *instrumentally*. That is to say, technological artifacts, machines, infrastructures, and so on, are tools that we value for the effects they coerce in a mechanistic universe. Machines are the instruments by which we get things done.

Technological artifacts *are* tools for doing work. In this light, we rightly ask "What sort of work is being done or undone?" For example, some technology is plainly hazardous. One by-product of nuclear technology is so-called "depleted" uranium, which is valued for its armor-piercing and ballasting properties. There is a growing body of data that links depleted uranium to deleterious health effects in U.S. ground troops that served in the Gulf War.[1] The consequences of exposure to depleted uranium appear to be even more dire for Iraqi civilians. Because Iraq is still a war zone, the evidence is largely anecdotal, but pediatricians working around Basra, for example, report a 600–1200 percent increase in the incidence of childhood leukemia and other cancers in the decade after 1991.[2] Regardless of whether that statistic is inflated, its very plausibility is troubling. Christians rightly call the military to task for the indiscriminate effects of such "dirty" bombs. Their case is especially strong in

1. Simons, "Doctor's Gulf War Studies."

2. Caldicott, "Spoils of War." See also Burnham et al., "Mortality after the 2003 Invasion of Iraq."

view of research, already in hand, concerning nonlethal weaponry that is highly preferable to bombs that are neither non-nuclear nor smart. For example, electromagnetic pulse (EMP) and high-power microwave (HPM) sources promise the ability to cripple an enemy's war machine by wreaking havoc with its electronics while leaving people and physical structures intact.[3] Devices such as the so-called "roach motels" use polymer adhesives to glue advancing troops and armory in their tracks while anti-traction technologies incapacitate runways and roads by covering them with a stubborn Teflon-like coating. Unfortunately, the Pentagon has an off-again, on-again approach to nonlethal weapons research, drastically curtailing the program in 1997, only to reboot it later. Suffice it to say, it is proportionally under-funded in comparison to ongoing research into lethal weaponry.[4]

A second way in which the instrumentality of technology requires a response from Christians concern those instances when technology has aided and abetted social injustice, as when it has contributed to classicism and prejudice. As is painfully well known, the internet has overwhelmed its surfers with a glut of information. In earlier days access to knowledge was the privilege of those who had the leisure and wealth to pursue it. All this supposedly changed with the opening of the information super highway. But of course, the information super highway is not without its share of casualties. For example, the spread of internet technology has created a new class of marginalized and invisible people—the computer illiterate and the "unwired." The Pew Research Center has found that those who make less that $30,000 per year have (unsurprisingly) the lowest frequency of internet usage—a mere 18 percent.[5] What is this if not an example of technology *widening*, rather than closing, the gap between the haves and the have-nots?

Perhaps just as dangerous is the way internet technology has contributed to an increase in bigotry. Type the word "Nazi" into Google and in one-tenth of a second you will be directed to 5.4 *million* webpages. When I tried it, one of the first on the list is a site maintained by Calvin

3. Harak, "Supercaustics, Roach Motels and the Grime from Hell." The trick is finding a suitable non-nuclear generated power source for EMP.

4. Broad, "Report Urges U.S. To Increase Its Efforts on Nonlethal Weapons."

5. For full demographics see the "Internet and the American Life" Web site: http://www.pewinternet.org/. For a readable summary of the Pew study, see Greenspan, "Internet Not for Everyone."

College. Near it stood the American Nazi Party homepage. If one were conscientious and diligent, both sites could be studied and weighed for their respective merits. Two down, five million to go! Of course, nobody has time to adequately evaluate all the sites listed. Information is so ubiquitous and its delivery so blindingly fast that assessment of any given Web site's quality is de facto left to *consumers* who, looking for shortcuts, simply pre-select their favorite *sources* of information. Unfortunately, consumers unwittingly select sources that tend to conform to their already unschooled prejudices.[6] In other words, most people line up one or two favorite sites on their browser toolbar and then never bother to look further. (This poses an insuperable problem for "internet evangelism." If the Web page on which the Gospel is presented is treated as a news site, it will only be read by those who bother to bookmark it. If the Web site wants broader range of hits, it will have to imitate entertainment sites. But can the Gospel be presented as something amusing or entertaining without distorting its nature? But I'm getting ahead of myself.)

A third way that the instrumentality of technology invites theological reflection involves those cases in which so-called technological advances have altered the character of social life. W. P. S. Dias highlights a well known example when he notes that planes, trains, and automobiles "have created greater mobility and freedom, but have also contributed to the fragmentation of society, whether in the form of differences between suburbs and inner cities, or in the diminishing of extended family interactions."[7] We no longer stop and chat on the sidewalk en route to market because suburban shopping malls have no approaching sidewalks; they are accessible only by automobile. Even churches have turned their architectural backs, so to speak, on their neighborhoods. Newly constructed church buildings tend not to face the neighborhood, but are now oriented so that the front entrance faces vast parking lots.[8]

Each of these three venues for ethical and theological reflection open as a result of seeing the instrumental side of technology; human agents create technology to get something done, and sometimes the instruments of change have unintended negative consequences.

---

6. Sunstein, "Daily We."

7. Dias, "Heidegger's Relevance," 393.

8. Bess, "Building the Church." For a seminal article on the way the automobile has shaped theology, see Heitmann, "What Would Jesus Drive?"

The Danger of Instrumentalism

When we think about technology-as-tool, it is easy to mistake the tip for the entire iceberg. What lurks below the surface, eclipsed from view, is hugely important, not to mention enormously dangerous to Christian belief. Below the waterline is an all-encompassing claim about the way things are and how things work. It is called *instrumentalism*. Contemporary technology not only fosters our unwitting allegiance to instrumentalism, the inverse is also true: our allegiance to instrumentalism fuels our belief that technological innovation is always and inevitably a good thing and that, in the end, technology will save us.

A close friend and colleague—himself an atheist of the friendly sort (one open to conversation)—forwarded to me an article from *The Chronicle of Higher Education* entitled "The Virtue of Godlessness." The article was an extract from a book-length treatment of the question, "Is religion good for society?"

In the book, *Society without God*, sociologist Phil Zuckerman argues that religion is harmful to society and thus ought to be discarded. In this chapter, I will show that Zuckerman's argument is wrongheaded. My task is not to settle whether religion is either harmful or beneficial to society, but to show that the debate turns on an instrumental view of religion. I will speculate about the role technology plays in fostering instrumentalism as a world-picture but spend the bulk of my time trying to accomplish two things. First, I will argue that instrumentalism is fatally flawed when assessing human praxis, including the practice of religion. Second, I will argue that an alternative world-picture is exemplified by gift economies.[9]

Voices as disparate as Ann Coulter and Pat Robertson on the one hand and John Caputo and Keith Ward on the other say that religion is *good* for society. Zuckerman freely grants that the world seems as religious as it ever was—perhaps even more so:

> [F]rom Nebraska to Nepal, from Georgia to Guatemala, and from Utah to Uganda, humans all over the globe are vigorously praising various deities; regularly attending services at churches, temples, and mosques; persistently studying sacred texts; dutifully performing holy rites; energetically carrying out spiritual rituals; soberly defending the world against sin; piously fasting;

9. Thanks to Michael Cox for his many insightful suggestions and to Kelly Johnson for putting me on to the poetry of W. H. Auden.

and enthusiastically praying and then praying some more, singing, praising, and loving this or that savior, prophet, or God.[10]

But, he wonders, does all this religiosity result in real improvement?
Religious believers, conservative Christians in particular, expect that it
should. Zuckerman notes Bill Bennett as a typical voice:

> Bennett has argued that "the only reliable answer" for combating
> societal ills is widespread religious faith, and that without reli-
> gion, a society is without "the best and most reliable means to
> reinforce the good" in social life and human relations.[11]

Zuckerman disagrees, insisting that sociological studies have *proven* that
the very worst places on earth to live are those that are the most religious. Conversely, those countries that are least religious—his favorites
are Sweden and Denmark—turn out to be the very best places to live.

Zuckerman presents a broad array of data, ranging from personal
interviews to socio-demographic comparisons of hundreds of nations.
For example, *The Economist* rated 111 nations according to "income,
health, freedom, unemployment, family life, climate, political stability,
life-satisfaction, gender equality, etc."[12] Taken together, these rankings
give a composite score for the "best places to live." Most of the top twenty
are what Zuckerman considers "relatively irreligious societies."[13] Sweden
comes in at the number five spot; Denmark number nine. These find-
ings have correlation with an even larger study published yearly by the
United Nations. The Annual Human Development Report ranks 175
nations according to three clusters of criteria related to physical health,
education and literacy, and livable income. Again the Nordic countries
are in the top twenty.

Zuckerman continues in this vein for some two hundred pages.
Perhaps like me, you are initially suspicious as to whether his claim
holds any water. I particularly want it *not* to be the case that secular
countries exceed religious ones in national charitable giving: Denmark
and Sweden are ranked second and third, respectively. Of course there
are a number of possible holes we might look for in his logic. Let me

10. Zuckerman, "Virtues of Godlessness."

11. Ibid.

12. Zuckerman, *Society without God*, 29.

13. Ibid.

quickly tick through these in order to get at what is most worrisome about his book.

First, Zuckerman appears to conflate a country's religious population with its entire population. Countries earn their reputation for being religious from the behavior of a relatively small percentage of the population who actually practice their religion "religiously," as they say. But qualities such as "life-satisfaction" are drawn from surveys of the *general* population. This is a comparison of apples and goat cheese.

Second, causation may be confused with correlation. Arguments for cases of causation in the social sphere are notoriously difficult to make. While Zuckerman blames religion for lack in the category called "life satisfaction," the data can be interpreted differently. In 2009, Simon Chapple of the Organization for Economic Cooperation and Development explained that the OECD's recent study likewise investigated "life-satisfaction," and again the Scandinavian countries were highly ranked. However, in contrast to Zuckerman's conclusion, the OECD study drew attention to the very high correlation between life-satisfaction and *the ability to trust strangers* rather than irreligiosity.[14]

Third, Zuckerman's criteria are ambiguous. In the studies Zuckerman cites, "success" and "satisfaction" are defined in terms of external goods. But, as Kierkegaard has shown, what counts as "good" is a function of what sphere of life—the hedonistic/aesthetic, the ethical, or the religious—the *investigator* occupies. Leaving aside what Kierkegaard calls the religious sphere, we might imagine two countries, one populated in the majority by persons in the hedonistic/aesthetic stage and the other populated mostly by persons in the ethical stage. Does a higher life-satisfaction rating by a predominantly hedonistic/aesthetic population indicate that life really is comparatively better there? With no universal definition of "good," how are comparisons ever to be made?

Fourth, Zuckerman's central vocabulary are "weasel words" whose meaning readers think they know, but cannot quite pin down. For example, how is "religion" defined? Insofar as "religion" names a family resemblance rather than a definition with sharp boundaries, the concept "religion" cannot function as a sociological category without great risk.

Fifth, cherry picking and over-generalizing are risks that threaten any summary of sociological data. For example, Zuckerman constantly reminds us where Denmark ranks, and occasionally where the U.S.

14. Mullins, "Not Enough Time."

ranks by comparison. But mightn't a better point of comparison be South Korea, the missionary's dream, with something like 39 percent of its population now reporting engagement in Christian practice? What conclusions would he draw about living in South Korea?[15]

We might also press Zuckerman for a full disclosure of other unstated, though highly relevant causes. When was the last time Denmark was at war?

It may be that careful investigation will show that some or all of these objections—and more—cripple Zuckerman's argument. And yet *. . . and yet* there remains something worrisome about his observations. Are we not deeply saddened by the fact that, setting aside those arguably justifiable cases, the divorce rate among Christians is virtually identical to that of the general population? Is not marriage a community-constituting practice whose point and purpose is to witness to the loyalty of our covenant-keeping God?[16] And are we not rightly surprised that a religion that names hospitality as a central practice (Rom 12:9–18) can boast of a personal charitable giving average at or below 3 percent of annual income, again not far from the national average? If as a nation we trail far behind Denmark and Sweden in charitable giving to poor nations, ought not Christian believers be ashamed?[17]

In the space that remains, I wish to challenge Zuckerman's argument by going after his warrant. (A warrant is the presupposition that two sides of a debate share and on which their respective arguments depend.) That warrant, which he shares with his interlocutors, is that the

15. There is some discrepancy between Zuckerman listing South Korea among the world's most irreligious nations (See Zuckerman, *Society without God*, 25, 119) and the fact that the 2005 South Korean census shows 19 million South Korean claiming Christianity as their religion. In a country of 48 million, this constitutes 39 percent of the population. If, as the Pew Global Attitudes Project of 2007 shows, only 35 percent of South Koreans self-identifying as "Christian" take their religion very seriously, this is still a country whose religious index *exceeds* that of the U.S. See Vu, "S. Korea Presidential Election Highlights Christian Influence."

16. This is a common theme in Hauerwas's writings. See, for example, Stanley Hauerwas, "Why Abortion Is a Religious Issue," in *Community of Character*, 210. Hauerwas situates his moral argument against abortion in the context of marriage as a Christian practice and gives a number of reasons why Christians ought not abort their children. For example, having children extends our witness, namely, our faith is worth passing on to a next generation and that no matter how dare things are at present, our God gives us hope for the future. Children witness to Christian hope.

17. Zuckerman, *Society without God*, 28.

point of religion is to change society. I will call this the "instrumental"
view of religion. By "instrumentalism" I do not mean to question the
fact that a particular religion, say Christianity, is supposed to make a
difference: "you will know them by their fruits" (Matt 7:20).[18] But today's
instrumentalism has both *standardized* the fruit and *measured* its production in terms of efficiency. Efficiency is an intelligible metric only if
input and output are quantifiable with respect to time. Standardization
and efficiency are, in their own right, problematic concepts for any religion. That said, as I see it, the deeper problem with the instrumental
view of religion is that it makes the point of religion *externally related*
to religious practices. I shall argue in contrast that the *telos* (end, aim,
purpose) of religion is *internally related* to its practices such that "the
whole *weight* may be in the picture."[19]

Instrumentalism as a Weltbild

The trouble with instrumentalism is not so much that it is a theory about
religion or a category by which we sort religions. Rather, the tricky bit
is that instrumentalism itself is a picture, an aspect, a bewitching way
of seeing, that slips in unnoticed amid religious language and practice.
Instrumentalism is included in what Charles Taylor calls the "buffered"
mode in which moderns experience the world.[20] Like explicitly religious
world-pictures (*Weltbilden*), instrumentalism is itself a world-picture. In
other words, it is not a picture we can look *at*; but rather one we (inevitably) look *with*.

Saying that someone looks *with* a picture is a shorthand way of
drawing attention to a characteristic way of being in the world.[21] A central feature is the "readiness to hand" of certain descriptions. Through
the lens of some *Weltbild* or other, one does not cast about for appropriate descriptions; descriptions spring to the lips: "What an answer to
prayer!" Alternatively, "what a lucky coincidence!" What I call *Weltbild*,
Taylor calls a "lived understanding. . . . the way we naively take things to
be. . . . the construal we just live in, without ever being aware of it as a

18. Of course, if we are honest with ourselves, the fruits of our contemporary
Christianity seem altogether puny. As I shall argue below, perhaps they are puny because we are neglecting the centrality of gift in the practice of our Christianity.

19. Wittgenstein, "Lectures on Religious Belief," 72.

20. C. Taylor, *A Secular Age*.

21. Mulhal, *On Being in the World*, 1–32.

construal."[22] The grip of the picture is reflected both in the fact that the world-picture doesn't wander and that one fluently knows his or her way around within the terms of the picture. At bottom, it makes sense to say that a *Weltbild* amounts to a kind of orientation of the person doing the seeing, a reliable disposition to see the world one way rather than any other. This was driven home to me by my conversations with an atheist colleague—the very one who sent me Zuckerman's review. He readily *understands* Zuckerman and agrees, and he readily *understands* Ann Coulter but disagrees. Yet he is having a devil of a time understanding how religion evolved if it didn't make the life of the species biologically better! Both his understanding and his puzzlement are evidence of his instrumental *Weltbild*.

On the Origins of Our Present Bewitchment

I suspect that we have become susceptible to instrumentalism, at least in part, due to the influence of the sciences. Since the time of Thomas Hobbes's seventeenth-century essay on "bodies," *De Corpore*, if not before, etiology in physics has been exclusively the study of the effects on bodies by causes that were always and entirely external to those bodies.[23] In other words, physics concerns *mechanical* causation. Think of billiard balls ricocheting around the table. Even gravity (seemingly a clear a case of *internal* causality if ever there was one!) is described mathematically in terms of distance from some *other* body. Stones no longer fall because they "love" the earth as Aristotle explained. They fall because the earth pulls the stone. All forces are external and all causes mechanical.

While the scientific outlook has grown powerful in the centuries since Newton and Hobbes, the addition of science to high school curricula does not seem fully able to account for the way we in the West have come to internalize the *Weltbild* I am calling instrumentalism. If it did, we could expect the scientific curriculum to be more successful in inculcating other scientific knowledge and values. Sadly, I still meet intelligent lay persons and college students who are entirely unaware of the *scientific* reasons for "greening" their personal behavior. Some even claim that "global warming" is a hoax foisted on an ignorant public by malicious

22. Taylor, *A Secular Age*, 30.

23. Jesseph, "Hobbesian Mechanics," 119–52. Taylor dates the shift to instrumentalism further back, claiming that Francis Bacon (d. 1626) was the result of thirteenth-century nominalism. Taylor, *A Secular Age*, 97–98.

scientists. Admittedly, some scientists have been guilty of oversimplify-
ing the data. But that they felt compelled to do this can only be evidence
of how unscientifically minded the public is. The hit television series CSI
has convinced the public to demand a smoking gun. But environmental
science doesn't work this way. Nevertheless, notice that unmoved is the
skeptical public's assumption that if global warming *were* factual, then it
could *only* be an effect that was *externally* related to causes such as consumer behavior. Consequently, changes in *somebody's* personal behavior
would be required (of course, not mine). In other words, commitment to
instrumentalism is evident among those who concede human behavior
is warming the planet but seek to shift the blame onto others, such as the
populous Chinese or the poorest 42 percent of the world who earn less
than $2/day and cook food on open-pit fires.[24]

No, I don't think that we learn instrumentalism just from the science curricula. On my view, we also learn it from *technological scripting*.
The basic result has been the loss of richness in our language of causality.
Prior to the fourteenth century, the concept of "cause" was far broader
than mechanical, or *efficient,* causation we think of today. A well-ordered
cosmos was linked together by efficient, but also formal, final, and even
material causes. Material causality included the idea that things always
act according to their respective natures. For an agent to act in such a
world, whether human or divine, the agent must *cooperate* with those
other natures, for each thing bears in itself its own God-implanted self-
governing *telos*. Sometime after the fourteenth century, the language of
causation atrophied until now we take "cause" as exclusively efficient and
"matter"—even living matter—as passive, even inert, something sitting
around waiting to be acted upon by forces and designs external to itself.[25]
Thus instrumentalism. The subsequent explosion of technology in the
West runs parallel to this shift in vocabulary.[26] In effect, contemporary
engagement with technology reinforces our cultural bias to think exclusively in terms of efficient causes acting upon passive bodies whose only
purposes are those which are *imposed* on them from outside and whose
only value is their ability to fulfill these externally imposed purposes. By

24. Rosenthal, "Third-World Stove Soot," A1.

25. For a contemporary account of the grammar of "cause," see Wittgenstein, "Cause
and Effect," in *Philosophical Occasions*, 370–426.

26. For this connection, see the work of Lynn White. For example, White, "Cultural
Climates and Technological Advance in the Middle Ages," 217–53.

means of "technological scripting," we have come to assume that human beings themselves are passive and inert, waiting for something outside of us to happen to us.[27]

Technology has a way of scripting our lives in ways that, though invisible to us, change our expectations and desires so long as we are being so scripted. A myriad of artifacts and infrastructures trick us into behaving in particular ways. Not one of us can enter our own homes without some version of the *grasp-twist-push* action commensuate with doorknobs. In other words, doorknobs *script* our lives so that we cannot go through the day without grasp-twist-push. Similarly we generally make right-angle turns with our cars, because we move across the surface of the earth on a roughly orthogonal grid paved with asphalt. And so on.

Innumerable scripted patterns of behavior feel as comfy as old Levis. We conform automatically and seldom notice how deeply ingressed technology is in our lives. In March of this year I attended the funeral of a young woman, a music major who sang with our church choir, who had been tragically killed when she fell asleep at the wheel and her car collided with a tree. The funeral was performed just three days before her twentieth birthday. The minister from her childhood church had the onerous task of addressing a packed sanctuary whose silence rang with the questions, "Why death?" "Why Sarah?" "Why, God?"

But no one thought to question the acceptability of hurtling through space at 70 miles per hour. This *was* a live debate in the early 1900s, when autos were incapable of exceeding 25 miles per hour. To move faster than horseback was then considered unnatural, un-human. But not anymore. Technology has permanently scripted our travel, *and* our expectations about what is natural, in ways now invisible to us.

Interestingly, a number of invisible technological scripts have managed to *supplant* roles that at one time were more commonly filled by religious narratives. For example, there was good reason for the Requiem Mass to repeat the plea *lux perpetua luceat eis*: "let perpetual light shine on them." Humans aren't nocturnal; we are light-loving critters: "The LORD is God, and he has given us light" (Ps 118:27). Light is associated with honor, gladness, and joy as well as understanding, guidance, and safety (Esth 8:16; Ps 119:105, 130). Thus light and dark-

---

27. Perhaps the most common reinforcement of human passivity comes from image-based amusement. See Postman, *Amusing Ourselves to Death.*

ness play central roles in religious belief and practice. Listen to the words that Graham Greene puts into the mouth of Father Thomas who serves at a leprosy hospice in the deepest jungle of Africa and see if you can't feel his terror too.

> Father Thomas stood by his netted door staring through the wire mesh at the ill-lighted avenue of the leprosaria. Behind him on his table he had prepared a candle and the flame shone palely below the bare electric globe; in five minutes all the lights would go out. This was the moment he feared; prayers were of no avail to heal the darkness. [The distant town of] Liege might be an ugly and brutal city, but there was no hour of the night when a man, lifting his curtain, could not see a light shining on the opposite wall of the street or perhaps a late passer-by going home. Here at ten o'clock, when the dynamos ceased working, it needed an act of faith to know that the forest had not come up to the threshold of the room. Sometimes it seemed to him that he could hear the leaves brushing on the mosquito wire [above his bed]. He looked at his watch—four minutes to go.[28]

It was for this instinctive and proper fear of darkness that the *Book of Common Prayer* as late as 1789 include a morning prayer that, as we saw in chapter 1, begins with a cry of relief: "Almighty and everlasting God, in whom we live and move and have our being; we, Thy needy creatures, render Thee our humble praises . . . *especially for having delivered us from the dangers of the past night.*"[29] But not us. And not anymore. The fear of darkness has been scripted out of us—we simply flip on a light.

I must be clear—I am not saying that all techno-scripting is a bad thing, even if it could be avoided. That some cars trick us into wearing seatbelts is a good thing! But whenever scripting does take place, it can at best only *mimic* genuine human formation. Whatever changes to human behavior scripts engender, the scripting itself never achieves lasting moral transformation. Aristotle reminds us that the justice system (i.e., its laws and retributions) *forces* the bad person to approximate good. In contrast, among genuinely good persons, friendship can be formed. And among friends, there is no need for a justice system to coerce me to do what I *willingly* and happily do for a friend. Technological scripting is like the justice system: both technology and the justice system differ

---

28. Greene, *Burnt-out Case*, 88–89.

29. "Morning Prayer," in *Book of Common Prayer*, 577.

from virtue-builders as external goods differ from internal goods, and coercive causation differs from deeds done in the right way, at the right time, in the right manner, to the right persons and for the right reasons.[30] In this way, technological scripts are the veneer laid over second-rate lumber to improve its appearance. It *does* look better, but it isn't very deep.

For example, employers have turned to various forms of electronic monitoring in order to discourage employees from Web surfing and emailing on company time. Its not that all employers are heartless and unrealistic. Most companies plan for employees to waste an average of 56 minutes per day, though they suspect them of wasting closer to an hour and a half per day. Ironically, when employees are interviewed anonymously, they admit to wasting over two hours per day![31] With good reason then, more that three-quarters of all U.S. firms monitor employee Web site connections, about half retain and review employee emails, and some even monitor every keystroke![32] It turns out that so long as employees *know* they are being watched, their behavior is quite commendable. Of course, if the snoop-ware goes on the fritz or is down for maintenance, then all bets are off. As Aristotle reminds us, virtuous habits are only formed by those whose actions stem from knowledge, right intent, and a firm and unchangeable character.[33] Of course, technology isn't the only thing that scripts human lives. As we saw in chapter one, F. W. Taylor's theory of scientific management has been applied by corporations that have themselves treated employees as inert, unthinking, cogs in the corporate machine.

Instrumentalism Ill Fits Human Practices

To sum up so far: Zuckerman's warrant for claiming that society is better off without religion is an instrumental view of religion—religion is *for* changing society and can be evaluated purely by that measure. Clearly,

30. Aristotle, "Nicomachean Ethics," II.9.

31. The single biggest time waster? 44 percent say "internet use." Malachowski, "Wasting Time at Work."

32. Joyce, "Every Move You Make."

33. "But just because the actions that are in according with the virtues have themselves a certain character it does not follow that they are done justly or temperately. The agent must also be in a certain condition when he or she does them; in the first place he or she must have knowledge, secondly choose the acts, and choose them for their own sakes, and thirdly the agent's action must proceed from a firm and unchangeable character." Aristotle, *Nicomachean Ethics*, II.2.

instrumentalism is a pervasive stance in this secular age.[34] How did it arise? I suggested the scripting of humans by artifacts and infrastructure is one plausible contributing factor to instrumentalism's pervading influence.[35] On the one hand, I suggest technological scripting seems to alter in a semi-permanent way the manner in which those who are scripted see the world. We have come to think exclusively in terms of external cause and effect. So, inhabitants of the technological West naturally expect technology to figure prominently in the salvation of the social sphere. On the other hand, I insist that technology scripts lives in a manner that falls short of genuine, lasting, virtuous habits. The tension between these two claims is not as great as it sounds. If, as Iris Murdoch and others have argued, vision accompanies virtue acquisition, then scripted behavior is short-lived precisely because the accompanying vision of the world is instrumental, which is to say, religious practice is an action one takes only when one *has* to.[36] In contrast, true virtue (i.e., genuinely and habitually good character) requires a *non*-instrumental vision of the world. Thus virtue ethics is categorically different from those theories that are relied upon by legal positivism.[37] But onward to my main argument.

Zuckerman reasons that imitation of genuine virtue is better than nothing. A neighbor who grudgingly obeys the law is to be preferred to one who flouts it! Thus, Zuckerman puts religion into the category of law, insisting it is reasonable to expect religion to do at least as good a job scripting behavior in positive ways as do traffic lanes and automatic seatbelts.[38] On Zuckerman's terms, improving behavior is what religion

---

34. Taylor, *A Secular Age*, 83.

35. Because scripting convincingly imitates virtue it has been adopted as the ideal means of social interaction: most nefariously, the church growth movement advises pastors and priests to intentionally script the lives of their congregants in both technological and non-technological ways. This corporate model of running churches is a direct if unwitting application of F. W. Taylor's method of "scientific" management.

36. Murdoch, *The Sovereignty of Good*. See also Hauerwas, "Significance of Vision" and "Learning to See Red Wheelbarrows." In Hauerwas's mind, vision and virtue are iteratively connected as one improves, so does the other, and vice versa.

37. Legal positivism is the view that there is no right and wrong except that which has been codified into an actual law or policy.

38. Bruno Latour gives a humorous account of the way some automatic seat belts force us to comply. Latour, "Where Are the Missing Masses?" 225–58.

is for. But my worry runs deeper. I contend that instrumentalism is not a picture that fits the human religious impulse.

Zuckerman is not the first contemporary thinker to suggest religion ought to be assessed according to its empirically detectable benefits. A similar point was raised forty years ago by Kai Nielsen against Peter Winch who held that religious criteria for rationality are to be found *inside* faith and practice. Nielsen complained that this effectively insulates religion from criticism. Thus Nielsen sides with atheists who, like Zuckerman,

> see religion as a tissue of metaphysical errors and superstitions that yield no sound arguments . . . as being utterly incapable in any reasonable way of meeting the problem of evil . . . as a groundless and pointless bunch of beliefs and practices that *do more harm than good.*[39]

But what follows from this? What if harm is done in the name of religion? What if, further, the rational case for God is full of holes? What follows? Instrumental reasoning would seem to demand that religion be abandoned. Yet many people are simply incapable of kicking the habit. Bernard Williams, himself an atheist, has written that contemporary atheism "seems seldom to have faced fully a very immediate consequence of its own views: that this terrible thing, religion, is a *human* creation."[40] That's why we cannot give up religion: *religion is part of who we are as humans.*[41] Human beings seem to be irreducibly music-making, ritual-creating, ceremonious animals.

I am perfectly aware that I am speaking of religion and the religious impulse in general terms. In point of fact, such generality cannot be sustained for very long. I do so here not because I think there is much substance in "religion-in-general," but because I think that Zuckerman's totalizing instrumentalism neglects crucial aspects of what makes us each human: my Christianity, their Buddhism, her painting, his music. Each of these enterprises in its own way defeats Zuckerman's assump-

---

39. Nielsen and Phillips, *Wittgensteinian Fideism?* 266; emphasis added. His seminal essay is Nielsen, "Wittgensteinian Fideism."

40. Williams, *Morality*, 80.

41. I am using Taylor's notion of religion as a mode of being in the world. This *Weltbild* approach has also been evidenced by Wittgenstein, Geertz, and Lindbeck. See Springs, "What Cultural Theorists of Religion Have to Learn from Wittgenstein," 934–69.

tion that the human mode of being in the world can be subsumed under the canons of instrumental reasoning. (The point of good art is . . . good art; it is not primarily *for* anything else.)

Zuckerman's warrant fails because the instrumental reasoning that he advocates is incapable of fairly assessing all those human activities—music, art, religion, etc.—that are born of *non*-instrumental reasoning. If the full gamut of human activity is to be fairly assessed, we would do well to consider an alternative logic.

THE LOGIC OF GIFT

Human practices—art, music, carpentry, religion, and so on—are governed not by instrumentalism but by the queer logic of "gift."[42]

When I was seven years old, "best friends" were marked by the willingness to give gifts to each other. The quickest way to fall out of favor would be to take back a present. This act of treachery, as we all remember, was to be—forgive me—"an Indian Giver." As a seven year-old, I did not dream up this term on my own. Oh no—it was taught me by my parents. To be an Indian Giver was horrible because it undermined the very fabric of American-style friendship and property. What my parents failed to tell me—because they did not know it themselves—was where the pejorative label came from.

The term can be traced at least to 1764 in Thomas Hutchinson's history of the Puritan colony.[43] In the name of goodwill, gifts were given by native Americans to settlers from the Old World. After some months had passed, the settlers were shocked when the natives demanded that gifts be returned. But the greater horror belonged to the natives who were terrified of the evil consequences—e.g., "storm damage"—that were sure to befall the land because the dimwitted Europeans had killed the Life Spirit of the gift by pulling it out of circulation. Now I find myself a bit perplexed: who are the real primitives in this story?

---

42. Because I wrote this as a thought experiment in reply to a good friend who is an atheist, I intentionally opted for sociological sources rather than theological sources (such as St. Bonaventure, Meister Eckhart, St. Aelred of Rievaulx, etc.)

43. My account of gift economies is borrowed almost entirely from Lewis Hyde's important extension of Marcel Mauss's original study by the same title. See Hyde, *The Gift*, 3–142, esp. 3–31.

For the sake of time, let me blend together features of several gift cultures in order to portray their striking contrast to instrumental cultures.

Three Is Not a Crowd

As a Minnesotan born to descendents of Scandinavian immigrants, I was raised on good American principles. The gem "a penny saved is a penny earned" instilled in me the conviction that wealth was for accumulating. Another, "the early bird gets the worm," taught not only the value of hard work and timeliness, but also implied that perishable goods like worms were naturally scarce so that we each needed to get a jump on our neighbors in order to compete for limited resources. I was also taught that "Two's company, three's a crowd." The clear assumption here was that the fundamental unit of social transaction—whether conversational or economic—was evidently *two*. According to all these maxims I learned to do my work before I played, to be ashamed of my empty piggy bank, and to always host parties with an even number of guests. All such reflexes became for me what the philosopher Ludwig Wittgenstein called "primitive reactions."

We know that God's creation is such that biological reactions enable similarly disposed creatures to co-exist in social community.[44] Dogs with dogs, cats with cats, and, on rare occasions, dog with polar bear and moose with cattle![45] Likewise, biological reactions enable similarly structured creatures to co-exist in *linguistic* community. As human beings, we squint at bright lights and shy away, while deer do not. These biological reflexes are embedded in the concept "brightness" as the readiness to pucker is built into the grammar of "sour" and "lemon." Other primitive reactions have profound *social* consequences, such as our early instinctive trust of one another (distrust being a complicated skill that is learned much later[46]).

But many other primitive reactions from which our linguistic communication develops are not instinctual but *learned* reflexes or hab-

---

44. For an expanded treatment on the relation of bodies and language see my Kallenberg, *Ethics as Grammar*.

45. Dogs and polar bears at play has been immortalized on YouTube: http://www .youtube.com/watch?v=JE-Nyt4Bmi8. On the moosecow love affair, see "Crowds Flocking to See Moose Courting a Cow."

46. Hertzberg, "On the Attitude of Trust," 113–30.

its. When someone gave me a gift, my mom drilled me to say "Thank you!" But she also taught me to reciprocate. In other words, I *learned* to keep score. If someone did something nice, I'd return the favor *in kind*. Likewise, if I had grudgingly given someone a birthday gift, I made sure to invite him to *my* birthday, because we both knew that he *owed* me a gift. The binary logic of the exchange often went unnoticed, that is until it is time to repay. And so reciprocal exchange continues to be trained into children even into early adulthood: young women are taught to be wary of the expectations of the boy who all too eagerly drops $200 on dinner.

The fundamental unit of exchange in the world of my Midwestern upbringing was always two. Accordingly, I was emotionally distressed to be in anyone's debt "too long." When I received a gift, my socially-constructed primitive reaction could not exactly be called "gratitude" per se. More fundamentally it was a certain feeling of indebtedness to the giver. I was *internally compelled* to repay him or her because as we all know, "There is no free lunch."

But now imagine an alternative economy where the fundamental unit of exchange is not two, but three or four or more. In such a culture, there would be no way to keep track of who owed what to whom. In fact, score keeping could never get off the ground. Under these conditions a distinctive set of primitive reactions can be imagined to emerge: in such a culture the reflex is not to "repay in kind" but rather "keep the gift moving," like a game of hot-potato with no-backs!

A number of such gift cultures have been studied and described. Expanding the pioneering work of Marcel Mauss, Lewis Hyde describes the Kula ritual of the Massim, a people inhabiting the cluster of islands off the northeastern coast of New Guinea. Crucial to gift-giving for the Massim is that the gifts must never return to the giver through the same hands that received the gift *and* the journey of the gift must *not* be tracked. Hyde writes of two different kinds of handmade gifts that circulate among the thirteen island communities. When one tribe received a gift of necklaces (*Soulava*), it brought a sense of well-being between the tribes, especially in light of the fact that the giving tribe had traveled hundreds of miles of open sea by canoe just to deliver the gift! Just as important, the gift itself soon enabled the receiving tribe to foster goodwill with a different tribe on another island. Of course, the tribe that received the necklaces also took care to express friendship and gratitude to the giving tribe. Before the calendar year was up, the receiving tribe undertook the hundreds-mile journey to deliver a gift of handmade *armshells* (*Mwali*). Of course, the gift of armshells enabled the original giver of the necklaces to build friendship with yet another clan.

Thus the gifts keep moving, necklaces in clockwise rotation through the islands and armshells counterclockwise. Hyde points out that "it takes between two and ten years for each article in the Kula [gift exchange] to make a full round of the islands."[47] So long as these gifts keep moving, friendship, community, and peace are nurtured.

Hyde speculates that the nearest thing to Kula exchange in our culture is possibly a gag gift or "white elephant" that gets smuggled from house to house among friends during holidays and reunions.[48] But perhaps most surprising, the Kula does not suffer death by attrition. Jaded capitalists, we might fairly wonder, "As there is no fixed exchange rate between armshells and necklaces, what prevents one from skimming profits by giving a cheaper gift?" Yet these gift economies have *not* petered out, nor devolved into market economies . . . at least not to my knowledge. Of course, hoarding, an American virtue, and the intentional accumulation of material wealth, the American dream, are poisonous to gift cultures. As if anticipating these dangers, many gift cultures purposely give *perishable* gifts as a way of scripting nonaccumulation.[49] Moreover, durable goods "perished" in the passing on, because they "perished" to the giver once they left the giver's line of sight.[50] The real test of the gift economy is the case when the gift consists in durable goods that are physically impossible to circulate. Shockingly, recipients *treat them as if they were perishable.* Thus recipients of a house celebrate it by burning it to the ground! In our horror we mutter, "What a shame! The house might have been sold for three-hundred denarii and some of the money given to the poor" (Mark 14:5). In contrast, their response is to say, "What else is to be done with a gift but consume that which cannot be passed on?" For, "if money stays, death comes."[51] Hyde draws attention to a lesson

47. Hyde, *The Gift*, 17.

48. Ibid., 16.

49. Not unlike manna, which perished day by day (Exod 16:4–20).

50. Hyde, *The Gift*, 11.

51. As spoken by Dr. Aziz in *A Passage to India*. (177 in my copy. Admittedly, Dr. Aziz admits to making up this Urdu proverb! But he is able to make it up on the spot because it so aptly conveys the outlook of the gift culture.) Cited in Hyde, *The Gift*, 27.

to be learned from the native Americans of the Pacific Northwest who celebrate the "potlatch," a several-days-long feast put on by a single tribal member. This was very costly. Its explicit purpose was to convert individual wealth into communal shalom, friendship, and honor. In this spirit, one gift culture, the *Haida*, happily and aptly dubbed their potlatch festival "killing wealth." Since wealth is toxic to gift culture, it is better to kill it off. Much the same logic was required of the Israelites. Though rarely practiced, the Year of Jubilee[52] aimed at protecting Hebrew gift culture by returning property to original owners and boundaries and to cancel all debt every fifty years. Jesus claimed that his reign reinstituted the Year of Jubilee.[53]

Gift-giving is understood at the deepest level to prevent disaster. In the eyes of many gift cultures, the "spirit of giving" is an actual spiritual being (the Massim call it the *hau*) or lifeforce which animates community within and between tribes. (The notion of communal spirit seems odd to Western eyes. But a careful reading of Christian Scripture shows authors often referring to the soul of the entire community.[54]) To recall the Puritan settlers, when they hoarded wealth, their wiser native neighbors, for the sake of love, became "Indian Givers" in order to put the gift back into circulation in hopes of avoiding "storm damage" to be inflicted by the spirit-being (*hau*) of the gift.

Although we thoroughly Modern Millies have difficulty with all this primitive mumbo-jumbo about spirit-beings, we ought to remember that the body of Christ is said to be inhabited and animated by a Spirit-Being too, one marked by *kenosis* (self-emptying) and giving, one that inhabits and fills *not* the individual but the corporate whole (Eph 2:21).[55]

Perhaps I digress. I do not describe gift economies in order to chide us for individual wealth, however deserving we are of such chiding. Rather, I describe gift cultures in order to defeat Zuckerman's claim—

52. The practice of *jubilee* is mentioned twenty times in Leviticus 25 and 27.

53. Luke 4:18–19. Biblical scholars tell us that the "year of the Lord's favor" refers to the Year of Jubilee. For the social significance of the (non)practice of jubilee see the work of Yoder, esp. *Politics of Jesus*.

54. Even the book with the greatest individualistic bent, the Psalms, was meant to be used in corporate worship and therefore contains references to "our soul," the single soul of the community. E.g., Ps 33:20.

55. On corporate dwelling by the Holy Spirit, see Kallenberg, "All Suffer the Affliction of the One." 217–34.

one he shares with many of his detractors—that the secular world-picture marked by instrumentalism is the *only* and therefore *best* way to understand religion. In fact, I claim that there are in play at least two rival families of world pictures or *Weltbilden*. On the one hand is the technologically inculcated world-picture: that everything is linked by a network of causes and effects; that for every action there is an equal and opposite reaction; that economics is but an extension of this causal network and makes all exchanges predictable and all (binary) contracts binding. Thus economics studies society in the technological mode.

But on the other hand are all those human practices governed not by the logic of cause and effect but by the logic of gift.[56] The poet W. H. Auden writes of the pleasures of practices that cannot be calculated in terms of external, instrumental goods. Rather, these pleasures are *internal* goods because they can only be known inside the practice.[57]

> You need not see what someone is doing
> to know if it is his vocation,
>
> you have only to watch his eyes:
> a cook mixing a sauce, a surgeon
>
> making a primary incision,
> a clerk completing a bill of lading,
>
> wear the same rapt expression,
> forgetting themselves in a function.
>
> How beautiful it is,
> that eye-on-the-object look.
>
> . . .
>
> There should be monuments, there should be odes,
> to the nameless heroes who took it first,
>
> to the first flaker of flints
> who forgot his dinner,

56. Again, I do not mean to subsume Christianity under a more general category "religion." But since the case against Zuckerman can be made in his terms, I wrote this essay as an exercise in argument.

57. The analysis of "practices" and "internal goods" is from MacIntyre, *After Virtue*, 181–203.

> the first collector of sea-shells
> to remain celibate....[58]

Part and parcel of the enticing, self-involving, healthily "addictive" quality of practices is the fact that their respective internal goods come alive only in the circle of gift-giving that constitutes a practice. Ironically, science and engineering are inherently gift cultures. That is to say, before a novice can buy into the totalizing view that instrumental cause and effect explains every transaction, the novice must accept as a gift the mentoring of an expert. At the outset, the novice doesn't know enough to calculate the worth of the gift he or she receives. But the novice receives it anyway: gifts of knowledge, of inclusion, of friendship, of mentorship, naively accepted on no better grounds than a primitive, wide-eyed trust of others.[59]

CONCLUSION

Theology is a gift culture, as are the Christian belief and practices that theologians study. I have argued that Zuckerman is wrong to assess religion on the basis of instrumental value for bringing about, or failing to bringing about, positive change in society. Even if he is correct to say that more harm than good comes from religious belief and practice, we may find ourselves unable to kick the habit. But what of it? Christianity is governed by a quite different logic and operates according to a quite different picture.

Speaking about art, music, and religion, Wittgenstein once observed that "the whole *weight* may be in the picture."[60] By way of conclusion, let me make two applications. First, if their whole weight is in the picture, then practices cannot be evaluated in terms external to the respective world-picture these practices embody. This has been the main focus of this chapter.

Second, if the whole weight is in the picture, then those of us who wish to communicate with those *outside* the ambit of religious faith and practice have nothing to offer but the picture itself. Insofar as we do not share with Zuckerman and Robertson and Coulter and Caputo and Ward the warrant of instrumentalism, we depend upon a different

58. Auden, "Horae Canonicae: Immolatus Vicerit," in *Collected Poems*, 477.

59. Hertzberg, "On the Attitude of Trust."

60. Wittgenstein, "Lectures on Religious Belief," 72.

warrant. God, who was in Christ reconciling the world to himself also *gave* to us the ministry of reconciliation (1 Cor 5:18–19). And while we hanker after means by which others *must* believe us,[61] our real task is to keep the Gift in circulation by endlessly *giving* the Gospel away.

---

61. Yoder argues that while we hanker for means to compel assent from others, the Gospel must be offered in a rejectable manner, in order to remain good *news*. Yoder, "On Not Being Ashamed of the Gospel," 285–300.

5

Technology and Redemption

W HEN WE THINK OF technology as *merely* instrumental, we are bewitched into thinking of it as morally neutral. That is, we are inclined to regard the moral content of technology as an add-on; as if the morality of technology is entirely exhausted by (1) the *uses* to which technology is intentionally put and (2) the attending *effects* of these uses. Yet once we believe technology to be morally neutral, we are enslaved:

> Everywhere we remain unfree and chained to technology, wheth-
> er we passionately affirm or deny it. But we are delivered over to it
> in the worst possible way when we regard it as something neutral;
> for this conception of it, to which today we particularly like to do
> homage, makes us utterly blind to the essence of technology.[1]

So writes philosopher Martin Heidegger. It is ironic that Heidegger should warn against the evils of technology since he was a vocal supporter of the Third Reich precisely because he thought Nazism provided the best hedge against global technology.[2] Yet I think Heidegger's analysis brings to light two other domains for Christian reflection on technology. He writes that technology is more than instrumentation. In the second place, it is in every instance a human act. And third, technology is a "revealing." Since these terms are somewhat mysterious and take us into perhaps unfamiliar territory, let me unpack them one at a time.

#2. TECHNOLOGY AS HUMAN DOING

Prior to abandoning the Roman Catholic Church, Heidegger had trained for the priesthood and spent years studying neo-scholastic theology while being groomed for the Chair in Catholic Philosophy

1. Heidegger, "Question Concerning Technology," 4.
2. Sheehan, "Reading a Life," 70–96.

at Freiburg University. So when he says that technology falls into the class of "human doings," he means what Thomas Aquinas, the font of scholastic theology, means. Thomas distinguished between "human doings" which always involve deliberation, and "acts of man" which do not. The latter—for example, absent-mindedly scratching my chin—have no moral content. Scratching an itch is something all mammals do. Come to think of it, so do birds and reptiles. In contrast, every human doing whether trivial or monumental, is a *moral* act.[3] Human doings may be trivial or monumental in significance. But morally neutral they cannot be. It follows that if technology is a human doing, technology would likewise be irreducibly moral. To pick an obvious example, driver's side air bags are moral because (1) they are the *instruments* for saving lives (level 1: technology-as-tool) but also because (2) their design and production and installation and maintenance are humanly *intended* for the saving of lives (level 2, technology-as-human-doing). Even a hammer is not morally neutral. Sure, it can be used to build a house or cave in someone's skull. But setting aside these actual uses, the hammer is not in and of itself neutral. We only have hammers because humans need to construct shelter. Constructing shelter is morally good because it meets a genuine human need. (Thus Habitat for Humanity is a morally good program.) If constructing shelter is inherently good, then so is the hammer. Technological artifacts are *never* void of human intention, and each of the intentions embodied in the artifact has moral weight.

However, precisely because technology embodies human intention, human interaction with technological artifacts can mold or deform the dispositions and character of those who engage it every bit as much as interactions with other persons shapes our dispositions and character. Theologian G. Simon Harak explains that our habitual responses to the world around us has its roots in human biology. However, you and I are equally prone to form habits by repeated interactions with *abstractions* (e.g., ideas) and *nonliving things* (e.g., machines) as we are by repeated interactions with other people.[4] The fact that we are habit-forming critters gives technology a moral significance that is broader than its instrumentality. For example, think of a puppy. We in the West have instinctual affections for puppies. We pet them, we giggle at them, we cuddle them.

---

3. For a very important summary of Aquinas' thought, one that contrasts him to contemporary theoretical ethics, see Pinches, *Theology and Action*.

4. Harak, *Virtuous Passions*.

We speak of "puppy eyes" and of "puppy love." All in all, we find puppies irresistible. Now imagine canvassing a large auditorium looking for a volunteer to wring a puppy's neck here and now with one's bare hands. No special reason is given. Here is a week-old Golden Retriever puppy with huge brown eyes and enormous feet. Now kill it. We'd expect no takers. Quite the opposite, we'd be horrified if someone did volunteer!

Now let's insert technology into the experiment. Might not the task of killing the puppy be a tiny bit easier if one were allowed to club it with a baseball bat? No? What about shooting it with a rifle? In other words, tie the puppy to a tree and you, the shooter, stand far away—a painless death over in an instant. Still no? Of course, one must still sight down the barrel of the rifle. Ah, but what if one could aim the rifle without looking directly at the puppy? Perhaps one could acquire the target by aligning crosshairs with a blip on an oscilloscope screen. Then one could simply depress a button, rather than pull a trigger, and the blip on the screen goes out. Surely this would be a nearly painless way for a human subject to achieve the objective. In fact, one could probably terminate multiple targets in a short span of time so long as the targets weren't allowed freedom of movement. Constrain the targets and the task becomes as easy as "shooting fish in a barrel."[5]

This very phrase, "shooting fish in a barrel," was used by one American pilot in Desert Storm to describe the bombing runs on re-treating Iraqi troops.[6] We have to admit that warcraft technology, by enabling human subjects to act at great distances, has lowered the threshold of any aversion one might have to killing. Incidentally, this helps us understand why Augustine's requirement (namely, that killing in war be done "mournfully") was a realistic requirement for medieval combatants, since killing in his day could not be done at distances great enough to impersonalize the "target."[7] It also helps us understand why

5. The inverse relation between proximity of subjects to their targets and the self-divestiture of responsibility emerges in the famous people-shocking-people experiment. Stanley Miligram's experiment was drawn to my attention in Schinzinger and Martin, *Introduction to Engineering Ethics*, 86–87. See also Milgram, *Obedience and Authority*.

6. "Crisis in the Gulf."

7. For a discussion and citation of Augustine's "mournfulness" requirement, see Bainton, *Christian Attitudes toward War and Peace*, 139. It might be objected that ar-chers could acquire targets at a depersonalizing distance. But even contemporary hunt-ers using compound bows know that bow hunting gives deer a sporting chance. Not so for those who shoot deer from a tree stand using rifles equipped with high-power

since the invention of the cannon, the possibility of consistently fulfilling the "mournfulness" requirement in warfare increasingly becomes an exercise in futility. How can today's soldiers be expected to feel genuinely mournful for an action carried out by drones?

Please note that one doesn't need to object to warfare per se in order to understand the point. God has wired our bodies to have an aversion to killing. This inversion to inflicting pain is a wonderful gift because it makes us naturally motivated to care for babies, give aid to the injured, and generally help others.[8] This aversion is so strong that only 15 to 20 percent of U.S. soldiers on the front lines of WWII even fired their weapons![9] In subsequent years the Department of Defense implemented a series of strategies to overcome this natural aversion to inflicting pain. To date the most effective tool the military has found to simulate battle hardening appears to be video games.[10] Since repeated playing of a certain video game makes the gamer less reticent to kill, we cannot say the video game is morally neutral. If one's interactions with the game shape dispositions, the game already has moral content, even if the use to which it is put (amusement) seems harmless.

We see in these examples technologies that make some (im)moral acts more likely than others. Consequently, the technologies themselves cannot be regarded as morally neutral. As a human doing, each instance of technology is a *moral* act. Of course, technology also is a social enterprise involving the interplay of many people, many human intentions, many human doings. Anytime people relate to one another, morality is involved. But technology is a unique case. There is a fundamental difference between organizing parents to drive kids to their soccer game and the sort of highly complex cooperation that marks the enterprise of engineering technology.[11] The sophistication of this interplay of many

---

scopes. So I will grant that medieval archers may have acquired depersonalized targets, but the margin for error was clearly great enough that they could not have claimed full responsibility for hitting a distant object without the help of God. In contrast, modern weaponry both greatly increases the depersonalization factor (by greatly increasing the distance) and enables the triggerman to claim full responsibility for the hit.

8. Wade, "We May Be Born with an Urge to Help."

9. Grossman, *On Killing*, 1.

10. Vargas, "Virtual Reality Prepares Soldiers for Real War."

11. Michael Davis has argued that widespread cooperation is what distinguishes engineering from other branches of science. Davis, *Thinking Like an Engineer*, 5–30.

persons indicates that engineering exemplifies what Alasdair MacIntyre calls a "practice."

"Practice" is a technical term for MacIntyre. By it he refers to those cooperative human enterprises that have the feature of turning novices into masters through the pursuit of excellence under the watchful eye of qualified mentors.[12] Thus medicine is a practice, as are law, football, even chess.

One notable feature of practices is their coherence; they aim at some end (*telos*). Medicine, for example, aims at health. When I ask engineering students what engineering is for, at what does it aim, they invariably say, "to build cool stuff." If I press them, they will explain that engineering aims at assisting human living or at making human life "better." But better in what respect? How do we assess what is better or worse? From what do we get a sense of our "ends" or "goods"?

On the one hand, the practice-nature of engineering itself can function as a crude gyroscope that charts its own course for excellence in technology. Consider the fact that the U.S. government willingly funds scientific research so long as each research project has obvious future promise (most often for military application). Yet the inducement of this large pot of R&D dollars is not large enough to prevent some engineers from expressing the tension they feel between their role as city-builders and those military applications of their technology that make them city-destroyers.[13] Even the nefarious Albert Speer, the architect-cum-Minister of Armaments under Hitler, knew that he could not consciously contemplate *as an architect* well-crafted buildings that had been bombed out—be they synagogues or houses—without a deep sense of loss.[14] Why not? Because engineering and its sister, architecture, aim at *con*struction rather than *de*struction. Consequently, the technology of destruction cannot but be parasitic on practices that have as their point and purpose something other than destruction. But that means that there is real goodness *already in play* in the practice of engineering in order for these objectors to feel the pinch. To be sure, the misgivings of some individual

---

12. See MacIntyre, *After Virtue*, 187–94.

13. See e.g., Steffens et al., "Panel Discussion: Ideas for Better Code."

14. Thus Speer opted to turn a blind eye. For complementary accounts of Speer's moral failure, see Sammons, "Rebellious Ethics and Albert Speer," 123–60. See also Hauerwas, with Burrell, "From System to Story," 158–90.

practitioners derive from their religious faith. Importantly, not all dissenters are religious believers.

Or consider another example. Engineering students cut their teeth on co-op jobs and internships. By the time they are ready to graduate, some will have picked up from the business environment the notion that competitiveness in industry requires designing obsolescence into each product. Thus, products with short lives are "good" because they must soon be replaced. Here "good" is measured in terms of market value.[15] A university colleague in the School of Engineering tells the story of an engineering firm that proposed the following project to my friend's senior-level engineering design class. Students were asked to shave pennies off the production cost of a one-dollar engine part. After studying the project very carefully, the class countered with the proposal that if the firm were willing to *spend* an additional two cents (or so) per part, they could suggest changes in the design that would double and perhaps even triple the mileage of the part. Predictably, the firm declined.[16]

Now, old-school engineers (like my father) squirm at stories like these because business as an "enterprise" runs against the grain of engineering as a "practice." Consequently, engineers are pegged by business entrepreneurs as "glass-half-empty" sort of folk who must be commanded by their superiors to take off their engineering hats from time to time and put on their business hats. (That of course was the infamous advice taken under duress by Robert Lund when, against his better engineering judgment, he approved the immediate launch of the space shuttle *Challenger* for its final flight.[17] Lund's failure as an engineer, and thus his moral failure, lies in the fact that he took off his engineer's hat in the first place.)

15. Of course, "market value" is not *value* per se at all, but only a reflection of what market can bear when supply equals demand. This point is made clear in Whitbeck, *Ethics in Engineering*, 6–9.

16. Of course designed obsolescence is not always a bad thing. For example, no product ought to outlive its function (e.g., long lasting buggy whips!). Some products already last too long (e.g., candy wrappers). The important point is that engineering seeks to minimize wasted material and efforts on the grounds that every product fails eventually. Koen, *Discussion of the Method*, 82–83.

17. The order to Lund was just that blatant: "Take off [your] engineering hat and put on [your] management hat," cited in May, " Engineer," 89–128. There are numerous other accounts of this disaster. See, for example, Schinzinger and Martin, *Introduction to Engineering Ethics*, 96–104.

So then, engineering seems already to possess something of a built-in gyroscope for Good that is embodied in its own history of excellence. This trajectory for the Good counters the tangential impetuses of government and business interests. Yet, on the other hand, the centripetal force of this gyroscope, while necessary to engineering excellence, is not *sufficient* for engineering to maintain a moral trajectory. It is too vague. It is just not enough. MacIntyre argues that all moral vocabulary—words like "better" and "good"—are contentless unless at home within master stories that answer "what is human life *for*?" If human life is for increasing market share in a capitalist economy, then designed obsolescence is a reasonable engineering strategy. If human life is for the dominance of other people groups by one's own, then engineering's reliance on the Department of Defense for funding is a no-brainer. But Christianity is in a position to contest the allegiance of engineering to nationalism, capitalism, militarism, and all other "isms." In place of these "isms," Christianity offers a rival account of what human life is for, and thus a categorically different *telos* (end, aim, purpose) for the practice of technology. This rival account begins and ends with the story of Jesus.

#3. TECHNOLOGY AS A "REVEALING"

A third locus for Christian reflection stems from the fact that technology is a "revealing" (*das Entbergen*).[18] By this mysterious gerund, Heidegger is alluding to the fact that technology, in its cumulative effects, takes on a life of its own in that it is able to reveal a message or tell a story akin to a human teller. This makes technology almost alive and gives us reason to speak of the "essence" and "nature" of Technology with a capital "T." Perhaps Technology is not a "something." But it is not a "nothing" either. In Heidegger's words, the essence of Technology is seen in its "harboring forth," "opening out," its "blossoming" in time. In other words, all moments of technology—my use of a gadget, your invention of a gizmo—share a (narrative) continuity that unfolds in time. Thus we can speak of the *progress* of Technology as if it were an entity and of the *development* of Technology as if it had a life of its own. And of course, in an important sense, it does have a life of its own.

This feature of Technology, its "revealing," means that Technology ought to be classed with social structures, power relations, what some

18. Heidegger, "Question Concerning Technology," 11.

Technology and Redemption

Technology and Redemption

Technology and Redemption

theologians have identified as "principalities and powers."[19] The fact that by "technology" we are not addressing some dead set of mechanisms means that Christians ought not attempt to coerce the place of Technology as one might use a crowbar to dislodge a heavy object. Crowbars are dead. But Technology lives. Crowbars are external causes for producing external effects. But if Technology has taken on a life of its own, we must seek an organic mode both for describing it and dealing with it, and furthermore to take care in its use that Technology does not in turn use us.

It is difficult to tell the story of technological development without presuming some theory of development or other. In a seminal article, philosopher Messay Kebede argues that theories of development are self-stultifying.[20] One kind of theory is "idealism," roughly the view that ideas drive history. However, idealism cannot account for cultural development without presuming something about the *material* conditions for change. The obverse kind of theory is "materialism," roughly the view that culture ratchets forward along tracks laid down in the material conditions already in place. Ironically, materialists wind up explaining their thesis using *ideas* and so end up unwittingly employ the very *idealist* features that their materialist explanations are intent on excluding! Thus while it has long been held that materialism differs from idealism in ways just as intractable as the mind-body problem, when it comes to actual cultural development, material and ideal conditions are irreducibly interdependent. Ideas drive cultural change? Material conditions drive cultural change? Yes; both!

Look at it this way. If we follow materialist theories when thinking about high-tech culture, we arrive at something like "technological determinism."[21] Taken to the extreme, society will one day reach a tipping point after which machines will control human destiny. Over the past two generations, we have witnessed a sharp decline in the average citizen's ability to repair the things she or he owns—a skill set still possessed by my parents' generation. While practical knowledge continues to plummet, the world currently holds its collective breath for the "singularity," the moment of genuine artificial intelligence. From then on there will be no turning back, we will slide into the future of science fiction

19. The classic introduction to principalities and powers is Berkhof, *Christ and the Powers*. See also the works by William Stringfellow and Walter Wink discussed below.

20. Kebede, "Underdevelopment and the Problem of Causation," 125–36.

21. The following analysis owes much to Winner, "Do Artifacts Have Politics?"

films such as *Terminator* or *The Matrix* or *iRobot*. Of course, many—though not all—educated folks snicker at such a proposal.

On the other hand, if we try to explain development of techno-logical culture by adopting the motto that ideas drive culture, we end up with a form of "cultural determinism." This view insists that technology always follows the dictates of the humans in charge. Society demands it, technicians build it, consumers buy it, and that settles it. Those in charge might include government officials, financial speculators, scientists and engineers. Technological advancement doesn't happen unless someone pays for someone else to think it up and build it with the permission of someone else. (God is typically left out of this chain of causes.) On this alternative analysis, any moral evil or moral good appears traceable back to the sum total of all the intentions of all the humans involved. And since human intentions predate the building of artifacts, it is theoreti-cally possible to completely analyze the moral state of a culture by exam-ining human intentionality without ever looking at its high tech tools.

As we saw in chapter one, this second view is overly simple too. Some technologies have moral effects that outlive their artificer's inten-tion (recall Robert Moses's overpasses.) Other technologies have wider moral effect than can be comprehended by human builders.[22] One of the chief difficulties with both ways of thinking about culture lies in the assumption that human beings are one thing and that technology is something else, leaving the two to relate to each other in *external* terms of mechanical cause and effect. Human beings mechanically effect ar-tifacts by building, using and discarding them. Artifacts mechanically affect human beings by scripting their behavior and sometimes hurting human bodies.

What if there were a subtler mode of human–technology inter-action? What if, instead of externally or mechanically related cause to effect, the two interacted organically (what philosophers might call "in-

---

22. Staudenmaier gives a compelling case in his description of the "impact con-stituents" of the automobile industry. The "damages" of Ford's innovations include the entire livery industry that was displaced by cars, the workers who are injured on the job (e.g., repetitive motion injuries) or inadvertently ingest unhealthy doses of toxins (cleaners like trichloroethylene, etc.) in the factory, the property owners who lost land to highways by rule of eminent domain, truck drivers who suffer permanent kidney or back damage from endless hours behind the wheel, all those accidentally killed in crashes. Even the very poor who cannot benefit from owning a car still live in low-income housing that may be located overly close to smog-clogged roadways. And so on. Staudenmaier, "Politics of Successful Technologies," 150–71.

ternally related")? That would, in effect, make us *social cyborgs*. By this term I don't mean that some humans have robotic parts—although many people have artificial knees, metal fillings, hearing aids, pacemakers, and prosthetic limbs. I mean, rather, that our social life can only be what it is by the smooth integration of technology and human lives. Technologies are so embedded in everyday living that they defy us to imagine their removal. What would human existence be like without cell phones, asphalt, laptops, the Web, sewers, automatic air conditioning, window screens, electric lights, and so on? Surely life would be enormously different. Are all these examples still merely tools? I say no. No, because the interplay of all these technologies and their related infrastructures shape how we perceive, think, and imagine our world.

A child who has been given a hammer walks around *looking* for things to pound. This has never occurred to the child before. But once in possession of a hammer, the whole world becomes something to wham! Not just nails, but bugs, rocks, fence posts, trees. . . . Now give a culture television. Doesn't the whole world become something to *watch*? Neil Postman recounts how the West migrated from a print culture to an image culture as information transfer increased speed (telegraph, telephone, wireless telegraphy, etc.) and as pictures became commodified and reproducible (newspapers, television, the Internet, etc.).[23]

Postman compares today's culture to ordinary county fairs of the 1850s. Nestled in the schedule among competition for prize cows and prize jams would be a political debate of some kind, attended by virtually everyone at the fair. Postman reports that fair-goers were no country bumpkins, "these were people who regarded such [debates] as essential to their political education, who took them to be an integral part of their social lives and who were quite accustomed to extended oratorical performances."[24] Just how "extended" were these debates? When Stephen A. Douglas debated Lincoln in Peoria, IL (1854), neither was a candidate for major office like U.S. Senate or President. They were both ordinary debaters on an ordinary stage. Douglas spoke uninterrupted for three hours. Lincoln's reply—amicably postponed until after dinner—was four hours long. No pictures, no sloganeering, just seven hours of highly nuanced debate that presumed familiarity with historical precedent and

23. Postman, *Amusing Ourselves to Death*.
24. Ibid., 44–45.

employed "irony, paradox, elaborate metaphors, fine distinctions, and the exposure of contradiction."[25]

Now, I can imagine an audience languishing through Douglas's speech (perhaps too embarrassed to leave). What is hard to imagine is that everyone came back after dinner for an even longer rebutal!

Clearly, today we inhabit a quite different form of life. This is not necessarily to say that television has lowered our collective IQ. It does mean that we process our world in entirely different ways than our grandparents. Granted, the average length of primetime news stories (45 seconds) seems to imply highly truncated attention spans. But feature films can hold our rapt attention for four hours, or even longer. The difference is this: while our grandparents could attend to texts—both spoken or printed—we seem to *require* images. We have become the consummate consumer of images. The ease with which high quality images can be televised and digitally streamed has allowed professional sports to become an enormous financial enterprise. After all, if spectating images are essential to how we process the world (maybe even essential to who we are), then we do not balk at paying for a steady stream of images. A steady stream of images is now considered a fundamental human good. Only this explains the incredulity of the AT&T sales rep who was going door to door in our neighborhood. He cheerfully approached me and offered to sign me up for a wonderful bundle of services: digital television, cell phone service, and high-speed internet. When I told him that I didn't own a cell phone (though my wife does) and I watched only the local commercial TV stations, he looked at me with incredulity, as though I said I believed in pixie dust: "Then I can't help *you* at all!" and walked away.

Apparently to be human is to spectate. At least we live as if that were obvious. But what if image-based media (television, digital streamed video, etc.) cannot do justice to every message? Postman reminds us that smoke signals could never be used to discuss philosophy! So, perhaps we ought not be too hasty to assume that everything, including Christian worship, is "televisable." Søren Kierkegaard's nineteenth-century advice still applies today. He explained that congregations are not the audience for whom the minister performs. Rather, God is the audience, the congregants themselves are the players, and the minister is simply the stage

25. Ibid., 47.

prompt who reminds us of our lines. Proper worship is participatory, not a spectator sport.[26]

Examples of how technology scripts both how we see and interact with our surroundings could be multiplied. Technology is neither our dictator (technological determinism) nor merely our tool (cultural determinism) but something much closer to us, under the skin or in the blood, as it were. Langdon Winner has called this "political technology." We are social cyborgs. So closely is technology bound to our life together that we must conclude that all technology has moral, political, communal, even human properties. Although each of us as individuals interact with technological artifacts countless times every day, the character-shaping properties are especially clear when viewed at the level of community and society. At the level of community and society we begin to understand a bit of what Heidegger meant.

As we have noted, Heidegger calls technology a "revealing." It is so in two distinct ways: (1) a social fact with causal influence, and (2) as a teller of wordless stories.[27] We learned the first way from Intro to Sociology. It is the way that social facts influence members of the social group. Famously, Emile Durkheim (father of sociology) showed in 1897 that a complete account of why John Doe committed suicide has to include among the relevant facts John's *social group*. In addition to considering medical condition, financial condition, and the state of significant relationships, one must also consider whether the victim was Protestant or lived in the city! This is because there is—or was in 1897—a statistical difference between the suicide rates of Protestants and Roman Catholics, between civilians and military, between city folk and farmers. There is no way to account for these different suicide rates on a case by case basis. Rather, something about being in the group tips its members one way or the other. The mechanism of this causal property may be mysterious. Suffice it to say that *social facts*—like being "Protestant" or "city dweller"— *have causal influence*. This force does not overwhelm other causes. But neither can it be discounted.

Social facts, then, are an important part of the mix of influence that jostle us about. In addition, social facts also are able to propagate

26. See Kierkegaard, *Purity of Heart Is to Will One Thing*.

27. The story-telling ability of technology is mimicry of creation: "There is no speech, nor are there words; their voice is not heard; yet their voice goes out through all the earth, and their words to the end of the world" (Ps 19:3–4).

themselves without attention or intention by any individual. This is the reason the North won the Civil War but the South won the cultural war.[28] Though defeated both by battles and legislation, bigotry is alive and well, no longer just in the deep South, but also north of the Mason Dixon line and west of the Mississippi. The insidious way social facts propagate themselves mean that social facts—social properties and the structures that bear them—take on a life of their own.

None of this is lost on the New Testament. On the one hand, the New Testament tells us that "sin" is "law-breaking" (1 John 3:4). But this is not a definition that exhausts what the new Testament teaches about sin. Sin is also likened to stain, to disease, parasites, corruption, folly, addiction, and so on.[29] Importantly, the New Testament very often describes sin in *social* terms. Thus Jesus opposes the idolatrous claims of social facts such as citizenship, family, and class (Mark 12:17;[30] Mark 3:31–35; Matt 6:24). Even the Jewish Law, which Paul calls good (1 Tim 1:8), was capable of holding people in bondage. The Apostle Paul homes in on this kind of bondage with his writings on "principalities and powers."[31]

The New Testament uses a variety of terms to allude to the "principalities and powers": thrones, powers, authorities, dominions, princes, lords, names, angels, demons, gods, elements, spirits, etc.[32] A good shorthand contemporary list of what Paul means by "principalities and powers" would include institutions, images, and ideologies for the way that they get a grip on people, distorting the way we see and act. And of course, we thoroughly Modern Millies no longer have teeny statues on the mantel to whom we pray. But that does not mean we are impervious to idolatry! William Stringfellow paints a grim picture of how much

28. See Clapp, *Johnny Cash and the Great American Contradiction.*

29. See Plantinga, *Not the Way It's Supposed to Be.* Oddly, Plantinga restricts himself to those cases of sin that concern us only on the individual level. For a helpful counterpart, see O'Keefe, *What Are They Saying About Social Sin?*

30. For a helpful guide into Empire Studies, see Carter, *Matthew and Empire.*

31. We live today shot through with individualism, the idea that everything in society begins from below, with the intent and action of the lone individual. So, despite the social character of sin and the social character of the Gospel held forth by the New Testament, Hendrikus Berkhof's book on "principalities and powers" came as something of a breakthrough, despite the echo of powers language in Karl Barth's commentary on Romans. Berkhof's translator and Barth's student, John Howard Yoder, went on to give us what has become the theological classic: *Politics of Jesus.*

32. For a good introduction and exegesis of the biblical terms, see the trilogy of Walter Wink. This first volume is the best place to begin: *Naming the Powers.*

contemporary idolatry falls under the Pauline idea of "principalities and powers":

> they include all institutions, all ideologies, all images, all move-
> ments, all causes, all corporations, all bureaucracies, all tradi-
> tions, all methods and routines, all conglomerates, all races, all
> nations, all idols. Thus, the Pentagon or the Ford Motor Company
> or Harvard University or the Hudson Institute or Consolidated
> Edison or the Diners Club or the Olympics or the Methodist
> Church or the Teamsters Union are principalities. So are capi-
> talism, Maoism, humanism, Mormonism, astrology, patriotism,
> plus many, many more—sports, sex, any profession or discipline,
> technology, money, the family—beyond any prospect of full enu-
> meration. The principalities and powers *are* legion.[33]

To the extent that Technology is deeply entwined in our lives together, it needs to be understood as one of the "principalities and powers." And the "principalities and powers" in turn can only be rightly understood in the light of Christ.

The late James Wm. McClendon Jr. joins William Stringfellow in reminding us of crucial facts about the powers in light of Christ.[34] First, each of the powers is creaturely. Paul's list indicates that the Powers may be brute features of physical world or extensions of human-made culture. "He [Paul] speaks of time (present and future), of space (depth and height), of life and death, of politics and philosophy, of public opinion and Jewish law, of pious tradition and the fateful course of the stars. Apart from Christ man is at the mercy of these Powers."[35] As creatures, none of them, no matter how pervasive, how enduring, how powerful, pose much of rivalry to the Creator for supremacy. Because they are *creaturely*, they have their true origins and destiny in the goodness of God's creation. Unfortunately, second, each are *fallen*. Each Power exists in a state of perpetual confusion with respect to its origins, its own identity and its end. Their own disoriented state only adds to the confusion that we as human beings suffer in our own fallen state. One of our more pitiable weaknesses is our susceptibility to deception. Sadly, one of the more unfortunate features of the Powers is their penchant for twisted use of language in order to deceive: denials of truth, doublespeak, "overtalk,"

33. Stringfellow, *Keeper of the Word*, 205.
34. McClendon, *Ethics*, ch. 6, esp. 173–77.
35. Berkhof, *Christ and the Powers*, 16.

secrecy, impressions of expertise, surveillance and harassment, exaggeration, deception, cursing, conjuring, diversion, and demonization to name a few.[36] These habits collude to trick human subjects into kowtowing to their putative authority.

> The principality, insinuating itself in the place of God, deceives humans into thinking and acting as if the moral worth or justification of human beings is defined and determined by commitment or surrender—literally, sacrifice—of human life to the survival interest, grandeur and vanity of the principality.[37]

But it is all a sham! The Powers have been shown by Christ to have no power at all. The author of Hebrews tells us that "Since, therefore, the children share flesh and blood, he himself likewise shared the same things, so that through death he might destroy—*katargeō*, to render powerless!—the one who has the power of death, that is, the devil, and free those who all their lives were held in slavery by the fear of death" (Heb 2:14–15). Odd formula, that. We don't ordinarily say that the guy in the white hat wins if *he* is shot dead at the O.K. Corral. But that is what Hebrews tells us. By dying, Christ denuded the Powers of their powers. The earliest church fathers put it this way: the Powers *exhausted* themselves at the Cross.[38] Their energies were spent, and their so-called power was revealed for what it truly is: a lie. Only the One who has the power both to lay down his life and take it up again (John 10:18) lives to see another day. That is not to say that the Powers don't go on *pretending* to be our masters. But it is all bluster.

Finally, the Powers are redeemable. Now, this is hard to understand. The short account is this: Anything in creation is good prior to its being suspect (because its original existence was precisely the overspill of God's own goodness into creation). The evilness of the fallen power is an *absence* rather than a presence, a "nothing" rather than a something. Of course, the only way to destroy an absence is to fill it. To fill the absence of a Power would take an act of grace that returned to the Power its original purpose, or *telos*. Granted, some powers seem irredeemable. But we are not going to concern ourselves with those. But we do need to explore the possibility that some of the powers are, in some sense and to

---

36. Stringfellow, "Strategems of the Demonic Powers," 214–22.

37. Stringfellow, "Traits of the Principalities," 207.

38. See Aulén, *Christus Victor*.

some extent, redeemable. This possibility gives Christians qualified hope for the redemption of some technology.

In other words, Christians are not expected to throw in the towel when facing enormous structural evils such as the pornographic use of the Internet or the commodification of religion by television. Rather, Christians are called to imagine and enact the reign that began in Christ, even if the task will not be completed until the Eschaton. Our job is not to change the world. Our job is, as always, to witness. Even Technology can be turned to this godly purpose. And in the ever-incomplete turning, technology becomes a "revealing" in the second way: if redeemed, Technology can reveal the Goodness that is in Christ.

We saw in the previous chapter that technology is a tool. In this present chapter we learned further that technology can be fruitfully understood as a *human doing*. And Technology has become deeply embedded in our social life together. In that it has "blossomed forth" since the Industrial revolution, it has taken on a life of its own. We naturally speak of technological progress and have a hard time imagining extricating it from our lives. Heidegger was astute enough to see this and label it a "revealing." The New Testament also anticipates this, but would label it more darkly as a "principality and power." As a "principality and power" Technology belongs to the fallen, creaturely realm. But it may, at least in some cases, be redeemable. Part of this redemption involves getting a clear answer to "What, in the eyes of God, is Technology *for*?" The historical practices of engineering design and technology can only give incomplete answers to this question, and thus engineering's internal gyroscope needs help from the outside. Fortunately, centuries prior to the technological revolution of the modern period, a few Christians were returning the *telos* (ultimate end, purpose, aim) to technology. It is to their witness we now turn.

AND NOW FOR SOMETHING COMPLETELY DIFFERENT: HUGH OF ST. VICTOR[39]

Technologists have not always been highly esteemed. The awe with which one speaks of BMW's "German engineering" could not have been

---

39. The following account is a compressed version of Kallenberg, "The Monastic Origins of Engineering."

spoken in the nineteenth century.[40] And American engineers had to stage something of a "revolt" in the twentieth century to get the social standing and widespread respect that allows Intel nerds proudly to boast "Our jokes aren't like your jokes!"[41]

But things were far worse in the twelfth century. As for all agrarian societies, mechanical artisans in the medieval period apparently shared life at the bottom of the pecking order. Part merchant and part unclean, mechanical artisans were at the bottom and periphery of the peasant classes.[42] Their alienation was not so much a function of the artisan's perennial poverty as it was a misunderstanding of what their crafts involved. The widely shared stigma against the earliest technologists came first from the mouth of Socrates. Plato's contemporary, Xenophon (d. 354 BCE) makes it clear that according to Socrates no true gentleman practiced "mechanical arts." Xenophon reports Socrates' exclamation:

> [N]ot only are the arts which we call mechanical [*banausikai*] generally held in bad repute, but States also have a very low opinion of them,—and with justice. For they are injurious to the bodily health of workmen and overseers, in that they compel them to be seated and indoors, and in some cases also all day before a fire, and when the body grows effeminate, the mind also becomes weaker and weaker. And the mechanical arts, as they are called, will not let men unite with them care for friends and State, so that men engaged in them must ever appear to be both bad friends and poor defenders of their country. And there are States ... in which not a single citizen is allowed to engage in mechanical arts [*banausikas technas*].[43]

Mechanical arts, in other words, were for slaves.

Less than a generation later, an equally influential philosopher, Aristotle, perpetuated the pejorative sense of "mechanical." If you wanted to "dis" someone in ancient Athens, you called them "mechanical" using the same tone of disgust my mother's school friends (ca. 1940) would have used to spurn someone as a "farmer." So uncontestable is the slur against all things "mechanical" (*banausos*) that in the *Nicomachean*

40. Gispen, *New Profession, Old Order*.

41. The Intel "Nerd Prank" commercial has been immortalized by YouTube: http://www.youtube.com/watch?v=RXZ1Qg-k3Xc. On the revolt by American engineers, see Layton, *Revolt of Engineers*.

42. Lenski, "A Graphic Representation," 284.

43. Xenophon, *Economist of Xenophon*, IV.2, 22–23.

Ethics the term is simply translated as "vulgar"! Similarly, in the *Politics* Aristotle writes that

> . . . any occupation, art, or science, which makes the body or soul or mind of the freeman less fit for the practice or exercise of excellence, is "mechanical"; wherefore we call those arts "mechanical" which tend to deform the body. . . for they absorb and degrade the mind.[44]

Yikes! Technical artisans labor under this stigma for the better part of fourteen centuries. A tiny light momentarily breaks on the scene in the seventh century. When Isidore of Seville (d. 636) compiles his "encyclopedia," he approvingly brings to light several disciplines that lay outside the classic seven that constitute liberal arts.[45] Here is a positive upturn in public opinion: Isidore includes mineralogy alongside the eminently reputable enterprises of medicine and agriculture. But unfortunately, Isidore did little to improve the social standing of mechanical arts as a whole. His blundering fascination with etymology led him to mistake the Latin *mechanicus* as derived from the Greek *moichos* meaning "adulterer" rather than from *mechane* (i.e., machine) or *mechos* (i.e., a means, something expedient, a remedy). Martin of Laon (d. 680) takes Isidore to mean that the ingenuity of a mechanism was akin to the secret doings of an illicit sexual affair:

> from "moechus" we call "mechanical art" any object which is clever and most delicate and which, in its making or operation, is beyond detection, so that beholders find their power stolen from them when they cannot penetrate the ingenuity of the thing.[46]

In the end, Isidore's genealogy could not help but accentuate the stigma that afflicted artisans and remind them of their proper place at the bottom of the feeding chain.

And now for something completely different. Hugh of St. Victor (d. 1142) presents the first and lasting positive picture of *ars mechanicus* by explaining how proto-engineers fit into the redemptive plan of God.

It is a little surprising that it takes Christian theology until the twelfth century to give this account. After all, we know that the so-called

---

44. Aristotle, "Politics," 8.2, 1337b; emphasis added.

45. The classical *quadrivium* was comprised of arithmetic, music, geometry, and astronomy while the *trivium* was comprised of grammar, rhetoric and logic.

46. Hugh of St. Victor, *Didascalicon*, 191.

"Dark Ages" were not at all dark. In fact, the church was not the op-
pressor of learning, it was the preserver of knowledge. This fact may
sound surprising in pop culture that delights in depicting Christianity
as primitive and backward. But unlike Dan Brown's *The Da Vinci Code*
and Umberto Eco's *The Name of the Rose*, serious scholars have shown
monastic orders to be havens of learning.[47] Important for my story is
that the first water mill in the West shows up, and put to good use, in
the Monastery of St. Ursus of Loches in the sixth century. For his part,
historian Lynn Townsend White insists that many of the technological
advances originated in the East (countries like Iraq, Arabia, India and
China). But these cultures were incapable of sustaining many new gadgets in any lasting way. In contrast to the East, White argues that it was
the Christian theological outlook that enabled technological advances to
take firm root in the West.[48]

Hugh of St. Victor was one of those theologians who helped make
technology stick in the West. He lived in the age between "mandatory"
Christianity (Emperor Theodosius, ca. 391) and "voluntary" Christianity
that was to grow from Martin Luther's 95 Theses (1517). Hugh shared
with Luther a close alliance with one of the greatest theologians to be
claimed by both Protestants and Catholics, Augustine of Hippo (d. 434).
For Augustine, as for Hugh and Luther, "theology" denoted the academic
discipline that encompasses all other disciplines. (When people referred
to theology as the "queen" of the sciences and philosophy as her hand-
maiden, they were not making a recommendation; they were simply
describing how things were in this age.) For Augustine and his followers, the master discipline, theology, had four important marks. First, all
disciplines are unified in theology, because truth, goodness, and beauty
are unified in God (*theos*). So, theology is not inherently at odds with any
academic discipline. However, not everything that bears the name "theology" is worthwhile. Theology may be "worldly" or it may be "graced."
These two modes of doing theology are incommensurable.[49] Thus is
Hugh quick to caution against conflating graced theology (a theology
that moves from knowledge of God to human experience) with worldly

47. For an important account of how the sciences, especially astronomy, were pro-
tected and financed by the Catholic Church before the Reformation, see Heilbron, *Sun
in the Church*.

48. White, "Technology, Western," in *Dictionary of the Middle Ages*, 650–54.

49. On the antinomy of grace and human effort, see Augustine's debate with the
Pelagian. Pelagianism was condemned at the Council of Carthage in 397.

theology "which lacked the lessons of grace" (a theology that tries to move from human experience to the knowledge of God).[50]

What are these lessons of grace? For Hugh grace is not something added on top of nature, but something that permeates the world and with which human beings may keep step. "Grace," writes Hugh, is the powerful medicine perpetually offered by God "to illuminate the blind and to cure the weak; to illuminate ignorance, to cool concupiscence; to illuminate unto knowledge of truth; to inflame unto love of virtue."[51] In contrast, worldly theology is like tugging at one's bootstraps. It reveals little, and therefore has little to say to mechanical arts, precisely because it ignores God at the outset. Worldly theology begins with an empirical study of "pure nature" and then attempts to reason up toward the possible existence of a divine realm. But graced theology unblinkingly assumes that creation is already shot through with the presence of God. Wherever one points is God's world. Human beings live as creatures under a Creator whose divine Wisdom is the archetypal Exemplar of creation.[52]

Of course *Christ* is the wisdom of God (1 Cor 1:24). This fact means that all graced theology, and all her subdisciplines, have an irreducibly *incarnational* focus. What human life is *for* is said best and finally in the redemptive life and death and resurrection of Christ. The highest Good, indeed the "highest curative in life" is the pursuit of Wisdom, a.k.a. Christ. In this sense we come to know who we are and Whose we are through instruction, which is to say, through discipleship.[53]

In addition to the marks of grace and incarnation, a third mark of Augustinian theology is the theme of sin: We pursue Christ at the

50. In his *Exposition of the Heavenly Hierarchy*, Hugh writes, "Invisible things can only be made known by visible things, and therefore the whole of theology must use visible demonstrations. But worldly theology adopted the works of creation and the elements of this world that it might make its demonstration in these. . . . And for this reason, namely, because it used a demonstration which revealed little, it lacked ability to bring forth the incomprehensible truth without stain of error. . . . In this were the wise men of this world fools, namely, that proceeding by natural evidences alone and following the elements and appearances of the world, they lacked the lessons of grace." Cited in J. Taylor, "Introduction," in *Didascalicon*, 35.

51. Rydstrom-Poulsen, *Gracious God*, 206.

52. This point is made explicit by J. Taylor, "Introduction," in *Didascalicon*, 13.

53. Hugh of St. Victor, *Didascalicon*, I.1, 47.

invitation of God (John 6:44), but our pursuit of Christ who is Wisdom is, unfortunately and inevitably, hampered by our fallen state.

The ancient Greeks explained evil in the world as the residual effect of an eternal battle between the powers of good and evil. Evil was not only conceived as a something, it was an eternal something. Thus, in the beginning was chaos. But Augustine, writing almost a millennium after Socrates, could not dignify evil with substance, much less with eternality, for as Scriptures spelled out, "in the beginning, God. . . ." Evil was not there in the beginning. Rather, evil had a temporal starting point. And, in order to avoid the conclusion that God created evil, Augustine insisted evil wasn't a substance at all, but an *absence*; evil was a defect that entered the picture some time after God had created an entirely good world.

Whence evil? Evil was a distortion in the order of creation effected by a misuse of creaturely freedom.[54] How so? In order for creation to be a uni-verse (rather than a multi-verse), creation embodied a single hierarchy of value. (This view was nothing new; the Apostle Paul agrees with the ancient Greeks who pointed out that there must be some reason why it is easier to step on a cockroach than to put down a horse, namely, that horses have more inherent worth—are higher on the hierarchy of being—than roaches.[55]) The human soul operates correctly when it ascribes that quality and quantity of love appropriate to the object in light of its place on the hierarchy. Augustine (combining Paul and Plato) considered the order itself every bit as real as the tangible objects that populated the hierarchy of the created world. In short, evil entered when human beings re-ranked the hierarchy of creation, ascribing an inordinate quantity of love to one or more of the rungs of the hierarchy. In the Apostle Paul's words, "For they exchanged the truth of God for a lie, and worshiped and served the creature rather than the Creator, who is blessed forever" (Rom 1:25). In essence, human misvaluing was a distortion of the order of creation. The change was very real, even though it was a distortion they bore within themselves, for a disordered love is a disordered soul. Thus, disordered human love manifests itself sometimes as greed, other times as jealousy, covetousness, pride, and so on. This condition had the unpleasant consequence of being perpetual, because one could only make moral progress if one possessed a faculty for index-

54. Augustine's theology of the origin of evil is often studied in introductory courses in philosophy of religion. See, for example, Augustine, "Problem of Evil," 19–27.

55. See 1 Cor 15:38–41.

ing one's own moral progress. And it was this very faculty, namely love of the Good, that could no longer be trusted.

But the bad news does not stop with human depravity. Once human beings, viceroys of creation, became incapable of rescuing themselves (*non posse non peccare*, not able not to sin), the creation they were supposed to tend fell under a curse and was doomed to go awry. Christian Scripture aptly expresses its undeniable reality:

> For the anxious longing of the creation waits eagerly for the revealing of the sons of God. For the creation was subjected to futility... in hope that the creation itself also will be set free from its slavery to corruption into the freedom of the glory of the children of God. For we know that the whole creation groans and suffers the pains of childbirth together until now. (Rom 8:19–22)

Whether we call this curse "sin" or "entropy" makes little difference for my argument. The fact of the matter is: iron rusts, people sicken and die, and things fall apart.

Augustine himself was no advocate of technology. Therefore, Hugh's account of the redemptive role of technology is a brand new way of thinking.[56] By paying more attention to the doctrine of the human fall into sin, Hugh is able to include mechanical arts under God's plan of redemption. Mechanical arts have to do with countering the effects of the curse, just as theoretical and practical arts have to do with countering the effects of human depravity, through the knowing and following of a gracious God on a redemptive path.

Hugh's inclusion of the mechanical arts into God's plan for redemption is no small feat, for "mechanical arts" by his day had evolved into a very broad array of crafts. To be specific, the mechanical arts were comprised of seven classes of practices: fabric-making, armament, commerce, agriculture, hunting, medicine, and theatrics. (Granted, "theatrics" seems like a stretch, but Hugh purposed to make the list seven in number so that it matched the perfection of the seven liberal arts. Besides, under theatrics Hugh envisioned any coordinated activity of a group of people. Not just drama, but marching bands and gymnastics would fit under this heading. Had Hugh lived to see Ford's assembly line, he surely would have treated it as a type of theatrics.) These seven name *families* of practices. So, for example, hunting "includes all the duties of

56. Chenu, "Arts «Méchaniques» Et Œuvres Serviles," 312–15.

bakers, butchers, cooks, and tavern keepers" as well as those who actually do the gaming, fowling and fishing.[57] And "armament" included material science, even metallurgy: "To this science belong all such materials as stones, woods, metals, sands, and clays."[58] With this last move Hugh has managed to embrace even the grimy-faced smithy so consistently maligned for centuries.

In sum, the final end or *telos* of mechanical arts is reunion with God and others through Christian common pursuit of divine Wisdom as well as the alleviation of physical weakness stemming from the cursed state of the created world. It is important to see that technology has *both* functions. When a tree is blown over onto a neighbor's house, we need the technologies of crow bars and chain saws. As the world is prone to fall apart, *ars mechanicus* takes the form of protective charity, fortifying the body against harm, and contriving "remedies" for alleviating physical weakness.[59] But it also expected to be proactive in the activities of the Gospel. Thus building a truss bridge across the river that separated warring states was an act that made reconciliation easier.[60]

APOCALYPSE NOW?

Heidegger called Technology a "revealing," a term that gestures to the development or progress of Technology as something real, alive, and coming into its own. A number of Heidegger's contemporaries responded with pessimism to the idea that Technology is "progressing." Philosopher Ludwig Wittgenstein clearly considered the modern technological outlook as signifying the *death* of a culture. In the aftermath of WWII, he wrote in 1947 that

> The truly apocalyptic view of the world is that things do *not* repeat themselves. It isn't absurd, e.g., to believe that the age of science and technology is the beginning of the end for humanity; that the idea of great progress is a delusion, along with the

57. Hugh of St. Victor, *Didascalicon*, II.25, 77–78.

58. Ibid., II.22, 76.

59. Ibid., I.8, 55.

60. When a seventeen year-old French shepherd boy named Bénezet undertook to build the only bridge he ever attempted, a bridge between the warring countries of Toulouse (heretics) and the Kingdom of Arles (orthodox), his work of mercy earned him a new name: St. Bénezet the Bridge Builder. For my account of the significance of this tale see Kallenberg, " Descriptive Problem of Evil," 297–322.

idea that the truth will ultimately be known; that there is nothing good or desirable about scientific knowledge and that mankind, in seeking it, is falling into a trap. It is by no means obvious that this is not how things are.[61]

Jewish philosopher Martin Buber shared Wittgenstein's dark view. Writing prior to WWII, Buber lamented that the "I-It" mode of technological reasoning had eclipsed the "I-Thou" relationship of authentic human relating.[62] A half century before Buber, Oswald Spengler distinguished between scientific outlook (*world-as-nature*) that treated all its objects as dead things, and in doing so necessarily missed the presence of the life-force which pulsates through the *world-as-history*.[63] More recently, Pope John Paul II called the conflict in outlooks one in which the "culture of life" is pitted against the "culture of death."[64]

The view these thinkers are objecting to was the one spawned by the scientific revolution. It was the view that championed predictability, inevitable progress, standardized increments of time and space, inexorable physical laws, the repeatability of all phenomena, etc. These traits reflect the assumption that everything relates to everything else as pieces of a cosmic mechanism. Thus Wittgenstein lamented "the terrible degeneration that had come over the human spirit."[65]

However, for Christians the "technological" view is not totalizing. Only Christians hold a view that is properly "apocalyptic." Things *don't* always repeat themselves. There is the possibility of the in-breaking of God; always the possibility of resurrection.

These two outlooks—technological progress and Christian faith— seem irreconcilable. What are we to do? Is the apocalyptic view that constitutes Christianity so thoroughly incommensurable with the technological view that we can only stand by and wring our hands? On the contrary, Christian *apocalupsis*, which is to say, the "revealing" that is

61. Wittgenstein, *Culture and Value*, 56e.

62. The first edition was printed in 1923. The second edition was revised in 1958. Buber, *I and Thou*.

63. Spengler, *Decline of the West*.

64. Pope John Paul, II, "Evangelium Vitae."

65. "I was walking about in Cambridge and passed a bookshop, and in the windows were portraits of Russell, Freud and Einstein. A little further on, in a music shop, I saw portraits of Beethoven, Schubert, and Chopin. Comparing these portraits I felt intensely the terrible degeneration that had come over the human spirit in the course of only a hundred years." Rhees, *Recollections of Wittgenstein*, 112.

Christianity, indicates that the mode of the church's relation to technological culture is not mechanical. Anyway, the church rarely, if ever, has
been in a position to coerce culture in one direction rather than another
(though we hanker after just such means). But this lack is not problematic, because the church doesn't stand toward culture as an external
cause stands to its mechanical effect. The power of the Gospel is tied up
with the fact that the church stands toward culture as an *internal* cause,
as a catalyst, for change. The mode of this internal causation is "witness."
By "witness" I mean the testimony embodied in the concrete life of the
church. To the extent technology can be taken up into Christian witness,
perhaps it can be redeemed.

REDEEMING TECHNOLOGY

In this and the previous two chapters we have considered three distinct
modes of technology. Often enough each gadget we use functions as a
tool, just as I use a laptop to type these words or you use an electric
lamp to read them by. To the extent the gadget is useful we are pleased.
If forced to assess the tool, we equate its usefulness to us with its goodness and think no more about it. Perhaps the only time we rethink our
assessment is when we learn that old laptops end up in landfills in the
Third World where heavy metals found in all electronics leech into the
local drinking water and poor people rummaging through the landfills,
intent on reclaiming the semi-precious metals for resale, absorb the toxins through their skin.

    We also saw that technologies can embody human intention. A
common example of technology-as-human-doing is when a technology
serves as instruments of someone's power over others by restricting or
scripting how we behave. Often enough we are not bothered by being
scripted; not so much because we happily comply as the fact that we have
become so adept at cooperating with the script that we no longer notice it. (Only toddlers and the arthritic notice and object to doorknobs.)
Some scripts are episodic—such as automatic retracting seatbelts and
air bags—which restrict the motion of human bodies the most when
it is most beneficial for our safety. Since the human intention (restricting passenger movement during crash) aims at a genuine human good,
we laud certain scripts as morally noteworthy. Of course, not all scripts
are entirely good. Many are mixed. The assembly line reduced costs to
consumers while simultaneously reducing the knowledge that any one

worker had of the whole process, effectively reducing worker leverage for better conditions or better pay by making each worker expendable. Other scripts are even more insidious, as revealed by our examination of Robert Moses's two hundred overpasses in the New York City parkway system that were too low for busses, effectively keeping minorities off the posh beaches.

Yet Technology is more complicated than can be captured by the tool mode and the human doing mode. Technology has become an immense system, self-propagating, growing, living, causal, yet supremely indifferent to human suffering. Like a juggernaut, the wheels of Technology move forward crushing anyone and everything in its path. In the mode of Technology-as-Principality, the scale of technological evil is more like a tsunami than a homicide. A homicide, while tragic indeed, can in some sense be traced to the moral failure of the killer. But we look in vain for someone one which to pin the blame for a tsunami.[66] So too for Technology. While human beings are undeniably involved in technology, there is no way to affix blame, because too many humans are involved. But also because as a "power" Technology has become much greater than the sum of human intentions.

I am strongly of the view that evil—whether natural evils like tsunamis or technological evils like "sexting" by teenagers[67]—is not a problem to be solved so much as it is a practical problem that calls for an active response.[68] New Testament scholar, N.T. Wright has written a wonderful book entitled *Evil and the Justice of God*. After summarizing the biblical resources for thinking theologically about evil, Wright argues that evil in this present era (i.e., between the Fall and the Eschaton, yet after the decisive victory at Calvary), Christians must *respond* to evil using all the imaginative resources at our disposal.[69] In particular, Wright thinks that art and literature play an important role in fueling our imagination for an imaginative Christian witness against evil. His point is well taken, but could be taken further. For one thing, artists tend to be lone

---

66. For those tempted to make God the agent behind the tsunami, please consider Hart, *Doors of the Sea*.

67. The sending of explicit photos of one's genitals to schoolmates.

68. So-called "solutions" to the so-called "problem of evil" are called theodicies. Theodicies have the unhappy characteristic of making worse several features of the "problem" they purport to solve. See Tilley, *Evils of Theodicy*.

69. Wright, *Evil and the Justice of God*, 126–28.

individuals rather than groups. And an individual response to social evil hardly seems to scale. Of course, great art and great literature may have impact across broad swaths of a populace. But even then art and literature run up against the boundaries of trying to symbolize (in words, in stone, in paint, etc.) what can only be *shown*.[70] Thus Dostoevsky is a genius at describing a world *as if* bereft of God, prompting the readers to take the opposite position that God *must* exist. But like all great art, Dostoevsky's agenda is open to debate.[71] Consequently, I want to suggest that Wright's conclusion can be strengthened by calling for responses that are *social* rather than individual and *dynamic* rather than symbolic. The short answer is that the *church* is God's present response to evil. To paraphrase theologian Stanley Hauerwas, the church doesn't *have* an answer to the problem of evil, the church *is* the answer. For nearly forty years this important theologian has been pounding this theme.[72] In his work, Hauerwas has been something of a prophetic herald, echoing the insights of John Howard Yoder.[73] Together they claim that whenever the church is the church (i.e., wherever Christians actually follow and imitate Jesus rather than merely reflect a microcosm of civil society), we embody God's spirit in such a way that the very life of the church itself becomes the creative impetus for social change.

I conclude by suggesting what the Hauerwas-Yoder thesis might look like if technology were the means of our witness. Of course, as I argued in chapter 4, nothing can be accomplished unless the church is living her witness in our daily interactions and form of life. Part of getting our own house in order is improving our corporate witness by means of technology.

70. The distinction between *showing* and *saying* is often credited to the philosopher Wittgenstein, but in reality it is as old as Psalm 19 (vv. 3–4).

71. See R. Williams, *Dostoevsky*.

72. Hauerwas's original aphorism is "The church doesn't have a social ethic, it is a social ethic." A little reflection will show that my paraphrase says the same thing. This is repeated throughout his many books. See, for example, Hauerwas, *Community of Character*, 40; *Peaceable Kingdom*, 99; *Christian Existence Today*, 101; and Hauerwas and Willimon, *Resident Aliens*, 43. For a scholarly introduction to Hauerwas's theological ethics, see Kallenberg, *Ethics as Grammar*.

73. In addition to *The Politics of Jesus* mentioned above, see Yoder, *Christian Witness to the State*; *Original Revolution*; *Priestly Kingdom*; and *Royal Priesthood*.

THE GOSPEL BY DESIGN

It has been said that it is impossible to keep the boy on the farm once he's been to Paris. In other words, the hick is expected to shrug off his backward ways and embrace the bright lights and modern ways of the city. And secularists imagine the same holds for the Christian who goes to university: Pollyanna inevitably grows up. What is technology but an extension of Paris and of the university? But what if it is the other way around? What if technology is the farm boy; the church is Paris?! What if technology shrugs off its backward ways once it has met the bright light of the church?! When the church succeeds at being the church, it fires technology's imagination; the church becomes part of the "inventory" in response to which a technological culture finds its way forward. There was a time when *technē* belonged to *poiēsis*, when technology belonged to poetry.[74] Greek artists imagined themselves to be bringing the gods near through the exercises of their craft, their *technē*. But in Christianity the authorship is inverted. We, the church, are the *poiēma*, the poem, authored by the One whose body we are.[75] We rightly say that the Spirit of the living God is present through the poetry of our corporate life together.[76]

Hugh of St. Victor said that invisible things require visible expression.[77] Ultimately this means the incarnation of Jesus. But the Psalmist also said that creation though mute was not without voice! "There is no speech, nor are there words; their voice is not heard; yet their voice goes out through all the earth, and their words to the end of the world" (Ps 19:3–4). Can technology share in this kind of witness?

We get some inkling of how this played out in medieval times by considering the role that machinery played in the monastery. The requirement that monks devote themselves to work is widely acknowledged. What is contested today is whether the Benedictine motto, "work is prayer" (*laborare est orare, orare est laborare*), originally reflected a sacramental rather than an instrumental view of work. For his part, historian Jacques Le Goff maintains that monks worked hard, intentionally trying

74. Heidegger, "Question Concerning Technology," 12–13.

75. Eph 2:10: *autou gar esmen poiēma.*

76. Kallenberg, "All Suffer the Affliction of the One," 217–34.

77. In his *Exposition of the Heavenly Hierarchy*, Hugh writes, "Invisible things can only be made known by visible things, and therefore the whole of theology must use visible demonstrations." Cited in J. Taylor, "Introduction," 35.

to improve their efficiency with machinery (such as the water-powered mill constructed at Saint Ursus at Loches in the sixth century) so as to free up time for the essential thing: *opus Dei*, "the work of God," namely contemplative prayer.[78] Work was, well, work, and prayer was what one did when work was over. In other words, Le Goff can see water mills for saving time but not for worship. Does Le Goff get history wrong?

Le Goff's history is not so much wrong as it is monochromatic. Did water mills save time? Sure. But that doesn't mean the operation of man and machine might not also be a form of prayer. Where Le Goff sees in black and white, Hugh sees in resplendent color. For Hugh, mechanical arts yielded artifacts (and processes) that were inherently sacramental because they rendered visible the end of mechanical reasoning, which in its exercise was simultaneously natural (namely, the alleviation of physical weakness) and supernatural (namely the journeying toward reunion with Divine Wisdom).

As we have seen, the strength of Hugh's theological account is that it supplies what non-theological (what Hugh called "worldly") accounts could not as easily do, namely a thick description of the final end toward which all human activity aims. In sum, it was by the "lessons of grace" that Hugh was able to see the physical world under both the aspect of the supernatural and the aspect of the natural. Accordingly he described mechanical arts as guided by a dual end. The supervening supernatural end is this: the exercise of mechanical reasoning is part of the journey toward reunion with God. The subvening natural end is this: mechanical artifacts are for the alleviation of physical weakness that is the consequence of living in a fallen world.

Historian Lynn White has detailed numerous other medieval examples, many of which were employed precisely because of their role in worship. Silicon glass—from which spectacles were eventually to be made—was first developed to give clear view of the Eucharistic host while enclosed in its tabernacle (part of medieval Christian worship). Nano-sized particles of silver and gold were added to glass to give stunningly beautiful "stained" glass depictions of the Gospel for all to see, but especially useful to those who could not read.[79] Clocks were invented for reminding believers when it was time to pray. Pipe organs were made to accompany musical liturgy. Ogival arches (and the flying buttress) effec-

78. Le Goff, *Time, Work, and Culture in the Middle Ages*, 80.

79. "The First Nanotechnologists."

tively fireproofed the now much higher church ceilings.[80] Importantly, these technologies were not only nurtured by the church, they were considered good also because they contributed constructively to the ongoing ministry of the church.

In the eyes of pre-modern Christians, even one of the oldest technological artifacts of all, the lowly bridge, was *theologically* significant. Since rivers are natural political boundaries, the one who undertook the building of a bridge was considered to do *an act of mercy*. In the eyes of Hugh (and Theophilus, Jacopo Aconio, Eilmer of Mamesbury, and others[81]), *every* exercise of mechanical reasoning had the potential of bridge-like effects of reconciling nations, calming wars, and strengthening peace.[82]

The mercy-minded ingenuity of the medieval monk ought to be imitated today. If monks who were often mystified by mechanical things could champion bridges as concrete embodiments of the reconciliation won by Christ, how much more ought we utilize our Christian imagination to deploy technologies that are "revealings" of Christ's Gospel.

I was once asked by a colleague what I hoped students might gain from my Christian ethics and engineering course. I told her, in effect, I wanted my students to see the world like Dean Kamen or Joshua Silver sees. Dean Kamen has earned momentary fame for his recent invention of the Segway, a self-balancing two-wheel scooter for pedestrians.[83] But the technology behind the Segway has a more important application in motorized wheelchairs. The balancing mechanism is so precise and sensitive that it enables a wheelchair to rock back and travel only on the back two wheels. This enables a paraplegic to navigate staircases as well as curbs unassisted![84]

80. See White, *Medieval Technology and the Social Change*; "Theophilus Redivivus," 224–33; "The Legacy of the Middle Ages," 191–202; "The Expansion of Technology"; and "Cultural Climates and Technological Advance."

81. White, "Theophilus Redivivus."; "Jacopo Aconcio as an Engineer," 425–44; and "Medieval Engineering and the Sociology of Knowledge."

82. Hugh of St. Victor, *Didascalicon*, II.23, 77. Hugh's statement originally concerned "commerce." What he meant by "commerce," however, is not what we mean, the exchange of goods for capital, but rather what we would call "process engineering" and "logistics."

83. See www.segway.com.

84. A version of Kamen's invention is now manufactured by iBot and can be viewed in action at www.ibotnow.com/home.html.

Joshua Silver, an Oxford University physicist, has invented a pair of user-adaptive eyeglasses. The lenses are really polyester films that are filled with silicone oil. The curvature of each lens can be adjusted by a small knob on the frame that pumps a little more or a little less oil into the lens. Over 129 million of the world's poorest people suffer serious though correctable visual impairment. In Ghana, for example, there is only one optometrist for every four million people and the per-capita income is about a dollar a day.[85] Yet with Silver's device, for ten bucks a farmer can once again see well enough to work.

What is noteworthy about Silver's design is that it is unlikely to make tons of profit. Nor will it make Americans' lives more convenient. But the device is obviously *good*. It is good because of its positive social impact on a world in need. This device redefines "need" according to the vision of Hugh of St. Victor. (What the world needs is not a Coke, but a reduction in child mortality, clean drinking water, adequate food, environmental sustainability, and so on.[86]) It is caring for "the least of these." And in giving "a cup of cold water" to these, care is offered to Jesus himself (Matt 25:31–46). Additionally, this technology joins our Christian voice in proclaiming that which is better than the bottom line, better than making convenient the lives of the wealthy. It speaks without words, but its message, and ours, is clear: this is *very* good.

I can go no further. Not that more and better examples can't be assembled. In fact, Emily Pilliton has assembled a hundred such ideas.[87] Do-it-yourself water-filtration devices, light-weight and extremely strong bicycle frames made of bamboo, charcoal made from local organic matter in areas devoid of wood, and so on. But an exhaustive list of "approved" technologies is impossible, immediately out of date, and besides the point. The point is not a list. The point is discernment nurtured by the hope that Technology, fallen though it is, is conquered in Christ and therefore redeemable (at least in part). As we attempt to "keep

85. Nicholas Thompson, "Self-Adjusted Glasses Could Be a Boon to Africa."

86. On these kind of goals we can agree with nonbelievers, see the United Nations Millennium Development Goals at http://www.un.org/millenniumgoals/.

87. A humorous interview by Stephen Colbert is helping bringing these technologies to light, including Joshua Silver's self-adjustable glasses: http://www.colbertnation .com/the-colbert-report-videos/262000/january-18-2010/emily-pilloton. For obvious reasons, Christians ought to rally behind many of the products in Pilliton's new book. Pilloton and Chochinov, *Design Revolution*.

in step"[88] with God's Spirit in this ongoing work of redeeming technology, we may discover to our chagrin that our faculty of discernment is underdeveloped or atrophied from disuse. If so, we do well to take notes from those whose skills are sharper than ours. This is the subject of the next and final chapter.

88. Gal 5:25: *pneumati stoichōmen.*

6

What Can Christians Learn from Technologists?

I'VE ALWAYS ADMIRED MARTIN Luther. His statement of justification by faith was a timely gift to Christian theology. Surprisingly, and despite stereotypes to the contrary, Luther became increasingly concerned with the positive role that doing good works played in Christian discipleship. There is some evidence that "Luther's early conviction—that 'good works' spring spontaneously from faith—was, over time, modified by experience." His later views on discipleship envisions Christians capable of incremental transformation by means of, crudely put, good habits.[1]

Since we will be considering Christian formation and habits, it seems fitting to remind ourselves of our desperate need for grace by calling to mind Luther's own prayer:

> Behold, Lord, an empty vessel that needs to be filled. My Lord, fill it. I am weak in faith; strengthen thou me. I am cold in love; warm me and make me fervent that my love may go out to my neighbor. I do not have a strong and firm faith; at times I doubt and am unable to trust thee altogether. O Lord, help me. Strengthen my faith and trust in thee. In thee I have sealed all the treasures of all I have. I am poor; thou art rich and didst come to be merciful to the poor. I am a sinner; thou art upright. With me there is an abundance of sin; in thee is the fullness of righteousness. Therefore, I will remain with thee—of whom I can receive but to whom I may not give.[2]

---

1. See Gaebler, "Luther on the Self."
2. Appleton, *Oxford Book of Prayer*, §137.

DIVINE COMMAND, GROUP THINK,
AND MORAL RESPONSIBILITY

Evangelical theologian Wyndy Corbin Reuschling has argued convincingly that evangelicals' vision of divine command ethics has made them in danger of a particular sort of a group-think that is an extension of their allegiance to the duty of obedience.[3] The trouble arises not with our strong sense of duty to obey but with a kind of virus that has sneaked in from philosophical circles, namely, the notion of moral agents as those who are "charged with maneuvering in a world whose features are neutrally open to view."[4] This view has been perpetuated endlessly through novels, television shows, and Hollywood films. The common storyline displays the protagonist as somebody wrestling mightily with questions of personal sacrifice: Should I risk X to achieve Y? However costly are the demands on him or her, the protagonist is never, *ever* in doubt as to what X or Y is.[5] Moral quandary in this storyline is not about personal confusion about what is good or what is due. The only "quandary" is how the hero will manage conflicting demands en route to discharging duties. (For example, the family breadwinner may be fired if he or she tells the truth, but knows that he/she is obligated both to tell the truth and to provide for the family. This is a conundrum, and depending on the story perhaps an unwinnable one. And while the breadwinner struggles to solve it, he or she is never confused about the twin demands of honesty and providing for the family.) Thus the moral life reduces to "decisionism"—how do I *decide* what I ought to do when faced with clear albeit conflicting demands?

Often enough, the telltale sign that decisionism is the mode of ethics in play shows up in one's appeal to black-and-white principles said to be deduced from definitions, laws, and theories. And of course, well intentioned Christians are as guilty as anyone on this score. When Christians appeal to the "plain" sense of Scripture it is a move that sometimes (often?) masks a social power play, a sinful will to win over others by preemptively shutting down conversations about the meaning of the

3. Reuschling, "Trust and Obey," 59–78.

4. Crary, "Introduction," in *Wittgenstein and the Moral Life*, 20.

5. A notable and intentional exception to this stream of stories are the novels intentionally crafted otherwise by Iris Murdoch. As a philosopher, she intent on displaying characters more real than the entirely imaginary and unrealistic modern protagonist. Murdoch, *Sovereignty of Good*, 1970.

text. If the sense is "plain" there is no need to talk about it; on this subject there can be no other opinion (except mine).

Of course, none of us is 100 percent godly! We are each some percentage "ungodly." Therefore, we fall under Psalm 36: "transgression speaks to the ungodly within their heart." Who among us can be absolutely sure we are not hearing the reasonableness of transgression rather than the "plain" sense of Scripture? We cannot tell. It is for this very real danger that David goes on to pray, knowing the ambiguous state of his own heart, "Let not the foot of pride come upon me" (Ps 36:10–11).

Regardless of whose ethics is under scrutiny (whether that of philosophers or evangelicals) the downside of ethics-as-decisionism is a corresponding tendency to neglect the rich resources of morally formative *practices* (such as Christian disciple-making), because it is commonly assumed that that which is to be obeyed is clear enough by itself to place the burden of duty on each *individual* regardless of the activities that filled this individual's yesterday, last week, or last year. In this chapter I show how Christian communities might avoid these twin dangers (i.e., individualistic decisionism in ethics and the neglect of morally formative cooperative practices) by describing something called *phronēsis*—which is to say, the skill of *practical*, rather than theoretical, reasoning. As we shall see, practical reasoning is constitutive of character-forming practices such as music, engineering, and medicine. More significant than the fact that novices must be *trained* to follow rules, is the fact that the *manner* by which they are so trained necessarily involves a transformation of the rules themselves, according to the progress of each novice.

In the first part of the chapter, I use an example of technological failure to ask the question of culpable ignorance: is one morally at fault for what he or she did *not* know? Admittedly, most of us are befuddled by technology. But it may surprise many that even expert technologists do not have complete knowledge of a given artifact. Their knowledge is quite bounded by unproven and unprovable heuristics. We can get a handle on the nature of heuristical knowledge by asking to what extent an expert is at fault when things go haywire. In the second part of the paper, I argue that Christian disciple-making shares a strong enough family resemblance with non-theological practices to make similar conclusions about the role *phronēsis* plays in biblical disciple-making. That being so, the danger to which Wyndy Corbin Reuschling alerts us is a particular threat for those communities whose discipleship process has seemingly become arrested at the novice stage. The upshot of my analysis will be the seemingly paradoxical remedy that in order for Christians to preserve the authority of the biblical witness we so prize, we must embrace a form of disciple-making whose goal is the eventual abandonment of the exceptionless nature of these binding principles.

Culpable Ignorance?

I begin with a story of technological failure in order to get at the question of *moral* failure.[6] In 1907, the City of Los Angeles voted to pass a $23 million bond for the building of a 233-mile aqueduct, four times longer than anything previously built, in order to meet the urgent water needs of a city whose population nearly doubled in just five years.[7] The drought of 1904 left the city in something of a water crisis. When the aqueduct opened in 1913, the aqueduct alone had the capacity to deliver 258 million gallons of water every day. The entire project had been put in the hands of fifty-two-year old William Mulholland—of Mulholland Drive fame. The complete project would extend for another fourteen years and was to include a series of eight enormous reservoirs in the mountains overlooking L.A. Together, these reservoirs were built for the purpose of holding in reserve at least one year's supply of water, a quantity that kept increasing because of the meteoric increase of L.A.'s population. The dams that held these waters were constructed in accordance with state-of-the-art engineering practice and were believed at the time to be three to four times stronger than necessary. Unfortunately, that turned out not to be the case.

Prior to 1923, Mulholland had honed his dam-making skills by constructing a number of large dirt dams. This is trickier than it sounds. A successful earthen embankment is semi-impermeable, holding back the water by means of the same sort of silt as can be found at the bottom of lakes.[8] In 1924, Mulholland changed medium, constructing the Weid Canyon Dam in Hollywood using concrete. Its capacity was two and a half billion gallons at a maximum depth of 183 feet.[9] It was hugely suc-

---

6. I want to thank Ethan Smith, Terry Tilley, Trecy Lysaught, Kelly Johnson, Dennis Doyle, and Aaron James for their insightful comments on an earlier draft of this chapter.

7. My account of Mulholland and the St. Francis Dam tragedy is taken largely from Petroski, "St. Francis Dam," 114–18.

8. Ibid. 115.

9. "Lake Hollywood Reservoir."

cessful. As the bronze plaque on the still-standing dam explains, Weid Canyon Dam was rechristened "Mulholland Dam" in 1923 by grateful residents in appreciation for its builder.

Another of the eight reservoirs planned, St. Francis Dam, was to be of similar size. Originally designed to hold 30,000 acre-feet of water (roughly half of L.A.'s yearly need), the design called for the dam wall to rise to a height of 175 feet above the San Francisquito Creek bed.[10] You can imagine how such a dam works by thinking of the mountains on either side as two giant cones. The creek flows along the floor of the narrow valley between the two mountains. From the dry side, the dam simply looks like a great concave wall wedged up against the sides of the mountain cutting off the flow of the creek. The weight of the water behind the curve effectively flattens the concave curve, pushing the walls horizontally against the mountain, while the weight of the concrete pushes the dam wall vertically down into the mountainside and valley floor.

Because of the triangular geometry of the mountains, the capacity could be increased an enormous 25 percent (bringing the total to approximately 38,000 acre-ft) by simply adding twelve feet at the top of the 175 foot wall.[11] At 187 feet, this dam was only four feet taller than the Mulholland Dam in Hollywood's Weid Canyon. The Hollywood Reservoir has been in good working order for 83 years. But just before midnight on March 12, 1928, the St. Francis Dam collapsed. Twelve billion gallons of water rushed down the canyon in an instant, laden with enormous sections of the dam wall, some of which weighed several thousands of tons, and destroyed everything in its path and killing in excess of 430 people. [12]

The question we need to consider is an ethical one: Is Mulholland culpable for 430 deaths and untold millions of dollars of property damage?

In retrospect, Mulholland might be faulted for failing to reinforce 130,000 cubic yards of concrete with steel rebar as is commonly seen

10. An acre-foot of water is the quantity of water needed to flood one acre of land with twelve inches of water. Petroski, "St. Francis Dam," 115.

11. Of course, because the mountains leveled out near their peak, the increase in height had to be accompanied by a large increase in the breadth of the dam wall at its top.

12. Petroski, "St. Francis Dam," 117.

in construction today. Moreover, Mulholland's designs included neither contraction joints nor inspection tunnels ("drainage galleries"). To be fair to Mulholland, he expected the St. Francis Dam to perform just as faithfully as its still-standing predecessor, the Mulholland Dam, for which the enormous weight of the dam closed up any cracks and held the thing in place. Who could have guessed that such a massive object could be rendered somewhat buoyant by a tiny amount of seepage under the dam and around the side walls? Today, having learned from the tragedy, contemporary designs for concrete dams reduce seepage by means of "cut-off walls" and "grout curtains." *But* this was 1925.

We return to the question: is Mulholland culpable? If *no one could have known* in 1925 what today is considered standard precautions in the construction of concrete dams, then Mulholland is "off the hook." And the failure of the St. Francis Dam must be regarded as simply a tragedy of nature.

Things are rarely so simple.

A moral haze surrounds complex human activities such as building a dam, for at least two reasons. First, human practices (such as engineering or medicine) deal with *unpredictable* systems. Consequently, the knowledge for which practitioners are held accountable will be a function of *the state of the practice* at the time in which they practiced.[13] There is no other source of knowledge except that which practitioners have accumulated and nurtured and tweaked through the ages. For example, physicians now know that bloodletting, a common treatment a century ago, failed to reduce fevers and tended to worsen the patient's condition. But medical ethicists would never suggest that eighteenth-century doctors were somehow morally at fault for prescribing treatments that today's doctors know are bogus. No, moral guilt is always measured against the protocols for best practice at that time.

Second, because individuals gain mastery of practices *progressively*, the working knowledge for which a *novice* is culpable is far less than the working knowledge expected of an expert practitioner. So, the degree to which Mulholland is culpable for the disaster is in some sense a function of the state of engineering in 1925 *and* of his own relative progress towards expertise in early twentieth-century civil engineering.

Taking the second point first, I'm not suggesting that ignorance automatically shields the novice from blame. I do believe there are

13. Koen, *Discussion of the Method*, 51.

cases of excusable ignorance. However, not all instances of ignorance are of the same kind. Thomas Aquinas identified three kinds of ignorance. "Accidental ignorance" describes cases in which we didn't know something at the time we acted, but, had we known we would have done the same regardless. Automakers didn't foresee that cars would create massive air pollution. But even if they could foresee this, they probably would have been justified in producing cars simply because of the enormous health problems, not to mention the stench, engendered by omnipresent piles of maggot-bearing horse manure. The second kind of ignorance is called "antecedent ignorance." It's the kind of ignorance that precedes action no matter who we are. Even expert doctors are never 100 percent sure of the results of their treatments. But they must act anyway. In fact, they must act even when probabilities are only a shade better than 50–50. The point is that real contingency accompanies every moral act.

The third kind of ignorance is called "consequent ignorance." Thomas argued that a person is culpable for genuine ignorance in cases where the person's lack of progress was consequent upon deficiencies in his or her character.[14] If she was arrogant . . . if he was greedy . . . if she was lazy . . . if he was stubborn . . . ignorance may follow. And if it follows, "consequent" ignorance is blameworthy as well as ignorant. (Incidentally, Aristotle uses similar logic to defend the Athenian law that assessed *double* penalty for crimes committed while drunk. Not a bad idea, it seems to me.) Any practitioner is responsible for the outcomes precisely to the extent one is responsible for the present state of one's character. As I shall argue below, Christians ought to imitate the way practitioners form the character of the next generation. However, before I do so, I want to think more carefully about the unpredictable state of the world. So, let's leave aside Mulholland for the time being. Rather than ask whether Mulholland was on schedule in his character formation and professional development, I want to ask what it is about building dams that makes it so difficult to determine guilt when they fall down. This difficulty is crucially important because it is not restricted to dam-building, or to civil engineering in general, or to all of engineering for that matter. This difficulty also marks politics, law, economics, medicine, and many others. So, let's think about my claim that practices such as engineering or medicine or psychiatry, etc., deal with unpredictable systems. A more

14. Aquinas, *Summa Theologica*, I–II.6.8.

precise way to put it would be to say that human practices deal with *dynamic*[15] rather than *linear* systems. As we shall see, it is this distinction that makes all the difference for a proper reading of Christian ethics, especially the kind of Christian ethics which claims that the moral force of any obligation traces to the command of God.[16]

Linear systems are those we dimly recall from high school physics. Billiard balls colliding on a pool table conserve momentum and ricochet at predictable angles. These kinds of systems behave predictably because the present configuration of the whole can be reduced to the behavior of the parts. The behavior of two billiard ball systems can be extended, enabling the prediction for collisions involving three, four, or five balls. At least that's what we were told.[17]

As the name implies, "dynamic" systems have the tendency to change. Dynamic systems can be relatively predictable or wildly unstable. When they are stable they are said to be "near equilibrium." When near a state of equilibrium, dynamic systems resemble colliding billiard balls and thus relatively predictable. But in sharp contrast to linear systems, dynamic systems can move far from equilibrium. And when this happens, the system can undergo enormous changes, *changes on the same order of magnitude as the system itself!*[18] This means that the dynamic system is capable of giving birth to an entirely new system, which is to say a brand new system whose relevant features cannot be anticipated and whose behavior cannot be predicted in advance.

15. For the sake of readers who are engineers, physicists or mathematicians, I am using the term "dynamic" to mean systems that are simultaneously non-linear *and* chaotic. I understand that many non-linear systems are fully predictable—for example, the motion of a pendulum. Unfortunately, the word "chaotic" has negative connotations that make it an ill-fitting terms to talk about human action. So, the convention is to use "dynamic" to mean systematic unpredictability. For an accessible introduction to this topic see Juarerro, *Dynamics in Action*.

16. For a very good introduction to divine command ethics, consider Mouw, *God Who Commands*.

17. In point of fact, there is a hidden upper limit to the predictability of even linear systems. Henri Poincaré proved that a system involving the collision of n balls, became utterly unpredictable if there were error in the nth significant figure of the starting position. Conversely, an error in the fifth decimal place, 0.00001, means that the positions and speeds of the final ball will be unpredictable after only five collisions. Polkinghorne, *Science and Providence*, 28–29.

18. A standard road for theologians to take regarding dynamic systems is Russell, Murphy, and Peacocke, *Chaos and Complexity*.

For this reason the study of these sort of dynamic systems has been dubbed "chaos theory."[19] The most famous case of a chaotic system is weather. Somewhat fancifully, chaos theoreticians illustrate chaos with the "butterfly effect": the claim that the mere flap of a butterfly's wing in Brazil may yield a hurricane in Polynesia . . . or not. And that is the point; we simply cannot know.

All Human Practices Deal with Dynamic Systems

In Mulholland's case, despite his skill, St. Francis Dam was built under dynamic, complex, chaotic conditions. The geometry of the valley, the composition of the hillsides (and valley floor), not to mention the behavior of the March weather, all conspired to make for a situation that was far enough from equilibrium to be unpredictable.

This sounds ominous. If we can never fully predict outcomes, then is not everybody off the hook? And if everybody is off the hook, then does it follow that anything goes?

If you grant me two presuppositions, I think we can sort this out and make some important applications for Christian discipleship.

PRESUPPOSITION 1: *All human "practices" deal with dynamic systems.* (By the way, it'll take a while to get to the second presupposition. So, if you're watching for it, don't panic.) I am using the term "practice" in by now a familiar way. I mean every sort of cooperative human activity that, despite dealing with dynamic systems, has managed to make slow progress over time, both in the sense of producing skillful craftspersons and also in the sense that the skillfulness of each generation *in toto* surpasses that of its forebears.[20] Medicine is such a practice. As mentioned above, a hundred years ago, fevers were reduced by bloodletting. Today physicians use Ibuprophen. A hundred years ago engineers thought airplanes could not be steered until they were made stable. But then the Wright brothers showed that instability can be harnessed to make planes

---

19. Gleick, *Chaos.*

20. I am, of course, indebted to Alasdair MacIntyre's description of "practice." As famous as it is tortuous, MacIntyre's describes practices as "any coherent and complex form of socially established cooperative human activity through which goods internal to that form of activity are realized in the course of trying to achieve those standards of excellence which are appropriate to, and partially definitive of, that form of activity, with the result that human powers to achieve excellence, and human conceptions of the ends and goods involved, are systematically extended." MacIntyre, *After Virtue,* 187.

more maneuverable rather than less. In cases like these, changes in best practices can be given clear retrospective explanation. But not always; at least not to nonpractitioners.

Advancement in the face of dynamic systems is not made via acquisition of information but by means of embodied knowledge or tacit skillfulness. The fancy name for embodied know-how is *phronēsis*, the virtue of practical reasoning. Practices like medicine and engineering have made genuine progress through the ages by virtue of the practitioners' ability to skillfully roll with whatever punches chaotic systems could throw. In fact, practices have become the primary way humans cooperate to beat the odds that dynamic systems pose precisely because the wisdom possessed by the practice as a whole is real, although largely *tacit* (which is to say, cannot be completely described). Human practitioners, as biological creatures embedded in a chaotic world, are capable of attunement with the dynamic world around them. One's attunement is accelerated by one's participation in relevant practice because practices aim to train bodies as well as minds. Practices may justify their mode of training with glib answers such as "we've always done it this way." And of course, those methods sometimes do need changing. But very frequently, the real reason they've always done it this way is because "this way" turns out to be the best way of doing it. And it is simply not the case that best practices can be given justification on the spot.

This is enormously important. Consider very carefully Hebrews 5:14. I quote from the New American Standard because that's the version I grew up memorizing. "But solid food is for the mature who through practice have trained their senses to discern good and evil." Three observations. First, the word for training has obvious physical connotations. The "training" in question is the word from which we get the English "gymnastics." This lexical fact underscores the fact that spiritual training has a *physical* component. (Remember chapters 2 and 3: our bodies are important to God, and it matters what we do with them.) Second, the training in view was regular and repetitive. So regular and repetitive was the training that it has resulted in a habitual, more or less permanent state of the soul.[21] Third, discernment of good and evil is paired with a

---

21. Given the Greek options, it is significant that the writer of Hebrews does not employ the Greek word for choice, nor "disposition" nor even "habit." Rather the strongest term possible is used: *hexis*. For Aristotle, *hexis* is at the end of the chain: choice: deed: disposition: habit: state (*hexis*).

bodily rather than mental faculty. Sometimes one "smells" goodness and detects evil by a wrenching gut.[22]

This bodily faculty is not the property of a select few. Granted, there is a spiritual gift of discernment that we so desperately need in the Body of Christ. But what Hebrews is talking about applies to all Christians that are in pursuit of maturity. I maintain that physically trained discernment depends on a faculty that we share with all human beings. It includes all forms of *tacit* knowledge.

Is the term "tacit" familiar? Do you know what a clarinet sounds like? Yes? Could you write a paragraph describing what it sounds like to someone who has never heard a woodwind of any kind? No? Your knowledge is tacit knowledge: you know what it sounds like, but you cannot write it down. In fact, you'd stake your life on knowing the difference between the sound of a clarinet and the whistle of an oncoming train. "Oh, listen! A clarinet. . . . (crunch!)"

Tacit knowledge resides in our bodies. Take bicycle riding for example. Long before one is old enough to comprehend the physics behind why balance is more difficult the slower one goes, one *knows* how to ride a bike and knows to coach a child to ride "fast enough" in order to learn balance. Anyone who has tried to sit motionless atop a bicycle hoping for the stoplight to change can attest to the difficulty of balancing at slow speeds! What about high speeds? At high speeds, the trick is not so much maintaining balance as it is steering the contraption. At slow speeds you steer with the handle bars. For high-speed riding, steering requires shifting one's hips in the saddle and swinging the inside knee into the turn. (This technique is most easily observed when motorcyclists corner at high speeds.) The physics of steering a bicycle involves three-dimensional geometry. But my point is that the body learns the "feel" of balancing and turning long before, and entirely apart from, being able to do the physics.

We should not be surprised that tacit knowledge was the reason that the under-funded Wright brothers who solved the riddle of steering

22. There are twenty-one occurrences of cognates of *diakrinō*. Usually it is said to be the action of the whole person, rather than of a particular faculty. And one time it is used to describe a spiritual gift. But one time (1 Cor 6:5) *diakrinō* is linked to the skill of theoretical reasoning, which would be normal in classical usage. The fact that the author of Hebrews pairs it with the idea of bodily perception (*aisthēsis*, from which we get aesthetics, and the verb form, used in Heb 5:14, *aisthanomai*) is notable for being unusual in the Greek New Testament.

airplanes. Avid bicyclists, the Wright brothers instinctively approached steering an airplane as a problem in *three* dimensions. Because one steers a bike by leaning into the turn, Orville and Wilbur equipped their aircraft with a hip saddle so that the pilot, laying on his belly, could by shifting his hips, pull cables that torque the wings and lean into the turn. Inventors with far better funding failed where the Wright brothers succeeded, because the others were flatlanders who naturally assumed that planes could be steered like automobiles, which is to say, in two dimensions. Tacit knowledge matters.

Tacit, or embodied, knowledge is *not* a lamentable stop gap measure until the preferable theoretical modeling can be put in place. Rather, in the realm of practices and dynamic systems, *embodied knowledge is both chronologically and logically prior to theoretical reasoning.* Consequently, getting the "feel" for engineering or medicine or music, and so on, is as critical to the expert as it is to the novice. One never outgrows it.

In 1951, Roger Whitcomb solved a crucial problem for designing the cross-sectional shape of airplane wings to enable planes to overcome drag that prevented planes from breaking the sound barrier. Although mathematical data and models abounded, no one could predict the optimum wing shape by means of calculation. Come to think of it, nobody could even make the choice when turned into a multiple choice question. (Countless wing-shapes had been identified, grouped into families and cataloged.) In fact, the "data" that is the most necessary for assessing the limits of models turns out to be *hands-on experience* with wind itself. Thus Whitcomb spent *years* inside the wind tunnel. Eugene Ferguson reports, "As an apprentice to the wind, he learned a great deal, much of which he could neither verbalize nor describe in any meaningful way to a person whose background did not include similar visual and tactile experience."[23] After eight years "in the tunnel," Whitcomb reports that the design sort of "slipped into his mind," almost unbidden. (Surprisingly, it was not the wing shape that was the crucial design, but the shape of the fuselage.) The most technical account of this discovery came from a fellow aeronautical engineer who simply described Whitcomb as a person "who just has a sense of intuition about these kind of aerodynamic problems. He sort of *feels* what the air wants to do."[24]

23. Ferguson, *Engineering and the Mind's Eye*, 52–53.
24. Ibid., 54; emphasis added

In Aristotle's terms, the difference between mathematical description and "getting the feel for it," is the difference between theoretical
reasoning and practical reasoning. If I'm correct about this comparison,
then achieving excellence in moral reasoning will in some sense be more
similar to an individual's advancement in medicine and engineering than
to an exhaustive compilation of the all axioms of Euclidian geometry.[25]
For this reason, when a practice such as engineering is on its cutting
edge, theoretical explanations of a good design frequently *follow* rather
than precede the design. *After* Whitcomb designed the ideal wing shape,
engineers may be able to explain why that shape *had* to take the form it
did to minimize drag. Then again, maybe not.

This ought not surprise us. The lag time between skillfulness and
explanation is, in part, a function of the dynamics of the context. If the
dynamic system is near equilibrium, then connections between this
explanation and that one begin to be noticed, a theoretical framework
begins to emerge, and predictions begin to be possible. But when the
discipline is in its infancy (i.e., the paradigm underdeveloped) or the dynamic context is far from equilibrium, *theoretical* reasoning lags behind
skilled judgment.

Because embodied know-how is tacit, *the wisdom of human practices is trained into novices by means of "heuristics."* In other words, just
because knowledge is tacit doesn't mean that words aren't involved.
No, language still can be employed—but in a performative (rather than
constative) way. Not all sentences are descriptive. A great many, perhaps
the vast majority, perform some action other than stating a description.[26]
Consider the sentence: "Words cannot express how grateful I am." The
person who asks whether this sentence is true or false has already missed
the point of the sentence. That is because there is a difference between
"saying" and "showing."[27] The concepts of "true" and "false" apply to sentences that *say* what they mean. But sentences that *show* rather than say

25. It is not unimportant that the Austrian mathematician Kurt Gödel proved in
1931 that no propositional system could be both exhaustive (containing all true propositions) *and* internally consistent. If it was complete, there it was bound to contain a
flaw. If it was comprised of only true and consistent propositions, it was bound to be
incomplete.

26. See, among others, Austin, *How to Do Things with Words.*

27. I am indebted to Wittgenstein for this notion. First discussed in the *Tractatus,*
Wittgenstein's later views transformed the distinction into the sense that I am using. See
Wittgenstein, *Philosophical Investigations.*

demand a different order of fluency to be intelligible. When a sentence uses words to *say*, or depict, some state of affairs, the skill of the language user becomes transparent, because the fact of the matter arrests our attention. But other sentences and phrases, ones that perform actions such as showing, tell us as much about human skills as about the thing in question. For example, many people can recognize the distinctive smell of a wet dog. But how many could write a paragraph that completely describes it? In this sense, no one can *say* what a wet dog smells like. We *know*, but we give up trying to say. We simply use the phrase "the smell of a wet dog" to do all the work. And phrases such as "the smell of a wet dog," "the sound of a clarinet," "the squeak of snow underfoot at twenty below," "the sensation of zero-gravity," or "the color of twilight on a midwinter snowscape" reveal as much about the know-how of the speaker as they do about clarinets, dogs, snow, weight, and color. As a result, these phrases *show* rather than *say*. In particular, they manifest the very close link between the thing and the person with know-how.

Such link-phrases enable practitioners to construct heuristics that guide novices. Heuristics differ from stipulations as *showing* differs from *saying*. Stipulations are imperatives that explicitly say what ought to be done or avoided: "All cars shall pay $1.00 at the toll booth." In contrast, heuristics use link-phrases to *show* what they prescribe or proscribe. For example, here is an engineering heuristic: "At the appropriate time, freeze the design and go into production."[28] Obviously, the one who rushes into production prematurely will generate a faulty product. Meanwhile, the one who endlessly tinkers with improvements will produce nothing at all. But exactly *when* is "the appropriate time?" This phrase, "at the appropriate time" is the link-phrase that depends crucially on the know-how of the skillful engineer.

The allusion of the link-phrase is all but lost on the novice. Novices don't know when "the appropriate time" is. Beginners need concrete, black and white directives for which they can scarcely be mistaken. Black and white stipulations are very comforting; if you've been given stipulations, you don't have to think. And you don't have to sweat the consequences—you just do what you're told. But fledglings need to be booted out of the nest! So, the issuing of such clear-cut directives must be a *temporary* stage in the development of novices. Novices need con-

---

28. Koen, *Discussion of the Method*, esp. 25–57.

crete directives *until* they are fluent enough to enter the iterative loop of heuristic-guided training.

The concrete directives or stipulations work precisely because they are instances of saying rather than showing. Stipulations are more about the thing being commanded (or forbidden) than about the know-how of the hearer. Good thing, too! For novices lack know-how. By contrast, heuristics are about know-how that practitioners bring to bear upon dynamic systems.

Perhaps a more mundane example can illustrate the difference. Consider the following two commands:

C1 "Every day do not eat a quarter-pound stick of butter."
C2 "Every day run five minutes farther than is comfortable."

Both commands purportedly aim at health. But the first command is not a heuristic. It is a simple stipulation. It requires no skilled judgment to apply. It is tidily proscriptive; either one has or has not consumed a stick of butter. At life's end one can report with precision how success-fully one obeyed C1. The more frequently one disobeys C1, the greater one's health is at risk. But strangely, the one who slavishly keeps C1 is not guaranteed health. For, one can eat a pound of bacon, or a quart of ice cream while refusing to indulge in the butter.

By contrast, C2 ("Every day run five minutes farther than is com-fortable") is a prescriptive heuristic. It proposes a positive training regi-men that requires skilled judgment to determine just how many yards, blocks, or miles elapse before one is uncomfortable enough to start the five-minute countdown. But even more important for my illustration is the iterative nature of C2. In other words, the greater the number of interations, the more consistently one has previously employed C2, the greater the distance is required to reach discomfort. This is because, as a heuristic, the health-seeker is transformed by the application of the heuristic. Endurance is procured by the person (who is increasingly considering himself or herself a "runner"). And even more surprising: the person's very *desires* are transformed.[29] Distance runners rarely eat slabs of bacon or sticks of butter. (Though I've known some to consume quarts of ice cream!) Believe it or not, they sort of lose their taste for fatty foods. Running and eating well have become second nature. And

---

29. Ethan Smith has done much to help me see how central role that proper desire must play in accounts of ethics modeled after Aristotle and Aquinas.

here is the surprise: the heuristic is discarded. But it is not discarded in order to disobey it. It falls from memory because it has been *successfully internalized.*

What should we conclude? Simply this: heuristics, which can be identified by the presence of link-phrases ("the smell of coffee"), differ from stipulations by being *iterative, prescriptive* and *self-transformative*. Of course, this is just the problem, isn't it? On the front end of the learning curve, novices cannot tell the difference. Novices typically mistake heuristics for authoritarian directives. But because of their current stage of development, their mistake is entirely appropriate!

The World of Human Relationships Is Itself a Dynamic System

I've already asked you to grant me one presupposition: namely, that every human practice deals with dynamic systems. Now I ask to be granted a second:

PRESUPPOSITION 2: *the world of human relationships is itself a dynamic system.*

Moral philosophers from all across the spectrum tend to agree on at least one point: real moral obligation is always a function of actual social relationships.[30] So my claim that the social world is a dynamic system means that the fulfillment of moral responsibility (we might as easily say, "response-ability") is every bit as much a human "practice" as engineering or medicine. If so, then we ought to expect to find in moral practice the same two features we've already encountered in engineering. First, we are right to look for heuristics that show (rather than say) the way to go on. Second, we should expect to discover novices in the practice who mistake these heuristics for authoritarian directives, even divinely commanded ones.

Please do not misunderstand me. I am not making the Kohlbergian claim that divine commands are fictitious or childish or a kind of "Morality for Dummies."[31] Rather, the complexity and practice-nature of

---

30. This is true for a broad spectrum of thinkers, from Robert Adams to Alasdair MacIntyre, and many in between. Adams, *Finite and Infinite Goods*, 233. MacIntyre, *After Virtue*.

31. Some have thought Lawrence Kohlberg meant to restrict divine commands to level-two morality, much like a child learns to follow rules circumspectly. This has the disadvantage of implying that moral saints, such as Mother Teresa, are less mature in their moral psychology than say Immanuel Kant! However, in later years Kohlberg

Christian "morality" means that Christians ought slowly to gain nuance
over time. But the spirit of surrender and allegiance to God as well as
humility before the canonical scriptures that marks a life under the command of God is never outgrown. Rather, divine commands, as novices
understand them, are the limiting case for a more mature Christian ethics that thinks in terms of divine heuristics. Divine heuristics; how might
this conceptual shift assist evangelical ethics?

Some of us remember being told as children not to fear thunder.
If you grew up in the Midwest, where thunderstorms are both frequent
and spectacular, you'll also remember the magic formula that tells how
far away the storm is. We were told to count the number of seconds between the flash and the kaboom and divide by five to estimate how many
miles away the lightening had struck.

The math gets more complicated if one tries to take into account the
speed of light (a blistering 186,000 miles per second) or to explain that
we really should divide by 4.72933086 instead of five! Do we mislead our
own children if we fail to disclose these details? When we disregard the
speed of light, we are not being disingenuous. We are simplifying it for
the sake of children's child-sized comprehension. In the case of thunder,
the complicated calculation *includes* the simplified approximation *as
its limiting case*. So too, it seems at least plausible that a mature moral
practice does not discard simplistic authoritative directives but rather
contains them as their limiting case.[32]

How else can we explain evangelicals' ambivalent stance toward
the sixth commandment? "Thou shalt not kill." It is widely known that
the sixth commandment provides evangelicals a strong rationale against
abortion. But statistically speaking anyway, evangelicals consider deaths
incurred by self-defense, deaths incurred in protecting loved ones, and
deaths by means of capital punishment to be somehow outside the am-

---

considered expanding his moral psychology from six levels to seven in order to accommodate religious reasoning. See Kohlberg and Power, "Moral Development, Religious
Thinking," 311–72.

32. Servais Pinckaers makes a parallel argument. Ethics has a fundamental need for
the notion of obligation. However, ethics cannot be reduced to obligation without doing damage to other notions central to morality. For example, friendship and kindness
are cheapened if one acts "because I am obligated to"! Moral notions such as kindness
may begin in the form of a stipulated obligation. The mother commands the child,
"Share your toys!" But the object of childhood training is not the flawless fulfillment
of obligations but rather a voluntary heart of kindness. Servais Pinckaers, *Sources of
Christian Ethics*.

bit of sixth commandment. What should we make of this dissonance? I account for this "exemption" in the following way. Evangelicals have among their number, novices who as they advance toward maturity neither discard the sixth commandment nor disobey it. Rather, they learn to take the sixth commandment very, very seriously—but as the limiting case. Thus evangelicals' own position vis-à-vis the sixth commandment illustrates my claim that the limiting case—"don't kill!"—does not apply in a straightforward way every time.

As a theological pacifist (one who opposes all war for theological reasons), the previous comments makes it look as though I've painted myself into a corner. I've used the typical evangelical stance on capital punishment and warcraft and lethal self-defense to make plausible my claim that divine commands do not function as black and white stipulations but as tools for training the desires of novices until their primal reflex is on the side of life. Once their "senses have been trained" (in the words of Hebrews 5), they can handle more nuanced cases. How then can I maintain my own pacifism without turning the sixth commandment into what I've said it is not, namely an exceptionless stipulation? (The philosophy students are nodding! If I say Exod 20:13 is a stipulation, I apparently undermine all my talk about heuristics.)

Please note that I've *not* claimed that novices who advance toward maturity *outgrow* the divine commands. Nor have I said that capital punishment, et al, are in fact *exceptions* to otherwise plain-sense and universally applicable directives. There are some Christian ethicists who say such things. But not me. Rather, I claim that novices slowly gain skilled judgment, most importantly in the form of an increase in their fluency in the conceptual language of the scriptures. As new Christians must be *trained* to spot "sin" as "sinful," so too they must be trained to give the sixth commandment its proper *scope*. So then, here's my account.

As an evangelical pacifist, I take the sixth commandment to function as a limiting case. The limiting case involves two items, *bodies* and *slayings*: people's *bodies* ought never be *slain*. If this is the limiting case for novice comprehension, what would a more discerning read look like? As my own children mature, I pray that they will come to see more profoundly that people's bodies not only ought never be slain, they also not be slowly starved either. Thus, I hope they protest certain fiscal policies that make it nearly impossible for minimum wage-earners to afford nutritious food. "People's bodies ought never be slain" is a limiting case in a second way as well. In addition to their bodies, people's *souls* ought never be slain either, as happens slowly through structural evil—such as Third World debt or racism in America or dysfunctional relationships. That *too* is a form of killing. Third, I hope my children come to see the object of the verb "to kill" includes, besides people, animals, birds, perhaps even trees. Only with such an outlook will creation's anxious longing for the revealing of the children of God be fulfilled (Rom 8:19). For the pacifist, the sixth commandment, "do not kill," which is taken by novices to mean "do not slay people's bodies," is the limiting case for a much broader prohibition that will one day characterize the eschatological kingdom of Christ. In the meantime, Christian novices must grow into those who appreciate the sixth commandment as a powerful heuristic of discipleship.

CONCLUSION

How to conclude? There are two loose ends to be tied before I conclude. First, what then of Mulholland? Is he culpable or not? Surely *I* cannot render judgment one way or the other, for *I* am not a civil engineer. I suppose that sounds evasive. But it has been my point that Mulholland's guilt is a function of the state of engineering circa 1928 and must be rendered by technically skillful as well as historically competent engineers.[33] But we may get some inkling of his relative innocence from the fact that engineers and historians of technology have, by and large, remembered him kindly.

Second, I conclude that Wyndy Corbin Reuschling is largely correct. There *does* exist a danger of group-think among evangelicals whose ethics is nothing but a narrowly construed divine command ethics. However, if I am correct about the comparison of Christian moral life with other dynamic practices, then at least two things follow. First, moral maturation is as much a training of bodies as it is a training of the will, as Heb 5:14 makes evident: "Solid food is for the mature, who through *practice* have *trained* their *senses* to *discern* good and evil." Notions such as repetition, training, and the body's role in discernment have close kinship with what I have been calling dynamic practices.[34]

33. For an interesting treatment of the relation between excellence in engineering and excellence in humanities, see Soudek, "Humanist Engineer of Aleksandr Solzhenitsyn," 57–60.

34. A more sophisticated biblical argument for the progressive nature of moral maturation can be seen in *Mark's* puzzling account of the healing of the blind man in

Moreover, if Christian morality is itself a practice, evangelicals ought to expect that the novice stage of discipleship will always be present among us, as novices are present in every flourishing practice. Because the practice of moral formation is of such grave importance, we rightly employ divine command ethics in the training of our novices. This is not something to be embarrassed about. For, divine command ethics contains something profoundly correct, and this feature is retained throughout one's training in virtue of the fact that divine command ethics is the limiting case.[35] Yet surely we are correct to expect of every practitioner the ongoing development of nuance in their moral know-how precisely because, unbeknownst to them as novices, divine commands are *heuristics* in a more sophisticated practice than they are capable of perceiving at their current stage of maturation.[36]

Mark 8:22–26. The story is puzzling because this miracle apparently doesn't "take" in the first attempt. While some worry that this amounts to a ding against Jesus' record, Jesus appears entirely undisturbed by the fact that in the first pass, the blind man can only see men as trees! The mystery is dissolved when this story is juxtaposed to the pericopes that come before it and after it in Mark's text—remember, we are expected to read the string of stories as a *single* narrative. On either side of this story, Mark's Gospel gives accounts of the incompleteness of the disciples' understanding. After Jesus walks on water, the disciples are "astonished" because "they had not learned anything from the incident with the loaves." Following the two-stage healing of the blind man, Peter confesses Jesus' lordship . . . but does so incompletely. For Peter possesses only dimly glimpses *that* Jesus is the Messiah, but is unable to comprehend *what* Jesus' reign amounts to: suffering. For this reason, Peter receives a stiff rebuke from Jesus. (See also the disciples' incomprehension as reported in Mark 9:10, 32.) Apparently, wanting to see clearly is not enough to guarantee that one sees clearly. Read contextually, the story of the two-stage healing underscores a lesson in discipleship, namely, that human beings gain moral and spiritual eye-sight *progressively* or in stages, rather than all at once. Not even Jesus finds this troubling or lamentable, simply a given.

35. As mentioned above, the something that is "profoundly correct" is the reality of moral obligation. Morality without obligation ceases to be morality. But ethics does not reduce to obligation without losing other moral compasses such as the telos of human life, the role of suffering, the place of friendship, the need for progress over time of one's moral eyesight, and so on.

36. A topic I've neglected for sake of brevity is the logical possibility of a range of speeds according to which individuals experience stipulations transformed into heuristics. In other words, some novices develop a nuanced grasp of some stipulations very quickly and very early on, while other take much longer. Perhaps some novices *never* experience this transformation for some stipulations. So too, it is at least logically possible that a believer simply does not live long enough to experience the transformation as complete. Christ-followers are unified in the conviction that to a person perfect obedience is highly unlikely, even impossible this side of the Eschaton. But perhaps it is also possible that some (most? all?) fail even to arrive at a place of maturity from which all moral stipulations are seen as heuristics.

The real danger that my friend Wyndy poses is the danger of group-think for the community whose moral development has been arrested at the novice stage. This will remain a danger only so long as they forget the *dynamic* nature of Christian practices.[37] Christian ethicist Stanley Hauerwas summarized the hoped-for application of this chapter when he once said, "I want to be part of a community with the habits and practices that will make me do what I would otherwise not choose to do and then to learn to like what I have been forced to do." This is how the New Testament speaks of discipleship.

The Greek New Testament had three basic terms that might have been used for referring to that mode of reasoning that befits Christ-followers. One of the available terms is *theōria*. Ancient philosophers used it to signify high-level, sometimes abstract, theorizing culminating in contemplation of insights. The New Testament *never* employs *theōria* in this manner.[38] A second term had to do with devising clever works-every-time techniques for increasing productivity in a craft. In this vein one thinks of the recent spate of church-growth "manuals." But the New Testament *never* uses this word this way.[39] It is the third alternative that the New Testament uses again and again. It is the word for *practical* reasoning that we've met above. The skill of the practical reasoner is called "practical wisdom," or *phronēsis,* and the one who gets it right is called a "wise one," a *phronimos*. Forty-seven times it is used in the New Testament. To cite one famous instance, Jesus scolds Peter for not *thinking practically (phroneō)* about God's interests (Mark 8:33).

The Apostle Paul uses the *phron-* words more frequently than any other author (33 times). And for good reason: it is the term of disciple-ship, fitting well his hortatory letters. A full *ten times* he uses it in the short letter to believers in Philippi! These believers are given special

37. For more on Christian practices see Murphy, Kallenberg, and Nation, *Virtues and Practices in the Christian Tradition*. Of course practices alone won't do it any more than works alone! It is practices in the presence of Christ that matter. Willimon wonders if perhaps we have forgotten the centrality of Christ. Willimon, "Too Much Practice."

38. To be precise, the noun does in fact show up, but once (Luke 23:48). But Luke uses the term not philosophically but simply to express "physical eyesight." The verbal cognate to *theōria* is *theōreō* and is used 58 times which connotes observing, beholding, physical seeing, or looking.

39. The words "craft" and "craftsperson" shows up only descriptively, and then only six times: Acts 17:29, 18, 19:24, 38; Heb 11:10, Rev 18:22.

mention as those who "participated" in the Gospel from Day One and were "co-sharers" with Paul in the grace that is reserved for those who both defend and confirm the Gospel by living it with each other (1:5–7).[40] The term "practical reasoning" (*phroneō*) is translated variously as "the same mind" (2:2), "the same purpose" (2:2), "Christ's attitudinal mindset" (2:5), and "the perfect mind" (3:15). Just as revealing, Paul takes Christian practical reasoning to be antithetical to the reasonings of those "whose end is destruction, whose god is their belly, whose *practical reasoning is bent on earthly things*" (3:19). It is not about theory; it is not about technique. It is about following Jesus in all things practical.

The mindset of a disciple is analogous to the mindset of the engineer-in-training. To adopt this mindset is to take the posture of a novice and undergo the training paces. The training regimen is long, hard, sometimes tedious, and sometimes defeating. But Paul-the-trainer exhorts Christ-followers to take courage and pursue justice, faith, love, peace, and so on *with others* who like us have stumbled, perhaps fallen, but been cleansed and rejoined the training.[41] In short, the training process itself is a team sport. The hoped-for outcome of the team in training is that we and our fellow novices one day find ourselves "fully exercised"[42] and thus in possession of the tacit discernment of the expert practitioner, able to sense good from evil, especially when on the face of it, things are not so clear.

40. In 1 Cor 1:6 Paul makes explicit what is implied in Phil 1:7, "confirmed *among you all.*"

41. Paul's exhortation is in 2 Tim 2:22: "Shun youthful passions and pursue righteousness, faith, love, and peace, along *with* those who call on the Lord from a cleansed (*katharos*) heart.

42. The Greek of Heb 5:14 is very rich and may be translated this way: "But solid food is for the mature, those who have completed their training, who by means of a steady-and-practiced disposition have had all their senses exercised to the sniffing out of good from evil.

Bibliography

Adams, Robert Merrihew. *Finite and Infinite Goods: A Framework for Ethics*. London: Oxford University Press, 2002.

Aguilera, Enrique, and Jose Maria Arnaiz. *Enfleshing the Word: Prayer and the Marianist Spiritual Journey*. Translated by Joseph Stefanelli. Dayton, OH: North American Center for Marianist Studies, 2000.

Alter, Alexandra. "Is This Man Cheating on His Wife?" *The Wall Street Journal Online*, August 10, 2007. Online: http://online.wsj.com/public/article/SB118670 164592393622.html.

Appleton, George, editor. *The Oxford Book of Prayer*. Oxford: Oxford University Press, 1985.

Aquinas, Thomas. *Summa Theologica*. Translated by Fathers of the English Dominican Province. New York: Christian Classics, 1981.

Aristides. "The Apology of Aristides the Philosopher." In *The Ante-Nicene Fathers (First Series): Original Supplement to the American Edition*, edited by Allan Menzies, 9:276–78. Grand Rapids: Eerdmans, 1965.

Aristotle. "Nicomachean Ethics." In *The Complete Works of Aristotle*, Bollingen Series 71:2, edited by Jonathon Barnes, 1729–867. Princeton, NJ: Princeton University Press, 1984.

———. "Politics." In *The Complete Works of Aristotle*, Bollingen Series 71:2, edited by Jonathon Barnes. Princeton, NJ: Princeton University Press, 1984.

Auden, W. H. "Horae Canonicae: Immolatus Vicerit." In *Collected Poems*, edited by Edward Mendelson, 47–86. New York: Random House, 1976.

Augustine. "The Greatness of the Soul." In *Ancient Christian Writers*, edited by Johannes Quasten and Joseph C. Plumpe. Westminster, MD: Newman, 1950.

———. "The Problem of Evil." In *Classical and Contemporary Readings in the Philosophy of Religion*, edited by John Hick, 19–27. Englewood Cliffs, NJ: Prentice-Hall, 1990.

Aulén, Gustaf. *Christus Victor: An Historical Study of the Three Main Types of the Idea of Atonement*. Translated by A. G. Hebert. 1931. Reprinted, Eugene, OR: Wipf & Stock, 2003.

Austin, J. L. *How to Do Things with Words*. 2nd ed. Edited by J. O. Urmson and Marina Sbisà. Cambridge: Harvard University Press, 1962, 1975.

Bainton, Roland. *Christian Attitudes toward War and Peace: A Historical Survey and Critical Re-Evaluation*. Nashville: Abingdon, 1960.

Banerjee, Neela. "Intimate Confessions Pour out on Church's Web Site." *The New York Times*, September 1, 2006. Online: http://www.nytimes.com/2006/09/01/us/01confession.html.

Benedict, Pope, XVI. "Papal Message for World Communications Day" (Jauary 2010). Online: http://www.zenit.org/article-28139?l=english.

Bennett, Jana Marguerite. "The Thomistic Internet? Theological Questioning in a Web 2.0 Age." Paper presented at the Society of Christian Ethics. San Jose, CA, 2010.

Berkhof, Hendrikus. *Christ and the Powers.* Translated by John H. Yoder. Scottdale, PA: Herald, 1977.

Bess, Jennifer. "Building the Church: The Future of Catholic Church Architecture in Light of Narrative Virtue Ethics and New Urbanism." MA thesis, University of Dayton, 2003.

Borgmann, Albert. *Power Failure: Christianity in the Culture of Technology.* Grand Rapids: Brazos, 2003.

Bowlin, John R. *Contingency and Fortune in Aquinas's Ethics.* Cambridge Studies in Religion and Critical Thought 6. Cambridge: Cambridge University Press, 1999.

Brand, Madeleine. "Blog Tips for the Pope: Give Us This Day Thy Daily Post." *All Things Considered* (January 2010). Online: http://www.npr.org/templates/transcript/transcript.php?storyId=123024977.

Broad, William J. "Report Urges U.S. To Increase Its Efforts on Nonlethal Weapons." *The New York Times,* November 6, 2002. Online: http://www.nytimes.com/2002/11/06/national/06WEAP.html?ex=1037605720&ei=1&en=15ffca68c085155f.

Buber, Martin. *I and Thou.* Translated by Walter Kaufmann. New York: Scribners, 1970.

Burnham, Gilbert, Riyadh Lafta, Shannon Doocy, and Les Roberts. "Mortality after the 2003 Invasion of Iraq: A Cross-Sectional Cluster Sample Survey." *The Lancet* 368 (2006) 1421–28.

Caldicott, Helen. "The Spoils of War." American Friends Service Committee. Online: http://www.afsc.org/pwork/0212/021213.htm.

Carter, Warren. *Matthew and Empire: Initial Explorations.* Harrisburg, PA: Trinity, 2001.

Chenu, Marie-Dominique. "Arts «Méchaniques» Et Œuvres Serviles." *Revue des sciences philosophiques et théologiques* 29 (1940) 312–15.

Clapp, Rodney. *Johnny Cash and the Great American Contradiction: Christianity and the Battle for the Soul of a Nation.* Louisville: Westminster John Knox, 2008.

Clement. "The First Epistle of Clement to the Corinthians." In *The Ante-Nicene Fathers. Vol. 1: The Apostolic Fathers—Justin Martyr—Irenaeus,* edited by Alexander Roberts and James Donaldson, 5–21. 1885. Reprinted, Grand Rapids: Eerdmans, 1951.

Cohen, Noam. "A Translator Tool with a Human Touch." *The New York Times,* November 22, 2009. Online: http://www.nytimes.com/2009/11/23/technology/23link.html?_r=1.

Crary, Alice. "Introduction." In *Wittgenstein and the Moral Life: Essays in Honor of Cora Diamond,* edited by Alice Crary, 1–29. Cambridge: MIT Press, 2007.

"Crisis in the Gulf: Pilots Race to Hit Fleeing Armor in 'Killing Box.'" Online: LexisNexis Academic Universe.

"Crowds Flocking to See Moose Courting a Cow." *The New York Times,* November 3, 1986.

Davis, Michael. *Thinking Like an Engineer.* Oxford: Oxford University Press, 1998.

Dias, W. P. S. "Heidegger's Relevance for Engineering: Questioning Technology." *Science and Engineering Ethics* 9 (2003) 389–96.

Diaz, Sam. "A Little E-Mail Prank, and a $2.8 Billion Panic." *The Washington Post,* May 18, 2007. Online: http://www.washingtonpost.com/wp-dyn/content/article/2007/05/17/AR2007051701995.html.

Dickson, Virgil, and Catherine Rampell. "Worship Goes Big-Screen and Hi-Fi, with Direct-Deposit Tithing." *Washington Post,* September 24, 2007. Online: http://www

.washingtonpost.com/wp-dyn/content/article/2007/09/24/AR2007092401854_
pf.html.

"The Digital Divide." *The Washington Post*, February 28, 2009. Online: http://www
.washingtonpost.com/wp-dyn/content/article/2009/02/27/AR2009022702749
.html.

Dunne, Joseph. *Back to the Rough Ground: Practical Judgment and the Lure of Technique.*
Notre Dame: University of Notre Dame Press, 1993.

Ellsberg, Robert. *All Saints: Daily Reflections on Saints, Prophets, and Witnesses for Our
Time.* New York: Crossroad, 1997.

Eusebius Pamphilus of Caesarea. *Church History.* Translated by Philip Schaff and Henry
Wace. A Select Library of Nicene and Post-Nicene Fathers of the Christian Church.
Second Series. Grand Rapids: Eerdmans, 1979.

Ferguson, Eugene S. *Engineering and the Mind's Eye.* Cambridge, MA: MIT Press, 1993.

———. "How Engineers Lose Touch." *American Heritage of Invention and Technology*
Winter (1993) 16–24.

"The First Nanotechnologists." *The New York Times*, February 21, 2005.

Fiser, Karen. "Privacy and Pain." *Philosophical Investigations* 9:1 (1986) 1–17.

Friedrich, Gerhard. "*Euaggelizomai.*" In *Theological Dictionary of the New Testament*,
edited by Gerhard Kittel and Gerhard Friedrich, 2:707–21. Grand Rapids: Eerdmans,
1971.

Gaebler, Mary. "Luther on the Self." *Journal of the Society of Christian Ethics* 22 (2002)
115–32.

Gispen, Kees. *New Profession, Old Order; Engineers and German Society, 1815–1914.*
Cambridge: Cambridge University Press, 1989.

Gleick, James. *Chaos: Making a New Science.* Rev. ed. New York: Penguin, 1993.

Gowen, Annie. "Lack of Computer Access Hampers Some Students." *The Washington
Post*, December 6, 2009.

Greene, Graham. *A Burnt-out Case.* New York: Penguin, 1975.

Greenspan, Robyn. "Internet Not for Everyone." Online: http://cyberatlas.internet.com/
big_picture/demographics/article/0,,5901_2192251,00.html.

Grossman, Lt. Col. Dave. *On Killing: The Psychological Cost of Learning to Kill in War and
Society.* Boston: Little, Brown, 1995.

Hafner, Kate. "Seeing Corporate Fingerprints in Wikipedia Edits." *The New York Times*,
August 19, 2007. Online: http://www.nytimes.com/2007/08/19/technology/19wiki
pedia.html.

Harak, G. Simon. "Supercaustics, Roach Motels and the Grime from Hell: Moral
Reflections on Nonlethal Weapons." Paper presented at the Society of Christian
Ethics, Albuquerque, NM, 1996.

———. *Virtuous Passions: The Formation of Christian Character.* Mahwah, NJ: Paulist,
1993.

Harley, Danielle. "Bishop Daniel Payne: Educating Black Saints in Ohio." MA thesis,
University of Dayton, 2002.

Hart, David Bentley. *The Doors of the Sea: Where Was God in the Tsunami?* Grand Rapids:
Eerdmans, 2005.

Hauerwas, Stanley. *Christian Existence Today: Essays on Church, World, and Living in
Between.* Durham, NC: Labyrinth, 1988.

———. "The Church as God's New Language." In *Christian Existence Today: Essays on
Church, World, and Living in Between*, 47–66. Durham, NC: Labyrinth,1988.

————. *A Community of Character*. Notre Dame: University of Notre Dame Press, 1981.

————. "Learning to See Red Wheelbarrows: On Vision and Relativism." *Journal of the American Academy of Religion* 45 (1977) 225, 644–55.

————. *The Peaceable Kingdom: A Primer in Christian Ethics*. Notre Dame: Notre Dame University Press, 1983.

————. "The Significance of Vision: Toward an Aesthetic Ethic." In *Vision and Virtue*, 30–47. 1974. Reprinted, Notre Dame: University of Notre Dame Press, 1981.

————. "Why Abortion Is a Religious Issue." In *A Community of Character*, 196–211. Notre Dame: University of Notre Dame Press, 1981.

Hauerwas, Stanley, and William H. Willimon. *Resident Aliens: Life in the Christian Colony*. Nashville: Abingdon, 1989.

Hauerwas, Stanley, with David Burrell. "From System to Story: An Alternative Pattern for Rationality in Ethics." In *Why Narrative? Readings in Narrative Theology*, edited by Stanley Hauerwas and L. Gregory Jones, 158–90. Grand Rapids: Eerdmans, 1989.

Heidegger, Martin. "The Question Concerning Technology." In *The Question Concerning Technology and Other Essays*, 3–36. New York: Harper & Row, 1977.

Heilbron, J. L. *The Sun in the Church*. Cambridge: Harvard University Press, 1999.

Heitmann, John A. "What Would Jesus Drive? Catholic Literature and the Automobile, 1930–1970." Paper presented at the Humanities Faculty Colloquium, University of Dayton, 2003.

Hertzberg, Lars. "On the Attitude of Trust." In *The Limits of Experience*, 113–30. Helsinki: Hakapaino Oy, 1994.

————. "Primitive Reactions—Logic or Anthropology?" In *The Wittgenstein Legacy*, edited by Peter A. French, Theodore E. Uehling Jr., and Howard K. Wettstein, 24–39. Notre Dame: University of Notre Dame Press, 1992.

Holzmann, Gerard J., and Björn Pehrson. *The Early History of Data Networks*. Los Alamitos, CA: IEEE Computer Society, 1995.

Hugh of St. Victor. *Didascalicon*. Translated with an introduction and notes by J. Taylor. New York: Columbia University Press, 1961.

Hyde, Lewis. *The Gift: Creativity and the Artist in the Modern World*. 2nd ed. New York: Vintage, 2007.

James, Aaron, and Brad J. Kallenberg. "What Mega-Churches Can Learn from Catholics." *Christian Ethics Today* 12:3 (2006) 19–20.

Jenson, Robert W. "What Is a Post-Christian?" In *The Strange New World of the Gospel: Re-Evangelizing in the Postmodern World*, edited by Carl E. Braaten and Robert W. Jenson, 21–31. Grand Rapids: Eerdmans, 2002.

Jesseph, Douglas M. "Hobbesian Mechanics." *Oxford Studies in Early Modern Philosophy* 3 (2006) 119–52.

Joyce, Amy. "Every Move You Make." *The Washington Post* (2006). Online: http://www.washingtonpost.com/wp-dyn/content/article/2006/09/30/AR2006093000147.html?referrer=emailarticle.

Juarerro, Alicia. *Dynamics in Action: Intentional Behavior as a Complex System*. Cambridge, MA: MIT Press, 2002.

Kallenberg, Brad J. "All Suffer the Affliction of the One: Metaphysical Holism and the Presence of the Spirit." *Christian Scholar's Review* 31 (2002) 217–34.

————. "The Descriptive Problem of Evil." In *Physics and Cosmology: Scientific Perspectives on the Problem of Natural Evil*, edited by Nancey Murphy, Robert John

Russell and William R. Stoeger, SJ, 297–322. Vatican City: Vatican Observatory Press, 2007.

———. *Ethics as Grammar: Changing the Postmodern Subject.* Notre Dame: University of Notre Dame Press, 2001.

———. *Live to Tell: Evangelism for a Postmodern Age.* Grand Rapids: Brazos, 2002.

———. "The Monastic Origins of Engineering." Paper presented at the Role of Engineering at Catholic Universities, University of Dayton, Dayton, OH, September 22–24, 2005.

Katz, Steven T. "Technology and Genocide: Technology as a 'Form of Life.'" In *Historicism, the Holocaust, and Zionism: Critical Studies in Modern Jewish Thought and History,* 193–224. New York: New York University Press, 1992.

Kebede, Messay. "Underdevelopment and the Problem of Causation." *Journal of Social Philosophy* 22:1 (1991) 125–36.

Kelsey, David. "Spiritual Machines, Personal Bodies, and God: Theological Education and Theological Anthropology." *Teaching Theology and Religion* 5:1 (2002) 2–9.

Kidder, Tracy. *Mountains beyond Mountains: The Quest of Dr. Paul Farmer, a Man Who Would Cure the World.* New York: Random House, 2004.

Kierkegaard, Søren. *Purity of Heart Is to Will One Thing.* Translated by Douglas V. Steere. New York: Harper & Row, 1956.

Koen, Billy Vaughn. *Discussion of the Method; Conducting the Engineer's Approach to Problem Solving.* New York: Oxford University Press, 2003.

Kohlberg, Lawrence, and Clark Power. "Moral Development, Religious Thinking and the Question of a Seventh Stage." In *The Philosophy of Moral Development: Moral Stages and the Idea of Justice,* 311–72. San Francisco: HarperSanFrancisco, 1981.

"Lake Hollywood Reservoir." Online: http://www.hollywoodknolls.org/hollywood_reservoir.htm.

Latour, Bruno. "Where Are the Missing Masses? The Sociology of a Few Mundane Artifacts." In *Shaping Technology/Building Society: Studies in Sociotechnical Change,* edited by Wiebe E. Bijker and J. Law, 225–58. Cambridge, MA: MIT Press, 1992.

Layton, Edwin T. *The Revolt of Engineers: Social Responsibility and the American Engineering Profession.* Baltimore: John Hopkins University Press, 1986.

Le Goff, Jacques. *Time, Work, and Culture in the Middle Ages.* Translated by Arthur Goldhammer. Chicago: University of Chicago Press, 1980.

Lenski, Gerhard E. "A Graphic Representation of the Relationship among Classes in Agrarian Societies." In *Power and Privilege: A Theory of Social Stratification,* 284. New York: McGraw-Hill, 1966.

Lindbeck, George A. "The Church's Mission to a Postmodern Culture." In *Postmodern Theology: Christian Faith in a Pluralist World,* edited by Frederic B. Burnham, 35–55. San Francisco: HarperSanFrancisco, 1989.

———. *The Nature of Doctrine: Religion and Theology in a Postliberal Age.* Philadelphia: Westminster, 1984.

MacIntyre, Alasdair. *After Virtue: A Study in Moral Theory.* 2d ed. Notre Dame: University of Notre Dame Press, 1984.

———. *Three Rival Versions of Moral Enquiry: Encyclopaedia, Genealogy, and Tradition: Being Gifford Lectures Delivered in the University of Edinburgh in 1988.* Notre Dame: University of Notre Dame Press, 1990.

Malachowski, Dan. "Wasting Time at Work Costing Companies Billions." *The San Francisco Chronicle,* July 11, 2005. Online: http://www.sfgate.com/cgi-bin/article.cgi?f=/g/a/2005/07/11/wastingtime.TMP.

May, William F. "The Engineer: From Nature's Adversary to Nature's Advocate?" In *Beleaguered Rulers: The Public Obligation of the Professional*, 89–128. Louisville: Westminster John Knox, 2001.

McClendon, James Wm., Jr. *Ethics: Systematic Theology.* Vol 1. Nashville: Abingdon, 1986.

McDonough, William, and Michael Braungart. *Cradle to Cradle: Remaking the Way We Make Things* New York: North Point, 2002.

Milgram, Stanley. *Obedience and Authority.* New York: Harper & Row, 1974.

"Morning Prayer." In *The Book of Common Prayer, and Administration of the Sacraments, and Other Rites and Ceremonies, as Revised and Proposed to the Use of the Protestant Episcopal Church, at a Convention of the Said Church in the States of New-York, New Jrrsey [Sic], Pennsylvania, Delaware, Maryland, Virginia, and South-Carolina, Held in Philadelphia, from September 27th to October 7th, 1785,* edited by Episcopal Church. London: re-printed for J. Debrett, opposite Burlington House, Piccadilly, 1789.

Moulton, James H., and George Milligan. *The Vocabulary of the Greek Testament Illustrated from the Papyri and Other Non-Literary Sources.* Grand Rapids: Eerdmans, 1930.

Mouw, Richard J. *The God Who Commands.* Notre Dame: University of Notre Dame Press, 1990.

Mulhal, Stephen. *On Being in the World: Wittgenstein and Heidegger on Seeing Aspects.* London: Routledge, 1990.

Mullins, Lisa. "Not Enough Time." *The World*, Public Radio International, 2009.

Murdoch, Iris. *The Sovereignty of Good.* London: Routledge, 1970.

Murphy, Nancey, Brad J. Kallenberg, and Mark Thiessen Nation, editors. *Virtues and Practices in the Christian Tradition: Christian Ethics after MacIntyre.* Notre Dame: University of Notre Dame Press, 2003.

Nakashima, Ellen. "Harsh Words Die Hard on the Web." *Washington Post*, March 7, 2007, A01. Online: http://washingtonpost.com/wp-dyn/content/article/2007/03/06/A2007030602705_pf.html.

Ness, John. "Culture: Gamers' Good News." *Newsweek*, March 6, 2006. Online: http://www.lexisnexis.com.libproxy.udayton.edu/us/lnacademic/results/docview/docview.do?docLinkInd=true&risb=21_T8522071894&format=GNBFI&sort=RELEVANCE&startDocNo=1&resultsUrlKey=29_T8522073001&cisb=22_T8522073000&treeMax=true&treeWidth=0&csi=5774&docNo=1.

Niebuhr, Reinhold. *Moral Man and Immoral Society.* New York: Scribner, 1932.

Nielsen, Kai. "Wittgensteinian Fideism." *Philosophy* 42:161 (1967) 191–209.

Nielsen, Kai, and D. Z. Phillips. *Wittgensteinian Fideism?* London: SCM, 2005.

Noble, David F. "Social Choice in Machine Design: The Case of Automatically Controlled Machines." In *The Social Shaping of Technology*, edited by Donald MacKenzie and Judy Wajcman, 161–76. Buckingham, PA: Open University Press, 1999.

O'Reilly, Tim. "What Is Web 2.0." Online: http://oreilly.com/lpt/a/6228.

O'Keefe, Mark. *What Are They Saying About Social Sin?* New York: Paulist, 1990.

Patterson, Bryan. "Simple Truth in Power of Forgiveness." *Sun Herald (Australia)*, 2006, Extra-82. Online: http://www.lexisnexis.com.libproxy.udayton.edu/us/lnacademic/results/docview/docview.do?docLinkInd=true&risb=21_T8989442745&format=GNBFI&sort=RELEVANCE&startDocNo=1&resultsUrlKey=29_T8989442748&cisb=22_T8989442747&treeMax=true&treeWidth=0&csi=244784&docNo=1.

Petroski, Henry. "St. Francis Dam." *American Scientist* 91 (2003) 114–18.

Pilloton, Emily, and Allan Chochinov. *Design Revolution: 100 Products That Empower People*. New York: Metropolis, 2009.

Pinches, Charles. *Theology and Action: After Theory in Christian Ethics*. Grand Rapids: Eerdmans, 2002.

Pinckaers, Servais. *The Sources of Christian Ethics*. Maryknoll, NY: Orbis, 1995.

Plantinga, Cornelius. *Not the Way It's Supposed to Be: A Breviary of Sin*. Grand Rapids: Eerdmans, 1995.

Polkinghorne, John. *Science and Providence: God's Interaction with the World*. Boston: Shambhala, 1989.

Pope John Paul II. "Evangelium Vitae." (March 25, 1995). Online: http://www.vatican.va/edocs/ENG0141/_INDEX.HTM.

"Pope: Spread the Word Using New Media." (October 29, 2009). Online: http://www.zenit.org/article-27387?l=english.

Postman, Neil. *Amusing Ourselves to Death: Public Discourse in the Age of Show Business*. New York: Penguin, 1985.

———. *Technopoly: The Surrender of Culture to Technology*. Rev ed. New York: Vintage, 1993.

Reuschling, Wyndy Corbin. "'Trust and Obey': The Danger of Obedience as Duty in Evangelical Ethics." *Journal of the Society of Christian Ethics* 25:2 (2005) 59–78.

Rhees, Rush, ed. *Recollections of Wittgenstein*. Oxford: Oxford University Press, 1984.

Richtel, Matt. "Thou Shalt Not Kill, except in a Game at Church." *The New York Times*, October 7, 2007. Online: http://www.lexisnexis.com.libproxy.udayton.edu/us/lnacademic/results/docview/docview.do?docLinkInd=true&risb=21_T8521873212&format=GNBFI&sort=BOOLEAN&startDocNo=51&resultsUrlKey=29_T8521865437&cisb=22_T8521876484&treeMax=true&treeWidth=0&csi=6742&docNo=65.

Rorty, Richard. "Inquiry as Recontextualization: An Anti-Dualist Account of Interpretation." In *Objectivity, Relativism, and Truth: Philosophical Papers, Vol. 1*, 93–110. Cambridge: Cambridge University Press, 1991.

Rosenthal, Elisabeth. "Third-World Stove Soot the Target in Climate Fight." *The New York Times* (2009) A1.

Russell, Robert John, Nancey Murphy, and Arthur R. Peacocke. *Chaos and Complexity: Scientific Perspectives on Divine Action*. Vatican City: Vatican Observatory and the Center of Theology and the Natural Sciences, 1995.

Rydstrom-Poulsen, Aage. *The Gracious God: Gratia in Augustine and the Twelfth Century*. Copenhagen: Akademisk Forlag, 2002.

Saint John of the Cross. *Ascent of Mount Carmel*. Translated by E. Allison Peers from the critical edition of P. Silverio de Santa Teresa. Edited by E. Allison Peers with a general introduction. Garden City, NY: Image, 1958.

Sammons, Jack. "Rebellious Ethics and Albert Speer." In *Against the Grain: New Approaches to Professional Ethics*, edited by Michael Goldberg, 123–60. Valley Forge, PA: Trinity, 1993.

Schinzinger, Roland, and Mike W. Martin. *Introduction to Engineering Ethics*. New York: McGraw Hill, 2000.

Schultze, Quentin J. *Habits of the High-Tech Heart: Living Virtuously in the Information Age*. Grand Rapids: Baker, 2002.

———. *High-Tech Worship?: Using Presentational Technologies Wisely*. Grand Rapids: Bake, 2004.

Schwehn, Mark. "Identity, Liberal Education and Vocation." *The Cresset* (2006) Online: www.valpo.edu/cresset/2006/2006_Michaelmas_Schwehn.pdf.

Sheehan, Thomas. "Reading a Life: Heidegger and Hard Times." In *The Cambridge Companion to Heidegger*, edited by Charles Guigon, 70–96. Cambridge: Cambridge University Press, 1993.

Siegel, Robert, and Frank Langfitt. "Wholesale Price Jump Dampens Good Retail News." In *All Things Considered* National Public Radio, 2007.

Simons, Marlise. "Doctor's Gulf War Studies Link Cancer to Depleted Uranium." *New York Times*. Online: http://web.lexis-nexis.com/universe/document?_m=d62d595 eafdc802b8912c19dac3ec1a4&_docnum=19&wchp=dGLbVtb-zSkVA&_md5=27 7668ca38c9a082ccf4a9576ad1a4f9.

Sinclair, Bruce. "At the Turn of the Screw: William Sellers, the Franklin Institute, and a Standard American Thread." *Technology and Culture* 10 (1969) 20–34.

Smith, Merritt Roe. "Army Ordnance and the 'American System' of Manufacturing, 1815–1861." In *Military Enterprise and Technological Change: Perspectives on the American Experience*, edited by Merritt Roe Smith. Cambridge: MIT Press, 1985.

Soudek, Ingrid H. "The Humanist Engineer of Aleksandr Solzhenitsyn." In *Social, Ethical, and Policy Implication of Engineering: Selected Readings*, edited by Joseph R. Herkert, 57–60. New York: IEEE, 2000.

Spengler, Oswald. *Decline of the West, Two Volumes*. Translated with notes by Charles Francis Atkinson. New York: Knopf, 1926–28.

Springs, Jason A. "What Cultural Theorists of Religion Have to Learn from Wittgenstein; or, How to Read Geertz as a Practice Theorist." *Journal of the American Academy of Religion* 76 (2008) 934–69.

St. George, Donna. "Sexting Hasn't Reached Most Young Teens, Poll Finds." *The Washington Post* (16·Dec 2009). Online: http://www.washingtonpost.com/wp-dyn/content/article/2009/12/15/AR2009121502321.html.

Staudenmaier, John M. "Denying the Holy Dark: The Enlightenment and the European Mystical Tradition." In *Progress: Fact or Illusion?*, edited by Leo Marx and Bruce Mazlish, 175–200. Ann Arbor: University of Michigan Press, 1996.

———. "Perils of Progress Talk: Some Historical Considerations." In *Science, Technology, and Social Progress; Research in Technology Studies, V. 2*, edited by Steven L. Goldman, 268–93. Bethlehem, PA: Lehigh University Press, 1989.

———. "The Politics of Successful Technologies." In *In Context: History and the History of Technology; Essays in Honor of Melvin Kranzberg*, edited by Stephen H. Sutcliffe and Robert C. Post, 150–71. Bethlehem, PA: Leigh University Press, 1989.

Steffens, J. H., C. Barus, R. I. Bergman, J . C. Bennett, H. B. Koning, M. G. Salvadori, V. Paaschkis, H. Lehneis, N. Balabanian, D. H. Pletta, and R. W. Anderson. "Panel Discussion: Ideas for Better Code." Paper presented at the Conference on Engineering Ethics, Baltimore, MD, May 18–19, 1975.

Stringfellow, William. *A Keeper of the Word: Selected Writings of William Stringfellow*. Edited by Bill Wylie-Kellerman. Grand Rapids: Eerdmans, 1994.

———. "Stratagems of the Demonic Powers." In *A Keeper of the Word: Selected Writings of William Stringfellow*, edited by Bill Wylie-Kellerman, 214–22. Grand Rapids: Eerdmans, 1994.

———. "Traits of the Principalities." In *A Keeper of the Word: Selected Writings of William Stringfellow*, edited by Bill Wylie Kellerman, 204–13. Grand Rapids: Eerdmans, 1994.

Sunstein, Cass R. "The Daily We: Is the Internet Really a Blessing for Democracy?" Online: http://bostonreview.net/BR26.3/sunstein.html.

Taylor, Charles. *A Secular Age.* Cambridge, MA: Belknap, 2007.

Taylor, Jerome. "Introduction." In *The Didascalicon of Hugh of Saint Victor*, 3–39. New York: Columbia University Press, 1991.

Teague, Don. "Give Me That Online Religion: Virtual Religious Services Are Gaining in Popularity." (2007) Online: http://www.msnbc.msn.com/id/18789168/.

Terdiman, Daniel. "Study: Wikipedia as Accurate as Britannica." (December 15, 2005). Online: http://news.cnet.com/2100-1038_3-5997332.html.

Thompson, Nicholas. "Self-Adjusted Glasses Could Be a Boon to Africa." *The New York Times*, December 10, 2002. Online: http://www.nytimes.com/2002/12/10/health/10GLAS.html.

Tilley, Terrence W. *The Evils of Theodicy.* Washington, DC: Georgetown University Press, 1991.

Vargas, Jose Antonio. "Virtual Reality Prepares Soldiers for Real War: Young Warriors Say Video Shooter Games Helped Hone Their Skills; A01." *The Washington Post*, February 14, 2006.

Vu, Michelle. "S. Korea Presidential Election Highlights Christian Influence." *The Christian Post*, December 13, 2007. Online: http://www.christianpost.com/article/20071213/s-korea-presidential-election-highlights-christian-influence/index.html.

Wade, Nicholas. "We May Be Born with an Urge to Help." *The New York Times*, November 30, 2009.

Walsh, Jason. "England's Ebay for Sex." *Wired* (March 7, 2005). Online: http://www.wired.com/culture/lifestyle/news/2005/03/66800.

"Web 2.0." Wikipedia, the free encyclopedia. Online: http://en.wikipedia.org/wiki/Web_2.0.

Werpehowski, William. "Ad Hoc Apologetics." *Journal of Religion* 66 (1986) 282–301.

Whitbeck, Caroline. *Ethics in Engineering Practice and Research.* Cambridge: Cambridge University Press, 1998.

White, Lynn. "Cultural Climates and Technological Advance in the Middle Ages." In *Medieval Religion and Technology: Collected Essays*, 217–53. Berkeley: University of California Press, 1978.

———. "The Expansion of Technology 500–1500." In *The Fontana Economic History of Europe Volume 1: The Middle Ages*, edited by Carlo M. Cipolla, 143–71. New York: Barnes & Noble, 1976.

———. "Jacopo Aconcio as an Engineer." *American Historical Review* 72 (1967) 425–44.

———. "The Legacy of the Middle Ages in the American Wild West." *Speculum: A Journal of Mediaeval Studies* 40 (1965) 191–202.

———. "Medieval Engineering and the Sociology of Knowledge." In *Medieval Religion and Technology; Collected Essays*, 317–38. Berkeley: University of California Press, 1978.

———. *Medieval Technology and the Social Change.* London: Oxford University Press, 1962.

———. "Technology, Western." In *Dictionary of the Middle Ages*, edited by Joseph R. Strayer, 11: 650–64. New York: Scribners, 1982.

———. "Theophilus Redivivus." *Technology and Culture* 5:2 (1964) 224–33.

Wilckens, Ulrich. "*Stulos.*" In *Theological Dictionary of the New Testament*, edited by Gerhard Kittel and Gerhard Friedrich, 7:732–36. Grand Rapids: Eerdmans, 1971.

Wilkins, Michael J. "Christian." In *Anchor Bible Dictionary*, edited by David Noel Freedman, 1:925–26. New York: Doubleday, 1990.

Williams, Bernard. *Morality: An Introduction to Ethics.* Canto ed. New York: Harper & Row, 1972.

Williams, Rowan. *Dostoevsky: Language, Faith, and Fiction.* Waco, TX: Baylor University Press, 2008.

Willimon, William H. "Too Much Practice: Second Thoughts on a Theological Movement." *The Christian Century* (March 9, 2010). Online: http://www.christiancentury.org/article.lasso?id=8270.

Wink, Walter. *Naming the Powers: The Language of Power in the New Testament.* Philadelphia: Fortress, 1984.

Winner, Langdon. "Do Artifacts Have Politics?" In *The Social Shaping of Technology: How the Refrigerator God Its Hum*, edited by Donald MacKenzie and Judy Wajcman, 26–37. Philadelphia: Open University Press, 1985.

Wittgenstein, Ludwig. *The Blue and Brown Books.* New York: Harper, 1958.

———. "Cause and Effect: Intuitive Awareness." In *Philosophical Occasions, 1912–1952*, edited by James C. Klagge and Alfred Nordmann, 370–426. Indianapolis: Hackett, 1993.

———. *Culture and Value.* Translated by Peter Winch. Edited by G. H. von Wright and Heikki Nyman. English translation with the amended 2nd. ed. Oxford: Blackwell, 1980.

———. "Lectures on Religious Belief." In *Lectures and Conversations on Aesthetics, Psychology, and Religious Belief*, edited by C. Barrett. Oxford: Oxford University Press, 1966.

———. *Philosophical Investigations.* Translated by G. E. M. Anscombe. Edited by G. E. M. Anscombe and Rush Rhees. New York: Macmillan, 1953.

Woodhead, Linda. "Sex in a Wider Context," In *Sex These Days: Essays on Theology, Sexuality, and Society*, edited by Jon Davies and Gerard Loughlin. London: Sheffield, 1997.

Wright, N. T. *Evil and the Justice of God.* Downers Grove, IL: InterVarsity, 2009.

Xenophon. *The Economist of Xenophon.* Translated by Alexander D. O. Wedderburn and W. Gershom Collingwood. Bibliotheca Pastorum 1. New York: Burt Franklin, 1971.

Yoder, John Howard. *The Christian Witness to the State.* Newton, KS: Faith & Life, 1964.

———. "On Not Being Ashamed of the Gospel: Particularity, Pluralism, and Validation." *Faith and Philosophy* 9:3 (1992) 285–300.

———. *The Original Revolution.* Scottdale, PA: Herald, 1971.

———. *The Politics of Jesus.* 2nd ed. Grand Rapids: Eerdmans, 1994.

———. *The Priestly Kingdom.* Notre Dame: University of Notre Dame Press, 1984.

———. *The Royal Priesthood: Essays Ecclesiological and Ecumenical.* Grand Rapids: Eerdmans, 1994.

Zuckerman, Phil. *Society without God.* New York: New York University Press, 2008.

———. "The Virtues of Godlessness." *The Chronicle of Higher Education* 55:21 (2009) B4. Online: http://chronicle.com/temp/reprint.php?id=gqchf08syrq7qfcxqfzjh9d949ndm2k2.

Index